MEDIA OPTIONS FOR TEACHERS

Veena Kumar

Published by
ATLANTIC PUBLISHERS AND DISTRIBUTORS
B-2, Vishal Enclave, New Delhi -110027
Phones 5413460, 5429987

Sales Office
4346/4C, Ansari Road, Darya Ganj
New Delhi-110002
Phones 3272880, 3285873, 3280451
Fax 91-11-3285873
E-mail gupta.atlantc@axcess.net.in

ISBN 81-7156-700-2

Typeset at
APD Computer Graphics, Delhi
Printed in India at
Mehra Offset Press, Delhi

Foreword

This text, authored by Dr. Veena Kumar provides an informed and comprehensive guide for teachers, on all aspects of instructional media. It gives a detailed coverage to the entire range of media options (from chalkboard to the internet) available to a modern teacher. Each media option has been discussed in detail with optimum input regarding design, development and application of each one of them. Immensely readable, the book is of special interest to teachers who wish to seriously equip themselves with effective instructional tools for actual application in classroom.

The book benefits from author's experience of over 20 years in teaching and designing media based educational resources. She brings to her task a unique set of qualifications and perspectives. With expertise in the fields of Language, Communication and Educational Technology, in addition to her academic activities, she draws upon a wide range of international research and consulting experience. Extended time spent in studying and teaching in France and America gives her work a marked international perspective.

Dr. Kumar has been teaching at the Indian Institute of Technology, Delhi, since 1988. She is also the Coordinator of Educational Technology Facility which numbers among its facilities a state-of-the-art video studio. This book should be an invaluable tool for teachers and instructors at all levels: school, university and industry.

Dr. Steven Darian
Chairman
Department of Education
University of Rutgers
New Jersey, USA

Preface

Today, technology has become an active companion in the act of giving and receiving instruction and it has become imperative for a teacher to acquire basic knowledge and skills for using the vast range of media options available.

In the fast changing learning environment, the audiovisual technologies have assumed prime importance. In spite of living in a world surrounded by electronic media, an individual teacher experiences a sense of awe and hesitation while incorporating it in her classroom teaching-learning environment. This is mainly due to lack of fundamental usable know-how. This book intends to provide just that. An important philosophy guiding this book is that technology by itself has no power of its own and its importance and relevance emerges from its application by the teacher. The humanistic and technological aspects are equally important and the two must be integrated for arriving at perfect solutions.

The main thrust here is not only on what instructional tools a teacher can create herself but also on what she can get created at an affordable cost or better still how she can adopt and use existing materials. The main purpose of this book is to illustrate that technology products can help the teacher to extend herself and become an expert, explorer and creator.

The information provided in this book will be useful for educators and instructors who care for the learner and value learning. The book is addressed to the typical teacher who views herself as not being *technology oriented* with little or no exposure to designing or using media options. The main objective of the book is to motivate and encourage her to incorporate media tools for making instruction more effective and efficient. The information provided is equally useful for teachers working in schools or colleges. This book focuses on what media tools the teacher can design, develop and use comfortably.

A number of convictions form the basis of this book. To begin with, the ideas expressed here take into account the different learning theories: behaviourist, cognitivist and constructivist. The theory however, must be well integrated with methodology which must keep pace with the available tools.

A conscious effort has been made to link various technology-based strategies to well-researched theories of learning and throughout the book, educational technology is viewed as a process rather than a culmination of devices.

The arguments presented assess each media option from the point of view of its advantages, limitations and the range of applications. The author believes that none is *better* or *worse* than the other but each one is unique in its strength in a specific teaching-learning context. Therefore, traditional options have also been given equal importance.

HOW IS THE TEXT ORGANIZED

Writing a book on such a subject, one has to begin by exclusion rather than inclusion. So much needs to be said about the hardware as well as the software in the field. The information is to be sifted carefully so as not to intimidate the user but to motivate and generate sufficient confidence in her to make her actually pick up the tools and start working with them.

The text is organized into thirteen chapters. Each media option is discussed individually from the point of view of the hardware (equipment, its use and maintenance) as well as of software (design, development and application). Most chapters begin with details regarding the nature of the medium and its evolution, going on to its special advantages, getting to know the nuts-and-bolts of hardware, general advice on setting it up, using and maintaining it. Input is then provided on the design requirements of the usable software for a given media option, to be concluded by the live applications in different learning environments - individual, small groups, large groups, in classrooms or in remote learning places.

Each chapter begins with an advance organizer outlining the knowledge and skills featuring in it. For the convenience of the readers and future users of the media options information has been arranged for easy assimilation. Drawings, figures, illustrations and checklists have been used to make this a *how to do* companion text.

Chapter 1 - ***Instruction, Instructor and Technology*** deals with the basic concepts of educational technology. Most teachers do not regard themselves as technology people and remain in awe of technology. This chapter provides the background on technology's role in education and discusses major learning theories and methodologies in the context of technology integration. The chapter brings out the very intimate relationship between the methodology and the tools as used by the teacher who must take charge and learn to command both.

Chapter 2 - ***Perception, Communication and Learning*** begins by defining the three prime players in the instructional process - *perception, communication* and *learning.* After discussing the fundamentals of human perception and its impact on both communication and learning, the chapter moves on to discuss the communication process in detaii. Focus is placed on how a teacher can apply basic principles to enhance and sustain communication with learners. The chapter then discusses the basic domains of learning and the role that media can play in enhancing learning.

Chapter 3 - ***Designing Instructional Media*** commences with a formal definition of Instructional Design and its key components. Different models of instructional design are discussed. The chapter provides an in-depth discussion on the impact of instructional media on different teaching methodologies. Input is provided on developing scripts and storyboards. The chapter ends by categorizing different media formats.

Chapter 4 - ***Designing and Reading Visuals*** discusses what is visuality and how visuals, the soul of media, play a key role in serving diverse instructional functions. The chapter provides input on the different functions of visuals, types of visuals and how they are seen and interpreted. The importance of visuals in developing media. How visuals are created and used effectively.

Chapter 5 - ***Nonprojected Media Options*** discusses the more traditional media formats such as the chalkboard, charts, flat displays, maps, pictures and realia. Detailed information is provided on the special advantages and limitations of each one of these media options. The chapter discusses how to design the nonprojected media options and to use them effectively and in harmony with the more sophisticated and technologically advanced media formats.

Chapter 6 - ***The Print Medium***, accepted as the primary medium of instruction, is discussed from the instructor's point of view. Keeping in mind the popularity and easy access to DTP equipment and software, teachers are provided relevant information on how to design their own print support materials. Drawing upon the principles of visuality, the chapter provides information on elements of page layout, lettering sizes and types and how to add artwork or photographs to the material being generated.

Chapter 7 - ***The Audio Medium*** begins with placing the medium in its historical perspective and its gradual evolution to the digital format. Special advantages of the audio medium in teaching are discussed. After providing necessary input on the basic equipment and infrastructure, the chapter deals with the actual development of audio material by the teacher. The concept and the use of audio laboratories is also discussed.

Chapter 8 - ***Overhead Projection*** covers the potential of overhead projection as the most popular and dependable media format. Beginning with the special advantages of overhead projection, the chapter discusses the features and use of hardware. Design and development of different types of transparencies is covered. Innovative and special displays form an important part of the chapter.

Chapter 9 - ***Fundamentals of Photography*** deals with the essentials of photography which forms the basis of most of the projected media options. With the new automatic cameras, a teacher can develop rich and effective support materials. The basic essential knowledge regarding types of camera, lenses and films is provided along with input on how to compose good pictures and how photographs can be best used for instruction.

Chapter 10 - ***Teaching with Slides*** discusses the special advantages of using 35 mm slides. Input is provided on different types of slides (camera & computer generated), how to design good slides and how to prepare an effective slide-tape programme. The chapter ends with input on how multi-image presentations, the unclaimed ancestor of the multimedia concept, can be used effectively.

Chapter 11 - ***The Video Medium*** focuses on the potential of performing different instructional tasks for different learner groups. In this day and time, it is imperative that every teacher is familiar with the potential of this magic medium. Even though a teacher may not herself develop a video programme, it is important that she is able to design video clips or intelligently select material from the pre-prepared materials available. All relevant information is provided with figures and check lists.

Chapter 12 - ***Computers and Instruction*** covers the entire range of information that a modern teacher should have. Beginning with the history of this tool, the chapter proceeds to discuss how it can be used in different teaching modes - lecture, tutorial, drill and practice, discovery, simulation and problem solving. Necessary input is also provided on the integrated learning systems and computer laboratories. The topics of hypertext and multimedia are introduced and discussed to provide sufficient background and motivation for a teacher to further explore and experiment.

Chapter 13 - ***Using Available Media Options*** deals with how teachers can and should look for ready support materials. How to evaluate the available material and how to adopt pre-prepared materials for specific use alone or in combination with other materials developed for the purpose. Information is also provided on how to evaluate and validate selected media options.

The book ends with a comprehensive glossary. The glossary contains all the media related terms a modern teacher may have to cope with during her enterprise as a designer or user of media options.

It has taken a great deal of will power to resist talking about future trends in the light of emerging information superhighways, artificial intelligence and the media centres. Some very important developments of special interest and relevance to a teacher have been included in the chapter on *Computers in Instruction.* The argument has been in favour of sparing the technology-young teacher the flood of information. It is hoped that once this new teacher has been initiated into the realm of technology, she will find her own way to keep pace with the future technologies and their mindboggling applications.

ACKNOWLEDGEMENTS

Many different sets of people have contributed to the birth of this book. A book such as this takes years of `curing' and during those long years several people add *something little* which facilitates the curing process: Over ten years that I have spent in the field of educational technology, my path has crossed several such outstanding academicians who have added that *something little* to this book, people one hears address audiences, people one works with, people with whom one discusses problems and solutions. Similarly, several books, journals and articles have stimulated and churned the thought process. I gratefully acknowledge their contribution.

I must also thank my students at IIT Delhi and at Rutgers University (USA) who have been, at times knowingly but more often unknowingly, the source of much wisdom through their comments and feedback.

On a more functional plane, several people have helped me to put this book together. Thanks are due to S.S.Chauhan for generating the computer graphics, Narender Choudhry for preparing the sketches, Nalini Katara and Prashant Sharma for proofreading.

Another set of people whose help must be acknowledged are the silent supporters who make you feel that you are about an important business. They lend meaning to the entire exercise and help you to go on. Obviously, only those who care deeply for you and have some sort of conviction in your enterprise fall in this category. I am truly indebted to my wonderful family, particularly Kulbhushan, my husband who, I am sure had several occasions to complain. I thank him for his patience.

Veena Kumar

CONTENTS

1

INSTRUCTION INSTRUCTOR AND TECHNOLOGY

... *growing companions*

Instruction vs Education

New Learning Environments

New Challenges for the Instructor

Towards Greater Student Autonomy

Media Technology in Instruction

Evolution of Instructional Media

INSTRUCTION, INSTRUCTOR & TECHNOLOGY

In any given teaching-learning situation, the three prime players are instruction, instructor and technology. To achieve the best results, the three must be in complete harmony with each other, collectively working towards attainment of set objectives.

It is appropriate to begin with establishing a clear distinction between the terms education and instruction. Both deal with acquisition of knowledge but while education concerns itself with knowledge which may be general in nature, instruction is knowledge acquired for specific, measurable purposes. Education may include accidental learning for example, while walking down the street or watching one's favourite television programme or by merely observing things or people. Instruction, on the other hand, refers to learning that takes place in response to a planned effort.

Both education and instruction deal with acquisition and transfer of information. Technology facilitates and promotes this process. It guides and supports both the sender (teacher-imparting information) and the receiver (student - absorbing information). In other words, while instruction is to do with collating, packaging and disseminating information, technology is to do with the various *tools* (products and processes) used for transferring that information. And, in the midst of these two, holding the reins, is the *instructor* who, in best interest of the learner and learning, must control both instruction and technology.

Instruction is the arrangement of information and environment for the benefit of the learner. Environment in this context refers to not only *where* but also to *how* instruction is imparted. The relationship between instruction and environment is a close one and can vary from formal to very informal. Once again, it is the instructor who manages this delicate balancing act between the information and the environment by choosing the best strategy for collating, packaging and delivering information in a given environment.

In achieving the selected instructional objectives, the instructor needs to cope with the 3Ms - *Message-Medium-Method* of instruction.

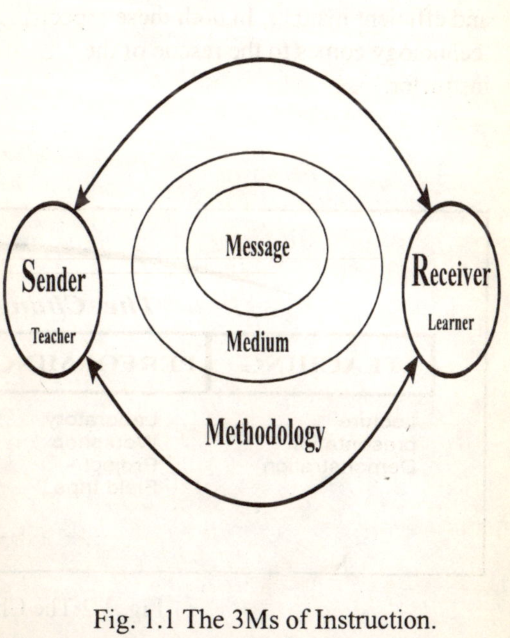

Fig. 1.1 The 3Ms of Instruction.

The Changing Student Profile:

What does a typical learner of this information age expect? A great deal ! The new learner wants complete autonomy in what to learn, when to learn and how to learn. There is a marked shift in focus from teaching to learning and from the teacher to the learner.

Two important factors are responsible for this change. First, the learner today is a product of the high technology environment. and grows up with electronics around her. To her, the audio-visuals are no longer a luxurious addition to her education but something to be taken for granted. The general standard of presentation skills has gone up and a teacher's classroom delivery has to meet some minimum standards.

The second, and more important reason is academic. The quantum leap in new knowledge to be imparted during the same time span imposes on a teacher new responsibilities of sifting, designing and delivering information in a highly effective and efficient manner. In both these aspects, technology comes to the rescue of the instructor.

The Changing Mandate of a Teacher:

One common apprehension that many teachers have is that technology is going to make their role minimal, even negligible. The reality, however, is that media actually underlines the need and the importance of a teacher. In this information age not only does a teacher have to cover the specified curriculum, she also has to teach the learners *how to learn* by themselves. Teaching the learners how to cope with their learning tasks, therefore, has become an important charter for the new teacher. Under this charter, the teacher has the additional responsibity to -

* Guide a student to identify her needs and means.
* Recommend sources of information
* Guide problem-solving
* Sharpen learner's capability to cope with hardware and software
* Encourage the student to develop her own learning materials.

In the new scheme of things, there is a definite shift of locus of control from the teacher to the student. To facilitate and promote this change, it is imperative for every teacher to be perfectly at ease with the *technological tools* available in the form of media options.

The Changing Focus

TEACHING	PERFORMING	DISCUSSING	STUDYING
Lecture presentation Demonstration	Laboratory Workshop Project Field trips	Tutorials Student presentations Group discussions interactive learning Q./A. Sessions	Projects Study guides Video CAI/CAL Self-learning Materials

Fig. 1.2 The Changing Focus in Instruction

The most important contribution of media is perhaps the facility it offers to recapture, present and simulate experience from the real world. This lends concreteness and relevance to the experience of learning.

In one of the earliest texts on the use of audio-visuals, the authors, Hoban,Hoban & Zissman claimed that the value of audiovisuals is in function of their ability to present realism. The authors arranged various teaching methods and aids to be used in a hierarchy of progressive abstraction.

In 1946, Edgar Dale, drawing upon the same constructs, developed the famous *CONE OF EXPERIENCE.* Dale tried to identify experiences required by a learner and the media sources likely to provide those experiences.

Starting with the direct, purposeful experiences, the learning experience moves twelve levels towards the most abstract.

Activities grouped under three main sections: Doing, Observing and Symbolising can all be enhanced by the use of media. Later, an attempt was made to link these

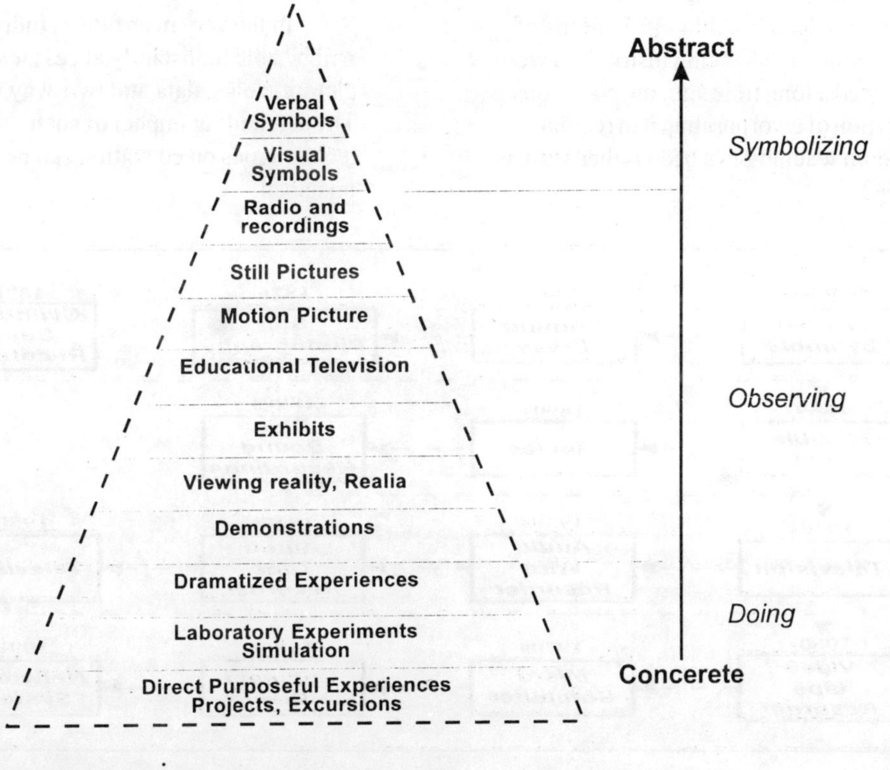

Fig. 1.3 Dale's Cone of Experience and Media Sources

The intricate interplay of *instruction, instructor* and *technology* has given rise to the concept of *Educational Technology or Instructional Technology* which includes technology of education, technology for education; and technology in education. In every combination, the inter-dependence of instruction and technology is ratified and acknowledged as ***Educational Technology.***

Speaking more formally, educational technology is the development, application and evaluation of systems, techniques and aids to improve the process of human learning. According to Council for Educational Technology, UK., educational technology helps to meet the challenges of the new learning environment.

Technology in the form of different media options, offers solutions to cope with all these challenges. Although benefits of using media for enhancing instruction were recognized a long time ago, the conscious application of incorporating it in regular classroom teaching has been rather slow in coming.

On the other hand, advances in telecommunications have metamorphosed instruction. It has now become possible to *time-shift* and *place-shift* instruction. New technologies using audioconferencing, computer and videoconferencing have almost wired the world up.

Two magical devices- *satellite dishes* and *fiber optics* have radically changed the education delivery systems. A satellite positioned over the Atlantic ocean can handle 30,000 phone calls simultaneously. Fiber optics, carrying digital signals as pulses of light generated by a laser device which is no bigger than a grain of salt, can link up homes, schools and universities into national and international networks.

In the very near future, individuals will be able to instantly access text, picture, voice, data and two-way video. The astounding impact of such technologies on education can be well imagined.

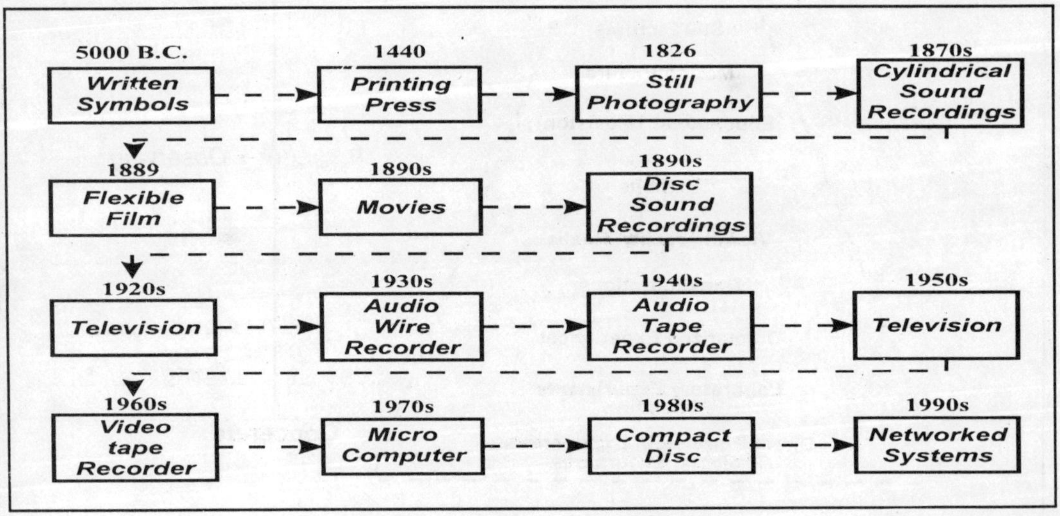

Fig. 1.4 Evolution of Instructional Media.

Media in Instruction - What Research Says!

Sufficient evidence is available to show that positive results can be obtained when carefully designed media- based materials are used for instruction both for group or individual learning. Some important benefits reported by research are -

* Media can *enhance motivation*. As the learning process becomes more interesting, the learner is motivated to continue to work. Assimilation of ideas and their retention also becomes very easy.

* Media forces *better content organization.* When a teacher plans to use media to support teaching, the contextual input becomes better organized and more focused. This is even more so when a teacher designs and develops her own materials.

*Media helps to *overcome constraints of time and pace*, opening the portals of instruction to a much wider and diverse learner community. Media sets the learner free to a certain extent by offering flexibility of making instruction available on *when* and *where* basis.

* Media helps to *enhance the quality of learning.* Using media-based support material promotes clarity of content by integrating multichannel communication. Well-designed media generally takes the wisdom of different accepted learning theories into account which results in active and effective learning.

* Media helps to make the *delivery process more sophisticated and standardized.* This feature is of great importance when learnerrs have to be grouped in several sections. replicated and used as training material with the help of media (video recording).

* Media helps to package information more intelligently ensuring active participation of the learner. With the help of media, the teacher can very easily include elements of interactivity, feedback and reinforcement.

* Media helps to reduce teaching time and offers the possibility of doing additional work with the learner. Complicated and time consuming drawings/sketches can be done well ahead of time. As instruction becomes streamlined, it requires less time to transmit and assimilate information.

* Media makes the act of *teaching more pleasurable and rewarding for the teacher.* The most important beneficiary is the teacher herself. She learns to innovate and acquire command over the content matter. She enjoys developing materials with the learners and thus becomes the real facilitator.

All these advantages, together or individually encourage the learner to adopt a positive attitude towards learning. She is guided towards a more efficient way of learning. Of course, the teacher has to be actively involved and must help the learner decide which of these advantages should take priority.

INSTRUCTION AND MEDIA

METHOD	FORMAT	MEDIA OPTIONS
• PRESENTATION	By one source. One- way communication	Models, Photographs, Overhead Projector, Slides, Video, Computer Projection
• DEMONSTRATION	Instructor shows activity. Two-way process, learner may be active or passive	Board, Charts, Models Realia, Slides, Video, Overhead Projector
• TUTORIAL	Information provided by instructor, peers, media	Slides, Video, Audio, Print, Computers.
• DISCUSSION	Sharing of information amongst different sources	Print, Video, Audio, Overhead Projector Computers.
• DRILL & PRACTICE	Series of practice sessions	Print, Audio, Video, Computer Projection
• COOPERATIVE LEARNING	Two or three students learning together	Print, Audio, Video, Computers
• DISCOVERY	Inductive, inquiry approach Learning through trial & error	Print, Audio, Video Models, Computers
• PROBLEM SOLVING	Higher order learning. Define, analyse & resolve a given problem.	Print, Video, Computers Overhead Transparencies
• SIMULATION	Experiencing a scaled down real life situation.	Models, Video, Audio Computers
• GAMES	Ensure deep knowledge of subject, problem solving skills	Print, Models, Audio Video, Computers

2

PERCEPTION COMMUNICATION AND LEARNING

PERCEPTION, COMMUNICATION & LEARNING

In order to comprehend and appreciate the actual contribution of media in the instructional process, it is imperative to clearly understand the three base processes by which human beings acquire new knowledge viz. the processes of *perception, communication* and *learning.* It is equally important to understand their inter and intra dependence.

Perception is a process whereby we become aware of the world around us. We use our senses : eyes, ears and nerve endings in the skin to establish contact with objects, events and our entire environment.

Communication, in the instructional process, refers to transfer of information from the source (teacher) to the destined receiver (learner).

Learning, is the development of new knowledge, skills or attitudes when an individual interacts with information and environment.

In recent times, the subject of human learning has received a great deal of attention. Many educational psychologists believe that a human being should be viewed not only as an organism making stimulus-related responses but also as a creature living in an information-filled environment, from which he absorbs some selected information and utilizes it in one or several different ways.

The human being absorbs information through *Perception* which involves more than mere recording of sensory experiences. Perceptual learning is the ability to extract information from the environment. We make contact with the external reality through the vehicle of perceptual process. It is a personalized world that we see. A number of variables intervene between the individual and the objective reality.

Information is collected by the nervous system from all sources surrounding the subject. The basic collectors of information - the sense organs, which are extensions of the nervous system, are particularly sensitive to changes in the surroundings.

Studies have been undertaken to understand how a human being handles information presented to him. Here, the subject is presented with some source of information (input) and the process through which information is utilized, transformed and stored (output) is studied. Discrepancies between the input and output provide knowledge of how efficiently the information is being handled.

Two important conclusions are of special interest: first, any perceptual event consists of many sensory messages that do not occur in isolation but are related and combined into complex patterns. Second, an individual reacts to only a small part of all that is taking place at any given instance. The part of an event to be experienced is *selected* by the individual according to her desire, experience etc..

Since the times of Aristotle, thinkers have been intrigued by the subject of sensory perception. Arguments have revolved around the question as to how many different senses are involved in the *perceptual system* on the whole. The sensitive cells that receive information are organized into five main systems (*Gibson, 1966). Within anyone of the systems, many different types of cells, may be involved. These are called *receptors.* The five major information systems related to the human being's orientation towards the external environment are :

* The visual system
* The auditory system
* The heptic system
* The taste-smell system, and
* The basic-orienting system.

Each one of these systems is an active system and collects information independently and spontaneously.

The Visual System is more than just the retina capturing the pictures from the outside world. It is an extremely active system designed for wide scanning. The system is supported by a strong muscular component and nervous network coordinating the entire system.

The Auditory system has limited capacity for scanning the environment. Animals are found to have far more sensitive auditory systems than human beings.

The Heptic system is a highly active system involving the touch receptors in the skin, joints and muscles. The learner (adult) acquires a great deal of information by visual examination of the shape and the texure of the object. The system is supported by muscle coordination which allows the individual to handle materials. The point becomes clear when one observes a human being inspecting a piece of delicate china.

The Taste-Smell System represents a single basic system which is relatively under developed in human beings.

The Basic-orienting System comprises mainly two sets of canals, one on each side of the head in the inner ear canal. These are not a part of the hearing machinary although they are located in the region. The principal function of these organs is to respond to sudden movements. The basic-orienting system has relatively little relevance in formal learning.

The perceptual process is very complex and involves elements such as -

* Receiving information
* Analysing the information received
* Coding of information at the sense organ level.
* Coding and classification of information at the central level

It has been established that much of what we respond to in the external world has structure and that perception involves recognition of that structure. The structure is not imposed by the individual though that is not impossible. Further, when an individual input is received and interpreted, the element perceived is classified as a member of a *set* of elements.

While designing media-based materials, it is important to remember that the user reacts to *only a small part* of all that is taking place at any given instance. The *part* to be experienced is selected by the user on the basis of desire and what attracts the attention.

Gibson, J.J., *The Sense Considered as Perceptual System,* Boston, Houghton Miffin, 1966.

Some Facts About Perception ...

* The experience of perception is individual and unique.

* An event is perceived in terms of an individual's past experiences, present circumstances and motivation.

* While a given perceptual experience is 'individual and unique', a series of perceptual experiences by a group of different people, can be related or almost identical.

* Instructional media commences with the assumption that people learn primarily from what they perceive.

A great deal of research has been undertaken to comprehend the perceptual process and its relationship to learning.

M.R.Moore, in his taxonomy of perception (1970) , proposes that the development of perceptual process follows a certain pattern moving from sensation to change in behaviour.

Moore's Taxonomy of Perception

- Sensation
- Perception of Figures
- Perception of Symbols
- Perception of Meaning
- Performance Perception:
  - Observation
  - Decision
  - Change in Behaviour

An active component in the learning process is *Attention.* A crucial subject which the educationists have found difficult to study. The term *attention,* as commonly understood, implies that there is a selective process of taking the information into the perceptual system. Some of the important factors which are known to promote attention are :

- movement
- complexity, and
- novelty.

A teachers can use these to ensure entry of information into the learner's perceptual system. Indeed, there are several other important factors which are yet to be fully understood. The stimulus *attended to* is in competition with many other stimuli and therefore the selected stimuli has to be stronger than the rest.

Movement is one way of adding strength to a stimuli. It is established that movement impacts attention of even a two day old baby.

Novelty is another important tool for strengthening the stimuli. A stimulus can have novelty attributes because it appears in an unfimiliar context and the learner has a low expectancy of finding it there. Novelty can be provided either in the 'content' or in the 'delivery' of the stimulus.

The *Complexity* factor, as the basis for attracting attention, is significant both from the practical and theoretical points of view. Research shows that if a simple visual is displayed along side a complex one, the latter commands greater attention. However, there is probably an optimum amount of complexity for individual learner and this optimum level increases with age.

Perception leads to *Communication.*

The success of the teaching-learning process is based almost entirely on ***communication.*** The word *communication* comes from the Latin root *commun* meaning *together*. It is a two-way process of sharing information indicating a relationship between the two individuals.

Communication may be defined as the art and science of conveying information without distortion to the intended meaning. Effective communication means getting the message across so that the meaning generated at both ends is identical.

Communication involves exchange, participation, adoption, sharing and interaction. No one can be ever accused of over emphasising the importance of communication, particularly in teaching,

HOW COMMUNICATION WORKS?

One of the earliest models of communication was developed by Claude E. Shannon.

Several other models of communication have been proposed but the Shannon-Weaver model retains its popularity because of its simplicity and its facility to identify and categorize the important steps in the process of communication.

The model which depicts the process of exchange of information, was later modified by Warren Weaver to include the overlap in the fields of experience of the sender and the receiver.

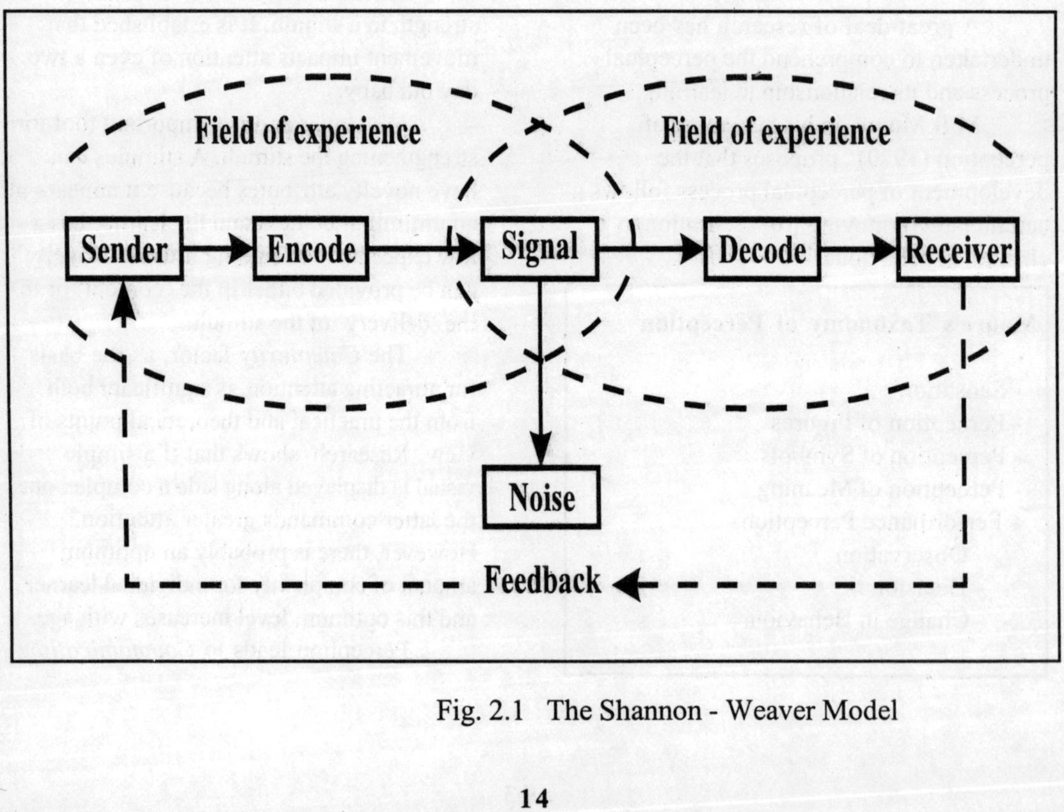

Fig. 2.1 The Shannon - Weaver Model

As is clear from the model, the process involves six distinct steps -

1. The sender selects the message.
2. The sender composes or encodes it in a transferable code (language, signs)
3. The sender selects the channel (written, verbal or nonverbal) and transmits the message
4. The message is received by the receiver
5. The receiver decodes the message
6. The receiver sends feedback to the sender.

It is clear that the cycle of constant feedback should be preserved with utmost care. *Media, if used effectively, can play a major role in facilitating all the different steps in the communication process.*

WHY COMMUNICATION FAILS?

An awareness regarding the vulnerable areas where communication can and often does breakdown, is very helpful in sustaining communication.

A number of factors - *physical, intellectual, background, linguistic and psychological etc.* can cause a breakbown in communication. Both the teacher (sender) and the learner (receiver) need to keep all these factors in mind.

It is essential that the teacher as the sender designs the message keeping the receiver in mind. Here too, media with its powerful tools - the visuals, graphics and symbols, can provide substantial help.

LOST COMMUNICATION ...

* ***Physical factors***	:	Noise, physical discomfort, hunger, ill health, fatigue, uncomfortable seating/working environment, poor lighting, spatial position between the sender and the receiver.
* ***Linguistic factors***	:	Lack of knowledge of the target language, unfamiliar terms and expressions, differences in pronunciation and images used.
* ***Intellectual factors***	:	Incomplete message, lack of authenticity in the message, lack of conviction, irrelevant context, redundancies, poor memory.
* ***Psychological factors***	:	Unpleasant/unrewarding experiences, unfulfilled curiosity, disinterest, prejudice, anxiety.
* ***Background factors***	:	Differences in educational, linguistic, cultural, conceptual or perceptual background.

Learning, as defined earlier is utilising the knowledge perceived or information communicated to achieve pre-defined goals. Though learning takes place all the time, here, the principal concern is with learning that takes place as a result of the instructional efforts.

For over a hundred years now the educational psychologists have been studying how people learn. A number of interesting theories help us to understand the process and in turn, guide us to enhance the process.

Most of these theories have, in their own way, influenced the way instruction is designed and consequently, the way media should be designed to enhance instruction. Therefore, it is important for a teacher who intends to design and develop media to keep in mind the key concepts propogated in these theories.

Some Well-Known Theories of Learning ...

- Operant Conditioning Theory
- Component Display Theory
- Elaboration Theory
- Information Processing Theory
- Social Learning Theory, and
- Attribution Learning Theory

Operant Conditioning Theory proposed by Skinner, views learning as a change in behaviour. Everytime a person acquires new knowledge, learns a new skill or experiences an event, the individual's behaviour is modified. When the *stimuli* (the message) and the *response* (the learning) pattern is repeated, the individual becomes conditioned to response and learning takes place.

Component Display Theory, proposed by Merill, classifies outcomes of learning in two dimensions - *Content & Performance.* According to this theory, each learning segment must have clear objectives and the selected content should be delivered in a planned manner using statement of rules, recall, attention-focusing devices, mnemonics and feedback.

Elaboration Theory proposed by Reigeluth, focuses on organization of content in terms of increasing complexity. It emphasizes that elaborations that relate to more than one single idea or concept are more effective in promoting learning. The theory emphasizes that at each step the learner should be informed about the procedure as a whole.

Information Processing Theory proposed by Norman, claims that the way an individual learns depends on his ability to select, encode and store information. The theory advocates the use of advanced organizers, instructional aids and cues to enhance learning.

Social Learning Theory proposed by Bandura, focuses on personality factors and the interaction amongst people. According to this theory, learning takes place through an individual's ability to observe and imitate behaviour. Most learning takes place through the three pronged interaction amongst, the *model,* the *learner* and the *environment.* This theory, indirectly recognizes the forceful role that media can play in enhancing learning.

Attribution Learning Theory proposed by Weiner, focuses on the different ways in which individuals understand events and messages. The search for understanding being the prime motivator in human behaviour, this theory lays a great deal of emphasis on motivation. Feedback from past achievements becomes a vital motivating factor.

Domains of Learning

In this context, it is also important to review input on the three major domains of learning. It was in 1948 that a system of using standard terminology for evaluating the goals of educational process and appraising learning was established. The three domins of learning were described as -

The Cognitive domain relates to acquisition of knowledge, information and other related intellectual skills.

The Affective domain relates to learning through emotions and feelings. Learner's interest, attitude and personal motivation become important.

The Psychomotor domain relates to learning skills through physical and motor controls.

Knowledge of these three domains and of the components involved becomes significant in the context of instructional media.

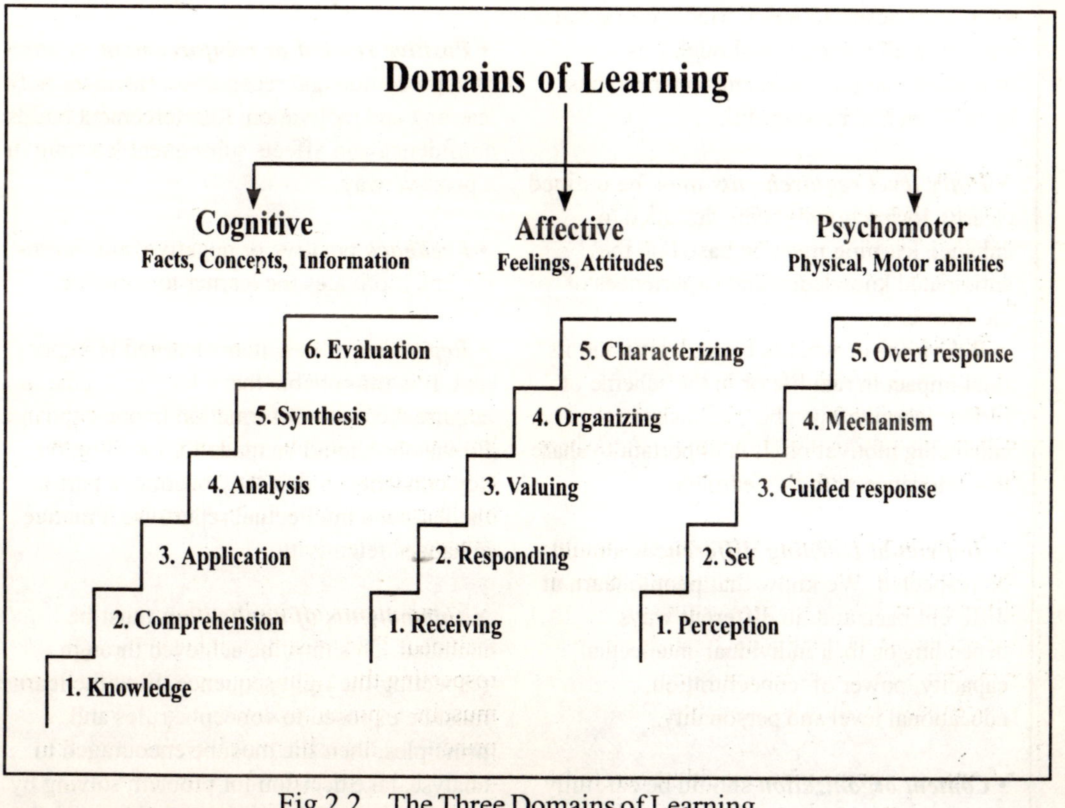

Fig.2.2 The Three Domains of Learning

RELEVANCE OF PERCEPTION, COMMUNICATION & LEARNING TO INSTRUCTIONAL MEDIA

A closer study of the various research findings related to perception, communication and learning provides certain important generalisation which are valuable while designing instructional media.

• ***Instructional objectives*** must be defined clearly as they come into play at several stages. The curriculum planners, teachers and the learners all need to be clear about the general as well as the specific objectives.

• ***Motivation*** is essential for learning. A learner is motivated when there is need, interest or desire to learn. Media can assist a teacher in all these areas though it is important that the media presentation must be relevant and meaningful.

• ***Entry level requirements*** must be defined clearly. Instructional media designed to enhance learning must be based on the anticipated knowledge and experiences of the learners.

• ***Relevance*** of what is being learnt and its final impact in real life or in the scheme of further learning must be established for enhancing motivation. It is important to share this relevance with the learners.

• ***Individual learning differences*** should be respected. We know that people learn at different pace and in different ways depending on their individual intellectual capacity, power of concentration, educational level and personality.

• ***Content organization*** should be carefully planned. Learning becomes easier when contents, procedures or physical skills to be learnt are organized in small meaningful segments. It is important to plan the flow of information in terms of complexity.

• ***Emotional involvement*** not only enhances learning but makes it more lasting. Instructional media can provide very powerful means of generating emotional responses. This aspect is equally important for motivation.

• ***Learner participation*** enhances learning and motivation. To learn, the information must be internalized. Participation enhances comprehension and retentivity.

• ***Positive reward or reinforcement*** in terms of appreciation and recognition enhances both learning and motivation. Reinforcement builds confidence and affects subsequent learning in a positive way.

• ***Feedback*** positive or negative, aids learning and motivates the learner to continue.

• ***Repetition*** of new items learned is important. It is improbable that a learner is able to acquire the entire information in one exposure. Provisions should be made for recalling the key concepts so that they become a part of the learner's intellectual repertoire. Practice enhances retentivity.

• ***Components of application*** must be included. This must be achieved through respecting the right sequence. First the learner must be exposed to concepts, rules and principles, then she must be encouraged to analyse, take decision for problem solving by applying the rules and concepts learned.

Guiding Learner Perception

Facts	Suggestions
1. Perception is relative rather than absolute	1. Break up information in small units 2. Provide pointers where the learner can attach new information
2. Perception is selective	1. Limit the breadth of information 2. Deal with one aspect at a time
3. Perception is organised	1. Use pointers & cues 2. Use listings
4. Perception is guided by expectation	1. Use advance organisers 2. Guide the learner to locate/ information and answers

Instruction and instructional media designed with the awareness of the fundamentals of *Perception, Communication* and *Learning* are bound to be more effective and efficient.

3

DESIGNING MEDIA FOR INSTRUCTION

Instructional Design defined

Elements of Instructional Design

Models of Instructional Design

Instructional Design & Teaching Methodology

Scripts and Storyboards

Types of Media: A Classification

DESIGNING MEDIA FOR INSTRUCTION

Any discussion regarding the design and development of instructional media must be preceded by a clear understanding of the term *instructional design*.

Instructional design refers to application of well-defined procedural steps for designing instruction and instructional resource materials. A number of related activities are involved which include: identification of objectives, formulation of instructional strategies, development of media-based components, evaluation of learning outcome etc..

Instructional design is meant to ensure effectiveness and efficiency of methods and materials used for delivering instruction. To achieve that it must incorporate inputs from theories of learning; fundamentals of perception, communication and learner motivation. The most effective way to study Instructional design, therefore, is through the *Systems Theory.*

The Systems Theory, perpounded by a biologist, Otto von Bertalanffy in 1968, broadly concerns with the 'organisation and structure of entire organisms'. It is founded on the exploration of *wholes and wholeness and their structure and stability.* The Systems Theory translates general principles into a procedure for application and finds wide applications in industry, business and education.

In education, the Systems's Theory has been modelled into a process called the ***Systems Approach***. The Systems Approach recommends application of rational procedures for designing instruction to

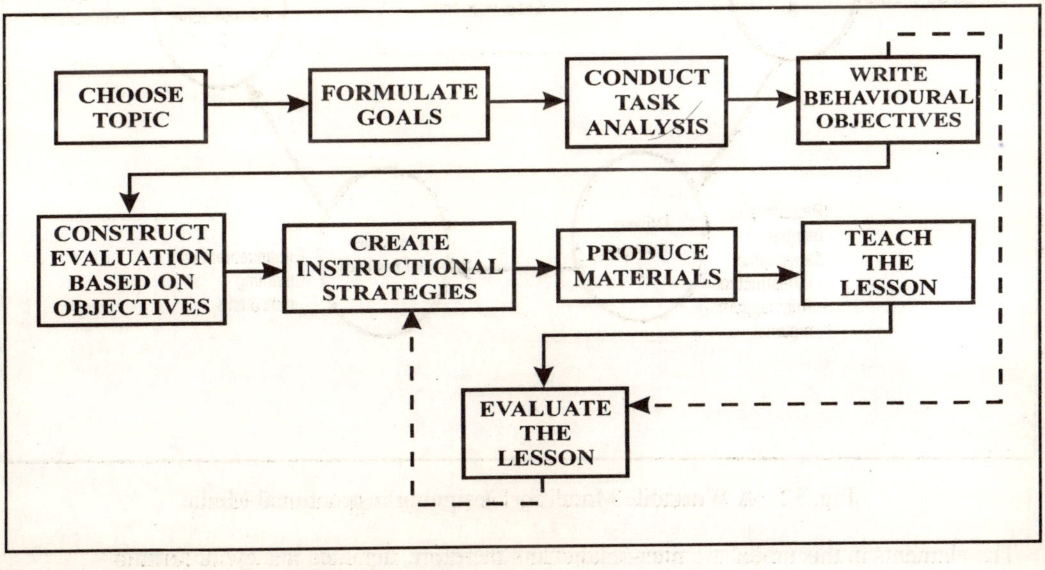

Fig. 3.1 Basic Steps to Designing Instruction

COMPONENTS OF INSTRUCTIONAL MEDIA

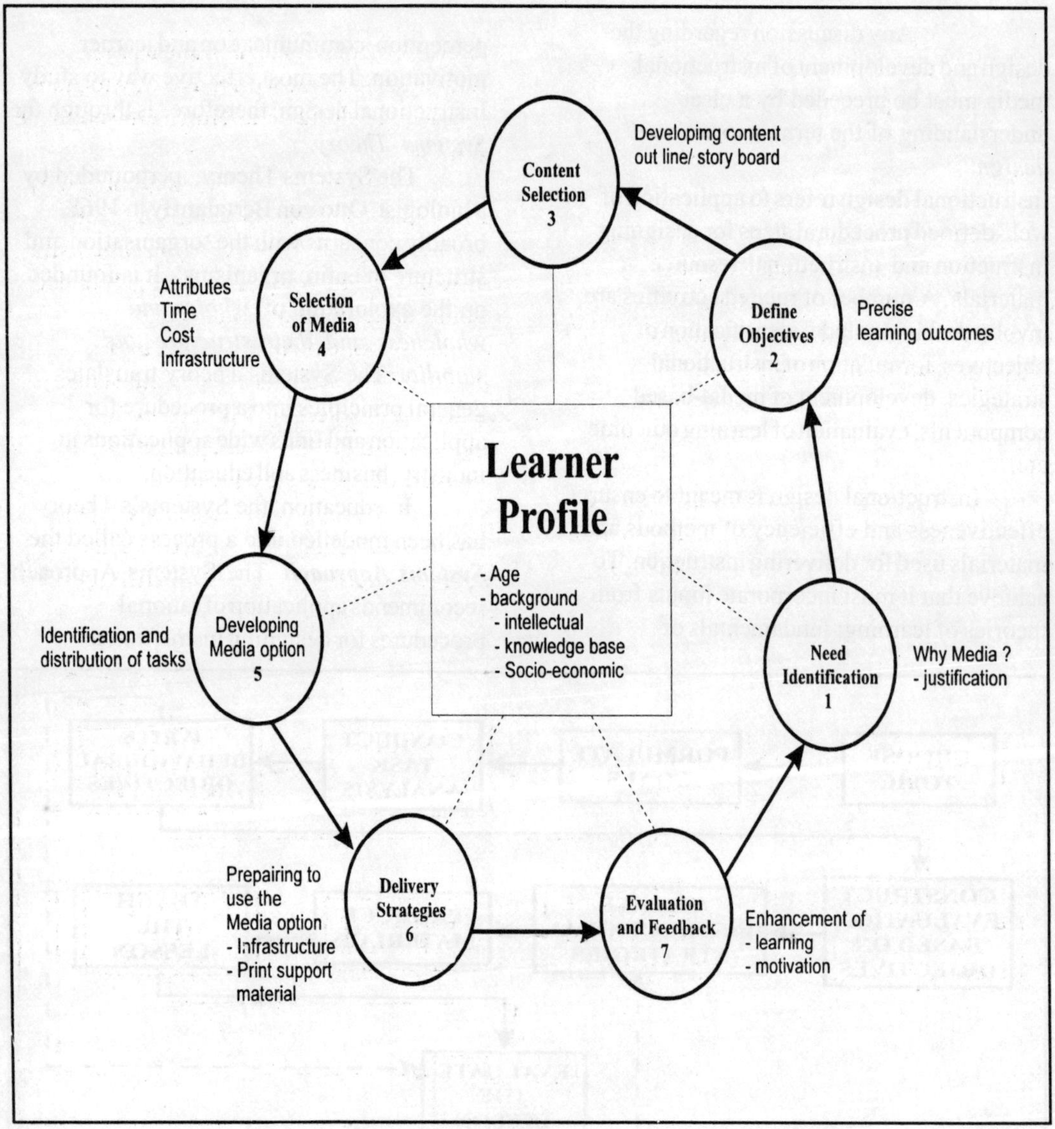

Fig. 3.2 A Workable Model for Designing Instructional Media

The elements in this model are inter-related and therefore, depicted in a cyclic form to indicate the ongoing nature of the various activities.

ensure attainment of specific behavioural objectives. *And, media becomes an important tool playing a pivotal role in the whole process.*

Instructional design does not always refer to an entire course, it is equally valid for a single unit or a module. Attention must be paid to specific learning tasks.

On the same lines is the **ASSURE MODEL** proposed by a group of acamedicians*. the acronym ASSURE stands for the six steps for designing instruction -

Analyze Learner
State Objectives
Select Methods, Media & Materials
Utilize Media and Materials
Require Learner Particpation &
Evaluate & Revise

While designing media-based instructional materials, it is important to keep in mind. not only the learner profile but also the mode in which instruction is proposed to be delivered. One must consider whether it is a -

* large group (lecture),
* small group (tutorial) or
* individual (self-paced study)

Other factors which must be taken into consideration are the availabilty of time and the availability of infrastructure both in terms of hardware and software.

But, irrespective of the model of instruction or strategy selected, the starting point is invariably the formulation of *instruction objectives* and one most begin with mastering the art and technique of writing them.

---

* Heinich R, M.Molenda, J.D.Russell, S.E. Smaldino, *Instructional Media and Technologies for Learning,* 5th Ed., Printice Hall, USA, 1996

Writing instructional objectives.

An *instructional objective* may be defined as a desired terminal outcome of an instructional programme, process or a resource material. Instructional objectives may be general or specific.

General objectives refer to information imparted for growth and for providing motivation. *Specific objectives,* on the other hand, aim at a defined learning outcome or *change in behaviour.* Obviously, a teacher is primarily concerned with the *specific* behavioural objectives. These objectives must be clearly written down using action- oriented verbs.

Verbs For Writing Objectives

...to be used	... to be avoided
list	comprehend
identify	get a feel of
draw	appreciate
define	understand
state	know

The principal advantage of using action verbs is that the objectives become *observable* and *measurable.* Instructional objectives must include three basic components:

a) the conditions under which the learner will learn (*on completion of* ..);
b) the expected performance (*will be able to ...);* and
c) the standard of the expected performance (*with percision etc. ...*).

Hence, the must accepted format for writing out instructional objectives - "*On completeion of these learning tasks, the learner will be able to .... with ...accuracy*" , has come to be universally accepted. A list of action verbs that a teacher can use for this purpose is given on the next page.

More Suitable Verbs for Writing Objectives . . .

arrange	analyse	apply	assemble	build	calculate	classify	choose
construct	compare	complete	compose	contrast	convert	demonstrate	deduct
define	derive	design	distinguish	explain	evaluate	estimate	fit
generate	identify	illustrate	indicate	install	label	locate	mark
measure	match	modify	multiply	name	operate	modify	plot

WHAT REASEACH TELLS US ...

MEDIA AND LEARNING

- While media-based component is important, sophistication of production (use of hightech special effects etc.) does not impact learning.
- Addition of music is appealing to the emotions but has little bearing on the instructional value of the media.
- Colour and dramatic presentation are good for gaining and sustaining attention but have no impact on actual learning.
- Simplified line drawings are equally, if not more effective than elaborate, shaded drawings.
- All action should be depicted the way a learner will see it while actually performing it.
- Lettering size plays an important role in the effectiveness of media.
- Narration/commentary should be in active voice rather than passsive voice generally used for writing.
- Generous use of subtitles, captions enhances and reinforces learning.

MEDIA & INSTRUCTION

* Media makes instruction more interesting.

* Media makes content selection more intelligent and better organised.

* Media optimises learning time.

* Media offers flexibilty of time and pace.

* Media improves the delivery of instruction and standardizes it.

* Media helps in extending learners' attention span.

* Media brings more satisfaction to the teacher.

* Media promotes retentivity.

* Media enhances the quality of instruction.

TEACHERS' GUIDE TO PLANNING INSTRUCTION & ITS DELIVERY

Although most teachers may not be involved in developing curricula, they still have a great deal of responsibility to design instruction at the delivery level. Every teacher must find her own best recipe. A simple and effective way may be to think of one's own favourite teacher and the startegies that worked well. These may be worth trying and even improving upon. Here are some general guidelines -

1. *Write out objectives*
This is fundamental. Objectives are critical at planning, teaching and evaluation stages. Objectives must be openly discussed and shared with the learners. This motivates them and optimises their learning effort.

2. *Go out of the way to understand the learner well.*
Expected entry level of a group is often very different from what it is in reality. An experienced teacher not only accepts these gaps but actually anticipates them. The pre-requisit level must be clearly indicated to the learner with an offer of additional help to the deficient students in the form of lists of books, tapes or other media-based learning material that the learner can use by herself,.

3. *Organize the content*
Break up the content into smaller units or learning points. Complex tasks should be broken up into simpler ones. The age old maxim of moving from "*the known to the unknown; from concrete to the abstract*" should be followed consciencíously.

4. *Give constant and immediate feedback*
The learner deserves clear, constructive and immediate feedback. This makes her more responsive and responsible for her learning.

5. *Design participative activities*
Effort made in this direction helps to stimulate thinking and works wonders for sustaining interest and extending the attention span of the learner. Demonstrations, group discussions and question sessions should become an integeral part of instructional planning.

6. *Include planned repetition and practice component.*
This motivates the learner and ensures proficiency of application.

7. *Organise content in terms of cue words or graphics*
This provides a hook for the new information to get linked to the existing cognitive map. This also facilitates retention and retrieval of information.

8. *Guide the flow of information*
Optimize the flow of information to the estimated comprehension ability of the learners. Extra rapid rate and high density of information leads to confusion while a slow rate of delivery often leads to decline in interest and frustration.

9. *Plan on using audiovisuals*
Visuals help to encode information effectively. They stimulate perception and promote schematisation, assimilation and retention. The interest of the learner is also sustained.

10. *Link information to real life experiences and examples*
This is the fastest way to assimilate and integerate new information. It implies that the teacher is fully aware of the learner's range of experience.

DESIGNING INSTRUCTIONAL MEDIA

Media meant to be used for instruction must be well planned, carefully prepared and then used effectively.

i) Planning:

Designing instructional media demands a great deal of planning. Planning is a structured procedure, requiring organization and logical sequencing of components to be taught. The components then must be integrated into a unified whole.

When one plans to develop some media-based resource material, the activity translates into answering a series of questions and taking valid decisions.

Some of the major concerns are -

- what are the the objectives to be served?
- what is the specific content to be treated?
- which medium suits the purpose best?
- what is going to be the planned sequences of visuals?
- What should be the format of the programme (story, drama, narration ...)?
- What is most appropriate - captions or sub-titles?
- Should there be graphics or photographs?
- Should anything else be included?

The inputs provided in the earlier chapters on perception, communication and laerning can help one to take these decisions.

To develop a useful resource of lasting value, one needs to put both *planning* and *creativity* into action. The two seemingly opposed processes are in fact, central to this activity.

Although most developmental work is planned, at times situations may arise that the work has to be done on the spot. In such situations, no original thought should be underestimated or ignored. Often the most unconventional ideas contribute significantly to the structure, appeal and effectiveness of the media being developed.To develop an effective and interesting media product, intermingling of both systematic planning and creative thinking becomes essential.

ii) Preparation:

Once all the questions have been answered and the initial planning is completed, one has to get started with the preparation for developing the materials.

At this stage, a different set of decisions need to be taken. It is important to decide how much investment in terms of money and time is justified; how much work should be done by whom; which are the areas in which expert help may be required.

The best way to begin here is to work out the different tasks involved and identify the the best person to do each one of them In the present age and times, it is often cheaper and more efficient to *outsource* i.e get work done commercially. These decisions are very important and should be taken objectively. For example, if you wish to develop a video clip/programme, typical tasks to be worked out will be -

1. Identification of content
2. Preparation of the scrtipt
3. Identification of format (documantary, drama, demostration etc.)
4. Identification of location/persons
5. Video recording
6. Editing
7. Generation of graphics/sketches
8. Narration
9. Validation

you will have to identify people or agencies who will take care of the different tasks.

The most important step in preparation of any media-based resource material is the development of a *Storyboard* or a *Script.*

Developing a Storyboard:

A **Storyboard** is a sequence of scenes, frames or units in which the desired media format is arranged for presentation. The technique essentially borrowed from the films, allows one to arrange and rearrange a whole sequence of small sketches or representations along with the verbal component.

Two fundamental components of media-based instructional materials are:

a. Visuals
b. The Story board

Designing and preparation of visuals will be dealt with in detail in the next chapter. Let us see what is a storyboard and how it is prepared.

In case of video or film production, a detailed **script** is prepared (page 144) which is like a storyboard with additional details and instructions for the cameraman/editor etc..

Several different methods can be used for developing a storyboard. The simplest one being the use of readily available index cards which can be procured from any stationery shop. Each card contains details for one frame or point.

These cards are then placed in the desired sequence on a flat surface such as large chart paper, cardboard or a folder. Once the cards are arranged, it becomes very easy to visualise the entire story. These can then be shuffled around or rearranged.

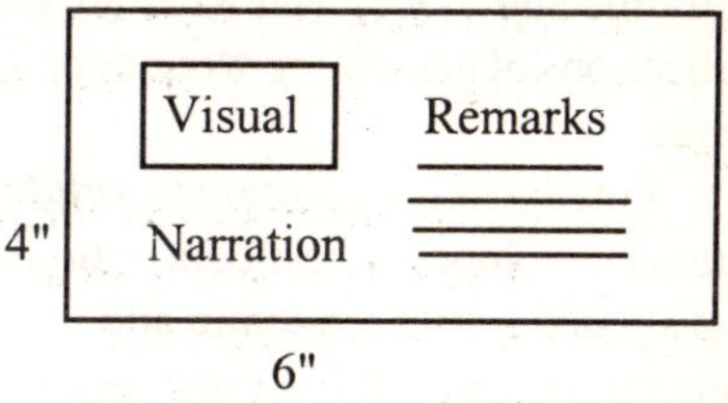

The Storyboard is like the blueprint of a building. It helps one to think clearly and take correct decisions. It saves time and cost, ensures continuity and puts the author/director in total command.

Now, an effective computer software - *Storyboarding Plus* is also available to facilitate the preparation of a storyboard.

Fig. 3.3 A Sample Storyboard Folder

Another advantage of preparing the storyboard is that the different tasks become clear and one is in a position to take decisions regarding identification of tasks and delegation of work.Often, it is cheaper and more efficient to *outsource i.e.* get things done commercially.

But, this also implies that the teacher should have a good idea about *where* and *how* to get things get done. She can only do so if she is sure of the precise requirements in terms of product specifications, availability of time and money and what are the implications of getting the work done from outside.

Finally, it is important to ***validate*** the material developed. The media option should be evaluated for its academic and motivational value. It is a good idea to preview the material with some colleagues mostly to identify areas which have not been included. It is always possible to create a handout to cover such points. The evaluation form provided on page 177 should prove to be very helpful for validating the media optiond developed.

iii) Using and Integerating Media with Instruction

Most often media options are used by teachers in an incidental manner. An instructor may decide to show a video clip or a set of 35 mm slides just because she happens to have one available with her. Or, a teacher may consider showing a film just to keep the group engaged. In such cases, media is hardly the learning tool it is meant.

The success of the media option lies in its effective use by the teacher. To begin with, it is necessary to review the instructional objectives. The concepts treated should be directly relevant to the objectives and should help in ensuring the learning outcomes.

A good practice is to prepare a pre-presentation plan which should outline the introduction, links, pauses and transitions. Focal points where questions should be asked or handouts should be distributed should be cearly worked out.

Questions must be invited immediately after the media option has been used. You need to be clear about the type of questions (closes/open ended) should be asked and what kind of feedback you are looking for. Good questions work wonders in promoting positive learning attitude.

To reinforce learning, it is always better to have some additional related follow up activity. These are also best planned at the initial stage and as an integeral part of the media.

Effective Delivery of Instruction

What a teacher should be sensitive about ...

* Quantum of information
* Flow of information
* Relevance of the examples
* Quality of media support
* Aptness of the media support
* Proficiency in using AV equipment
* Eye contact
* Voice modulation
* Pace of delivery
* Fluency in speech
* Effort to engage student participation
* Poise & Confidence

INSTRUCTIONAL MEDIA & MOTIVATION

One of the important functions of media is to motivate the learner. An effective and concerned teacher always tries to promote and sustain learner motivation. Motivation involves both direction and magnitude and its level is noticeable in the intensity of the learner's desire towards completing a learning task. While designing instructional media, special attention has to be paid to include cetain *motivation generating* devices.

Four key conditions have been identified for promoting motivation and the same are relevant when media-based resources are being designed. These are:

* Relevance
* Attention
* Expectancy
* Satisfaction

It is important to bring out the relevance of what is being taught. The learner should be able to appreciate the immediate and long term relevance of the content or skill being studied.

Motivation demands that the interest of the learrner is sustained throughout the instructional process. Media options prove to be excellent tools here.

A learner gets motivated by being involved in her own learning. It is important to share the instructional objectives as well as the strategies being adopted for achieving those objectives, with the learner.

Finally, motivation depends on satisfaction achieved by the learner in a given learning task in the specific environment.

To Enhance Learner Motivation ...

* Provide interest	- Move one step at a time (from the known to the unknown) - Use new events/example
* Maintain relevance	- Share objectives with the learner - Use simple language - Use concrete examples - Link to learner's range of experience
* Promote leaner expectancy	- Provide advance organisers - Provide prompt feedback
* Ensure learner satisfaction	- Provide reinforcement - Use constructive evaluation - Provide scope for personal achievement

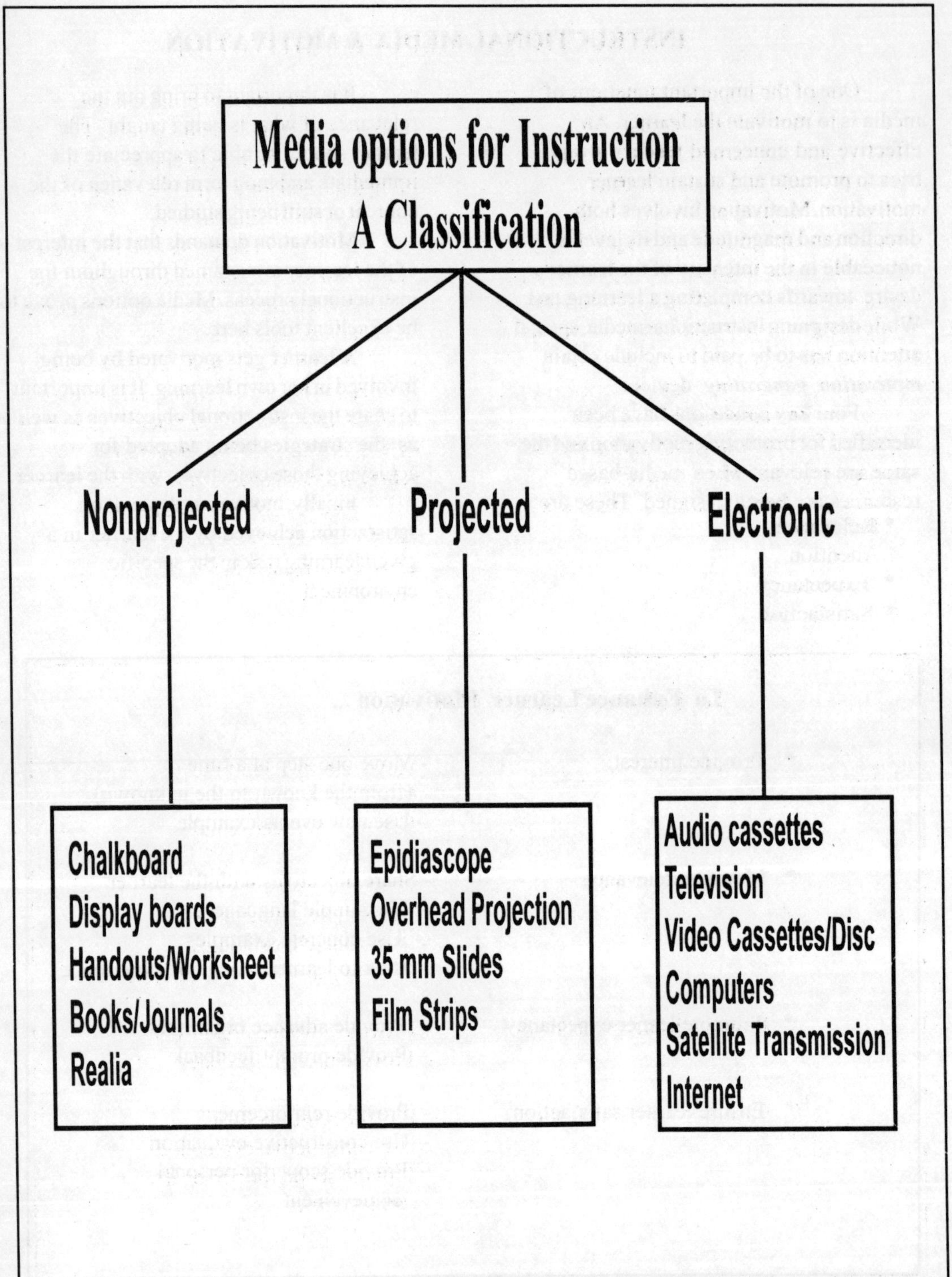
Media options for Instruction
A Classification
Nonprojected
Projected
Electronic
Chalkboard
Display boards
Handouts/Worksheet
Books/Journals
Realia
Epidiascope
Overhead Projection
35 mm Slides
Film Strips
Audio cassettes
Television
Video Cassettes/Disc
Computers
Satellite Transmission
Internet

4

DESIGNING & READING VISUALS

Visuality Defined

Functions of Visuals

Types of Visuals

How People Read Visuals

Tools for Creating Visuals

Designing Visuals for Instruction

Aspect Ratio for Visuals

DESIGNING AND READING VISUALS

Any discussion about media is incomplete and meaningless without comprehending and appreciating the real value of *visuals.*

Visuals in several different forms and formats fill the .the environment in which we live. We are surrounded by visual messages.Television, for example, is a potent channel for visual messages. The commercial world of advertisements, subtle or explicit, floods our lives with visuals. New technologies in printing have accorded visual attributes to texts in books, journals and newspapers.

In instruction, visuals play an important role. It is worth noting that only 83% of learning takes place through seeing as opposed to only 13% from listening . Moreover, people remember only 20% of what they hear as opposed to 50% of what they see. This makes the design and appropriate use of visuals an integeral part of successful instruction.

It is now commonly accepted that the two halves of the brain specialize in different functions: while the left side takes care of the linear, linguistic and rational; the right side processes the spatial, intuitive and holistic information. Evidence is also available to suggest that information aimed at both halves through text+visuals, aids the reader's comprehension, appreciation and retention.

Visuals and the Adult Learner

In instruction, we often associate visuals with young learners. Extensive studies have been undetaken on the impact of visuals on adult learners. They devised interesting experiments to test this and came up with some startling results. Their study showed that :

- Adults learn better when text is supplimented by visuals.
- They learn even better when they draw their own sketches or drawings
- Working with flow charts improves an adult learner's speed of performance and reduces the number of errors.
- Visuals help adults in problem solving

In instruction, the visuals do not have to be complex or sophisticated. They have to be well designed to suit a specific objective. Visuals in instruction can take different forms ranging from a plain sentence list to a table, a graph, a flow chart, an algorithm, a drawing, a scanned photograph or a complex computer graphic.

The importance of visuals has been formally recognised and a discipline *Visual Literacy* has actually emerged. The modern learner lives in a visual world and the ability to read, understand, create and analyse the p

Visual Literacy has been formally defined as the ability to perceive relationships or sense meanings; to be knowledgeable about such relationships and to be able to construct representations of these mental images. In other words, the skills an individual develops in interpreting, judging, responding to and using respresentation of reality results in what is called visual literacy.

The need for visual literacy is now gaining wide recoginition as is clear from the fact that a professional association - *The International Visual Literacy Association* (IVLA) now exists with its own set of journals and resource centres. Extensive research is being conducted in the areas of influence of visual processing system on the acquisition of knowledge, skills and attitude.

In instruction, visual literacy has become almost as important as print literacy and schools and universities now offer special courses in the discipline. The principal objective of visual literacy programmes is to introduce the learner to the concepts and skills related to interpreting visuals and communicating effectively through them. Learners are also encouraged to design and develop their own visual materials and to study and analyse different aspects of visuals .

> A visually literate learner is expected to :
>
> - Recognize and read graphic or photographic illustrations respresenting reality.
> - Sift and organize visual representation into patterns relationships that use the vocabulary of nonverbal visual expression.
> - Create and produce their own visual materials as an interpretation of reality.

To be visually aware, one requires to be familiar with the design principles and visual tools and elements of composition.

How individuals react to visuals is very interesting. A fact to be noted here is that *liking a visual* is not the same thing as *learning from a visual.* For example, most people prefer coloured photographs but are known to learn better with black and white drawings.

Encouraging a learner to be able to see and interpret visuals intelligently is an important concern of an aware instructor. The ability to *create* visuals is equally important. The learner has to be exposed to both the *encoding* and *decoding* skills.

Visuals are often viewed selectively. Cultural specificity is an important factor here. As the experiences and environments of people from different cultural backgrounds are different, their preferences in terms of patterns and impact are also different.

In instructional media, visuals can be created by using one or a combination of any of these three forms:

* verbals symbols .
* graphic and
* photographic,

Verbal symbols are descriptive in nature. *Graphic,* on the other hand are symbolic and artistic representation of reality. *Photographic* representations bear close resemblance to reality.

FUNCTIONS OF VISUALS

The mental pictures evoked to enhance comprehension and assimilation of the content, must be used by the teacher to facilitate her task. Visuals can be most useful in -

* Promoting Understanding
* Providing Motivation
* Providing Emphasis
* Summarizing
* Problem Solving
* Enhancing Retention

Visuals promote **understanding** by simplifying the verbal tangles. Often information presented in a long paragraph can become crystal clear by being presented through visuals.

Research shows that whenever information gets really complex the learner needs a non-prose alternative i.e. it is probably time to use a visual.

Visuals promote **motivation** by stimulating the learner's interest. They succeed in attracting and then holding attention. Visuals have the capacity to make dull material interesting. A teacher can identify major arguments, issues, themes or concepts for according special visibilty.

Visuals help to **Summarize** information. Long verbal descriptions can be presented easily through visual summaries which are more pointed and easy to remember.

Let us look at an example. Here is a description of the importance of the Public Relations Department in a typical firm.

A. The Verbal Description:

The Public Relations department in any major company is a very crucial link in the company's 'well-being'. Whatever the size or the nature of the business, most companies need to interact with several different sets of people.

First of all companies need to deal with people in the Government agencies such as the Departments of Revenue, Police, Commerce and Finance.

Then, companies have to deal with people in media. good press relations are vital and can increase sales while bad press relations can substantially hurt the sales.

The company also deals with people from the world of finance such as the banks, investment houses, brokerage firms and stockholders.

The company has to take care of general public. It's ultimate concern is about its reputation - what the public thinks of its products and policies.

Let us now try to summarize this information with the help of a visual.

B. *Visual Summary*

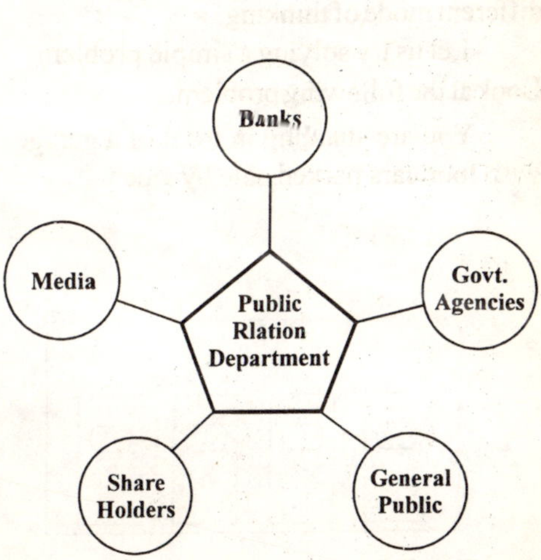

Fig. 4.1 The Public Relations Department in a Company

The visual is self-sufficient and does not require any explanation at all.

Visuals are excellent for **highlighting or emphasizing** the important points. A little time and effort spent in illustrating the key components or teaching points can be very rewarding for a teacher.

Visuals enhance **retention**. We know that in addition to words brain stores information spatially. So content presented in this mode becomes easy to retain and recall. The main purpose of Visuals, in words of graphic designer Jan White is, 'to catapult ideas off the page into the reader's mind.'

The most important function of visuals, however, is in **problem solving**. Once the information to be conveyed is translated into a visual, it becomes more explicit and hence more accessible for use. Scientists often report that their most important discoveries have come from visual insights while thinking about a problem. Words and sentences are not congenial to 'clear thinking' and graphic representations increase the learner's ability to use information. Visuals provide a different mode of thinking.

Let us try solving a simple problem:

Look at the following problem:

You are standing in front of a garage with four cars parked side by side.

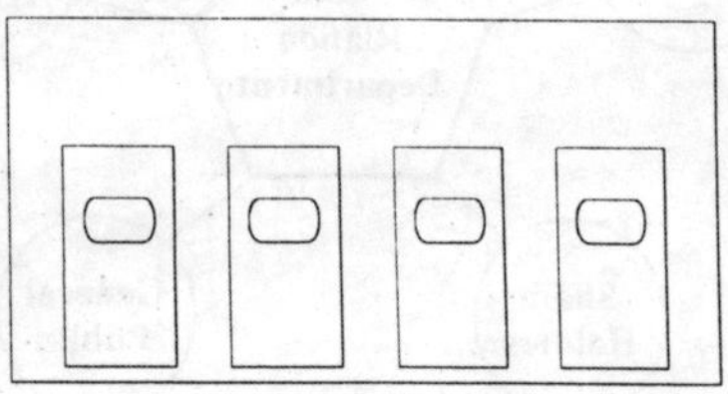

Fig.4.2 Visuals for Problem Solving

Using the information provided find out:

a) the colour
b) the make
c) the state of registration
d) the year of registration, and
e) the order in which they are parked

1. One of the cars is a 1965 model
2. The Maruti Van has a Haryana number plate.
3. The green car is from Punjab.
4. The Fiat is parked next to Contessa.
5. The Delhi car is between the 1991 and 1989 models.
6. The 1991 car is blue.
7. The Contessa is on the right (facing you)
8. The red car is from Bombay.
9. The Zen is parked next to the Van.
10. The car from Haryana is not parked next to the one from Punjab.
11. The Zen is green in colour.
12. The Contessa is a 1980 model.
13. The 1989 is from Bombay.

Could you have managed without using the visual?

TYPES OF VISUALS

Visuals do not always refer to large, bright pictures, complex drawings or photos. Text can also be represented visually. Visuals include -

- Sentence Lists
- Tables
- Graphs
- Line drawings
- Flow charts
- Algorithms
- Pictograms

Let us take an example and try representing it in different visual formats. This should also help in appreciating the criteria for choosing one format over the other. This is a message from the Transport Department -

If time is limited, send goods by plane. unless cost is a factor. In that case send them by train. When only cost is a factor, ship them by parcel post for distances under 500 kilometers and by State Truck Service for longer distances. When time and cost are not important factors use local Van Delivery Service for distances upto 500 kilometers. For distances longer than 500 kilometers, use the services of India Transporters.

Sentence List : refers to redesigning the message in short key sentences so that the reader can understand it quickly.

Sentence lists are very useful when decision-making is involved.

1. **Limited Time ?**
   Send goods by plane
2. **Limited Time & Cost?**
   Send goods by train
3. **Only Cost is Limited?**
   Use parcel post < 500 kms
   Use State Truck Service > 500 kms
4. **No Time or Cost Constraint?**
   Use Local Van Service < 500 Kms
   Use India Tranporters > 500 Kms

In comparison to the paragraph format, a sentence list is much simpler to understand and retain.

Tables: Once the criteria under discussion in the problem are identified, a table offers the most rapid retrieval time. Make sure all captions are brief and clear.

Choosing a Carrier

Table - I

Consideration	< 500 Kms	> 500 Kms.
Only Time is limited	Plane	Plane
Time + Cost are limited	Train	Train
Only Cost is limited	Parcel Post	State Truck Service
Neither Time nor Cost is limited	Van Delivery Service	India Transporter

Fig. 4.3 Information Displayed through Tables

Flow diagrams & Algorithms stand between prose and a picture. They contains words of prose and the spatial quality of a picture. Flow diagrams direct the reader to the desired information without having to sift through peripheral information. A ***Flow diagram*** helps the learner to comprehend the sequencing of an argument. An ***Algorithm*** is only an extension of the flowchart to the extent that the latter uses *if-then* or *yes-no* kinds of reasoning.

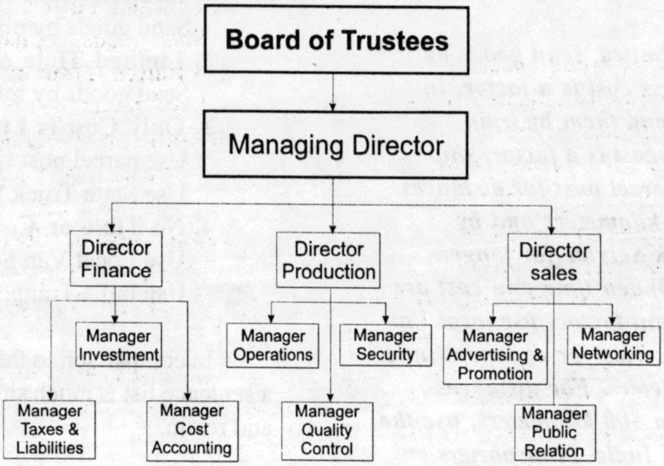

Fig. 4.4 A Typical Flow Diagram

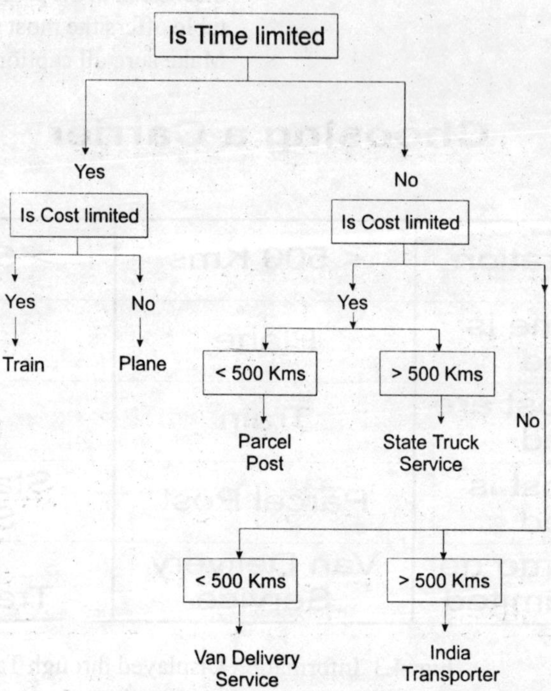

Fig. 4.5 An Algorithm for Choosing the Right Carrier

Pictograms are useful when the learner has low verbal abilities or when the information is being pesented to learners from a foreign country. Pictograms are of special value for mass instruction and young learners as pictures help in attracting and retaining attention. Pictograms are also very effective tools for motivating learners.

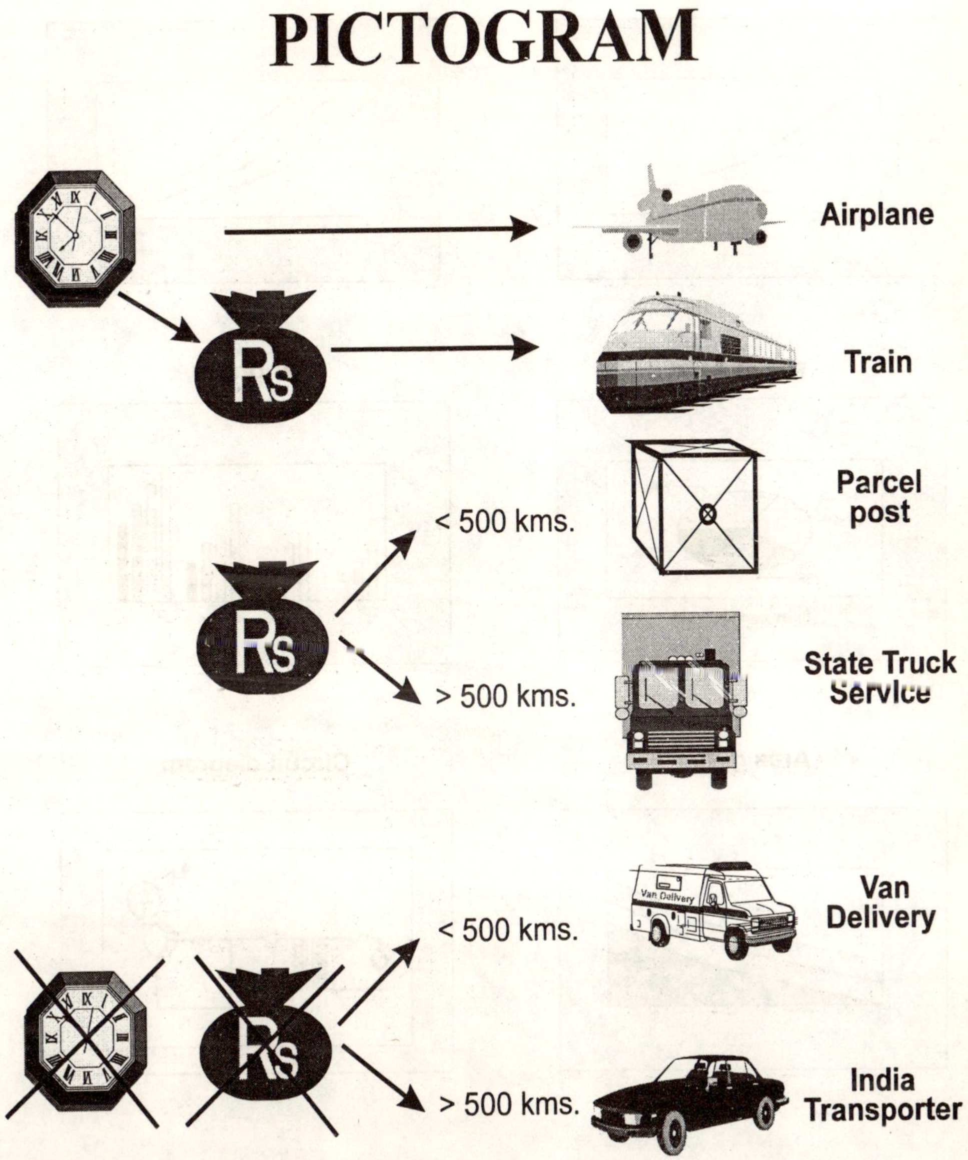

Fig. 4.6 A Pictogram to Represent the Choice of the Right Carrier

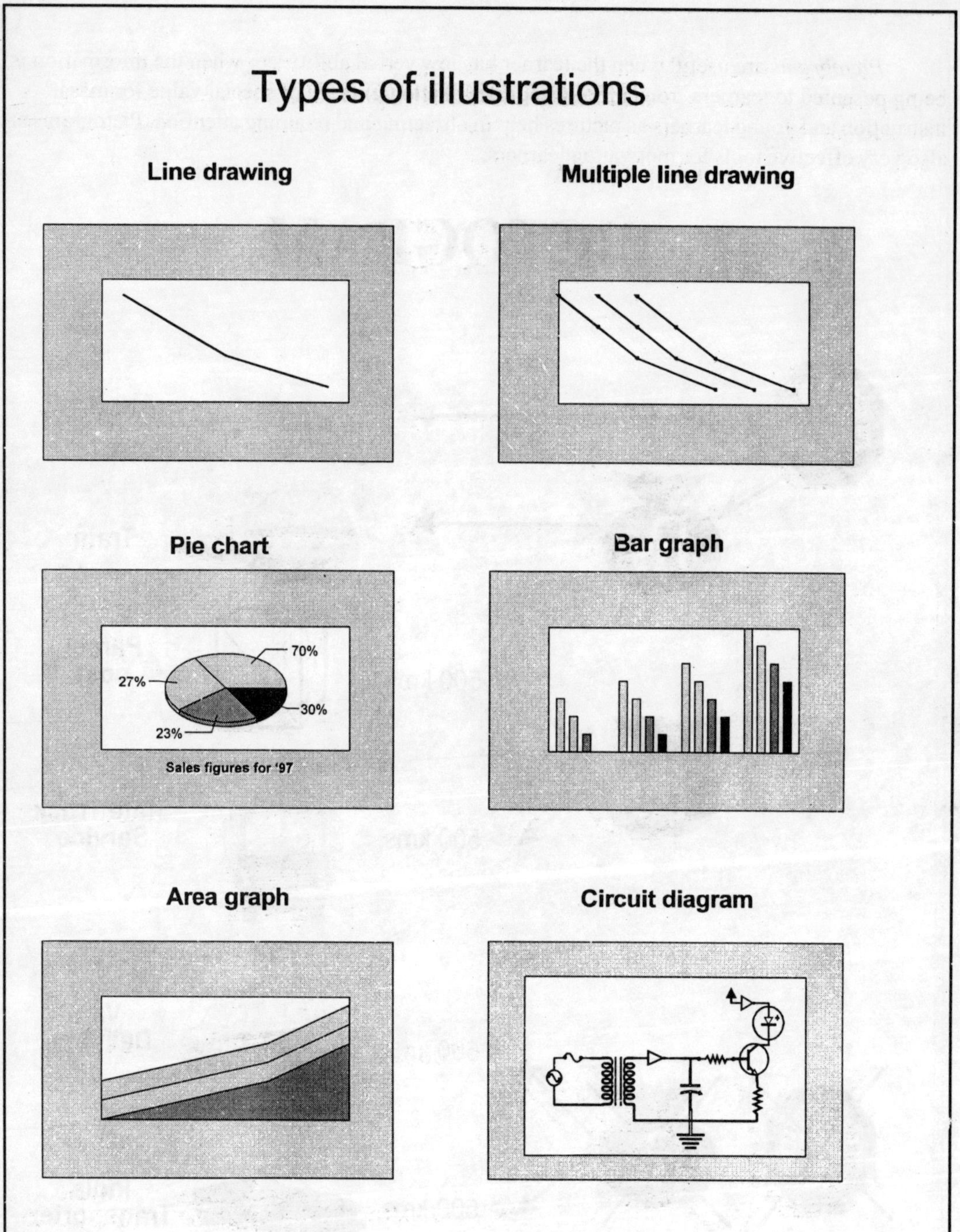

Fig. 4.7 Different types of Graphs for Illustrating Data

HOW PEOPLE READ VISUALS?

A number of factors intervene when an individual perceives a visual. While developing visuals one must kep in mind the manner in which people see and read visuals. Any teacher who is interested in developing media-based support material must keep this point uppermost in her mind.

The question has also been the subject of serious study. Two different approaches have been adopted. First, through the study of eye movements as different sets of people look at the same pictoral representation and second, through analysing learner response to the pictoral representations shown.

Some interesting findings reported in this area are:

* If text contains pictures, the reader first looks at the pictures.
* People with low mechanical ability to read learn better with pictures.
* Most readers tend to look first at the upper left hand portion of the picture.
* If an image is static, the reader loses interest shortly but if the image is changing denoting movement, the learner attention stays for a much longer period.

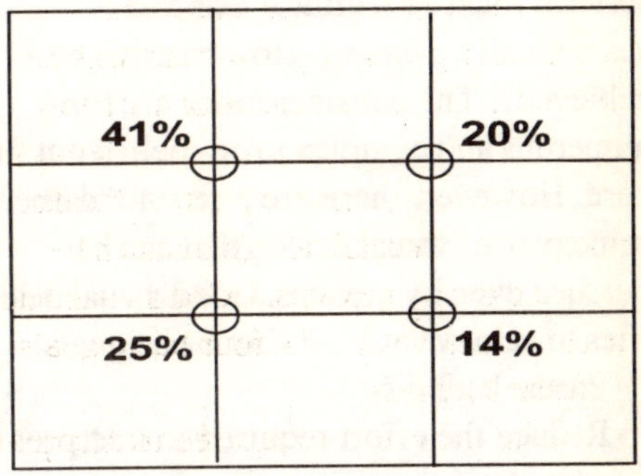

Fig. 4.8 The Rule of Thirds

If a visual were to be divided into 3x3 parts, maximum attention will be attracted at the intersections.

Fig. 4.9 How People See and Interpret Visuals

DESIGNING VISUALS FOR INSTRUCTION

Designing visuals for projected and non-projected media options involves management of several elements. Depending on the purpose the visual is expected to serve, it must be legible, clear and aesthetically pleasing. How can this be achieved? The considerations are too numerous and complex to be spelled out fully here. However, there are a few fundamental principles of visual design that can be pursued even by novices. Good visual design tries to achieve at least four basic goals:

- Ensure legibility.
- Reduce the effort required to interpret the message.
- Increase the viewer's active engagement with the message.
- Focus attention on the most important parts of the message.

Let us look at some of the key factors important for designing visual.

- **Simplicity** : While a large amount of information is acceptable in a manual or a report requiring detailed study, a visual needs to be compact dealing with one idea at a time. As a rule, lesser the number of elements laid out in a given space, the more pleasing will be the outcome. For projected visuals one should try to limit the verbal content to not more than fifteen words.
- **Unity** : It is essential that all different elements in a visual are laid out so that the visual is preceived as a whole. Unity can be achieved by using differnt visual tools such as lines, arrows, texture, shape & colour.
- **Balance** : A visual may be formally or informally balanced. Formal balance implies that the visual can be divided into two halves which are like mirror image of each other. Informal balance is more interesting and gives an impression of dynamism.

Fig.4.10. Informal & Formal Balance

- **Emphasis** : In addition to unity & balance, every visual requires some elements to be highlighted in relations to others. These must be clearly identified and emphasized with the help of visual tools such as shape, size, colour and space.

Visual Tools

Shape

A visual can be made attractive and interesting by using different shapes.

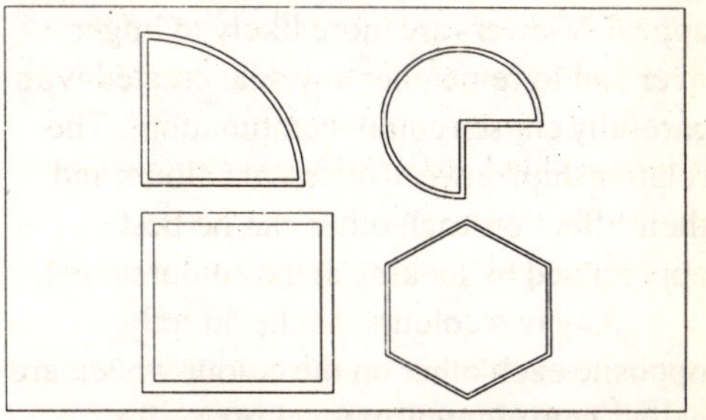

Space

Only when space is used carefully can the elements of design become effective. Open spaces around the visual and verbal elements facilitate comprehension by preventing cluttering.

Line

Lines in a visual assemble the different elements together and direct the viewer to study the visual in the intended sequence.

Texture

Texture is a visual element that serves as a replacement for the sense of touch. Texture like colour—can be used to provide emphasis, to separate elements, or to enhance unity.

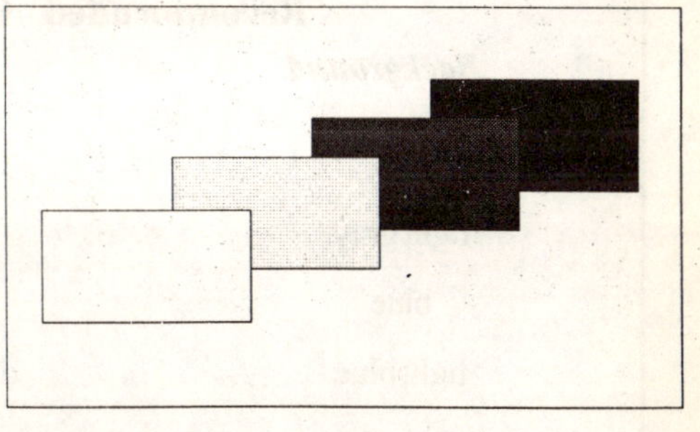

Fig. 4.11 Tools for Creating Visuals

The Use of Colours

Colours are powerful communicators. They have strong emotional and intellectual appeal. Viewers are more likely to linger over and to remember a visual created with carefully chosen colour combinations. The relationship between different colours and their effect on each other can be best appreciated by looking at the colour wheel.

Any two colours that lie directly opposite each other on the colour wheel are called **complementary colours**—for example, red and green or yellow and violet.

Complementary colours offer the best contrast so essential for highlighting or providing emphasis.

Colours that lie next ot each other on the colour wheel are called **analogous colours**—for example, blue-green, blue, and blue-violet. Analogous colours are more suitable to communicate depth or harmony.

When thinking about a colour scheme for a display, chart or a computer screen, it is necessary to think in terms of differnt colour combinations for *background, images* and *text.* Some suggestions are provided in the chart below.

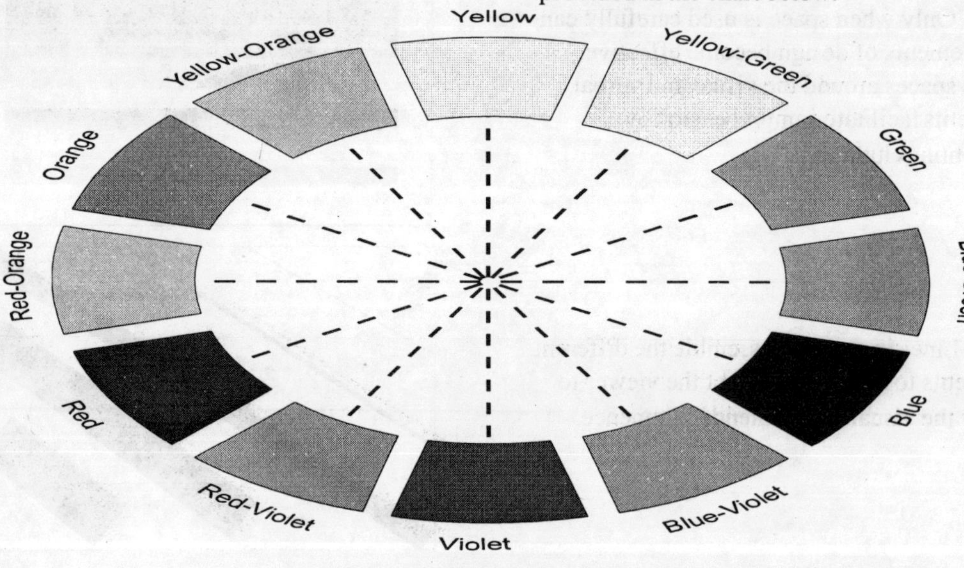

Recommended Colour Combination for Images and Text

Background	*Foreground*	*Highlights*
white	dark blue	red, orange
light gray	blue, green, black	red
blue	light yellow, white	yellow, red
light blue	dark blue, dark green	red-orange
light yellow	violet, brown	red

Fig. 4.12 The Colour Wheel and Recommended Colour Combinations

DESIGNING VISUALS - TIPS FOR READY REFERENCE

To Enhance Learning

- ❑ Use visuals as often as possible to explain complex concepts.
- ❑ Present a single concept in each visual.
- ❑ Break down complex visuals into simpler ones or build them up step-by-step.
- ❑ Minimize text on each visual.

Graphic/Picture Elements

- ❑ Create visuals that are neither too abstract nor too realistic.
- ❑ Eliminate distracting backgrounds.
- ❑ Use scale of common object to indicate size of unfamiliar objects.
- ❑ If feeling of depth is important, use another object to create the foreground.
- ❑ Use the "Rule of thirds".
- ❑ Avoid splitting visuals exactly in half with a horizontal or a vertical line.

Text/Lettering Elements

- ❑ Avoid using many different typefaces (styles of letters) on the same visual.
- ❑ Use features such as italics, boldface, underlining, or colour for emphasis.
- ❑ Compose text in lowercase lettering, adding capitals only for titles etc..
- ❑ Titles should be centered on top or bottom of the visual.
- ❑ Use short, concise, meaningful, descriptive titles that contain key words.
- ❑ Spacing between lines should be $1^1/_2$ times the word height

Choosing Colour

- ❑ Limit the number of colours on a visual.
- ❑ Use lettering and visuals that contrast with background colours.
- ❑ Use consistent background colours in a series of visuals.
- ❑ Use brightest and lightest colour to focus attention on important elements.

Layout of Visuals

- ❑ Make visuals as simple as possible; avoiding excessive details.
- ❑ Make sure your visual appears balanced.
- ❑ Lay your visuals horizontally particularly if they are to be used for overhead transparencies or slides.
- ❑ Use appropriate lettering size so that it can be read and seen comfortably.
- ❑ Leave sufficient blank spaces around the visual.

Proportions of Visuals

Finally, while designing visuals it is important keep in mind the required **aspect ration,** for each medium. Proportions for the most common forms of instructional media are given.

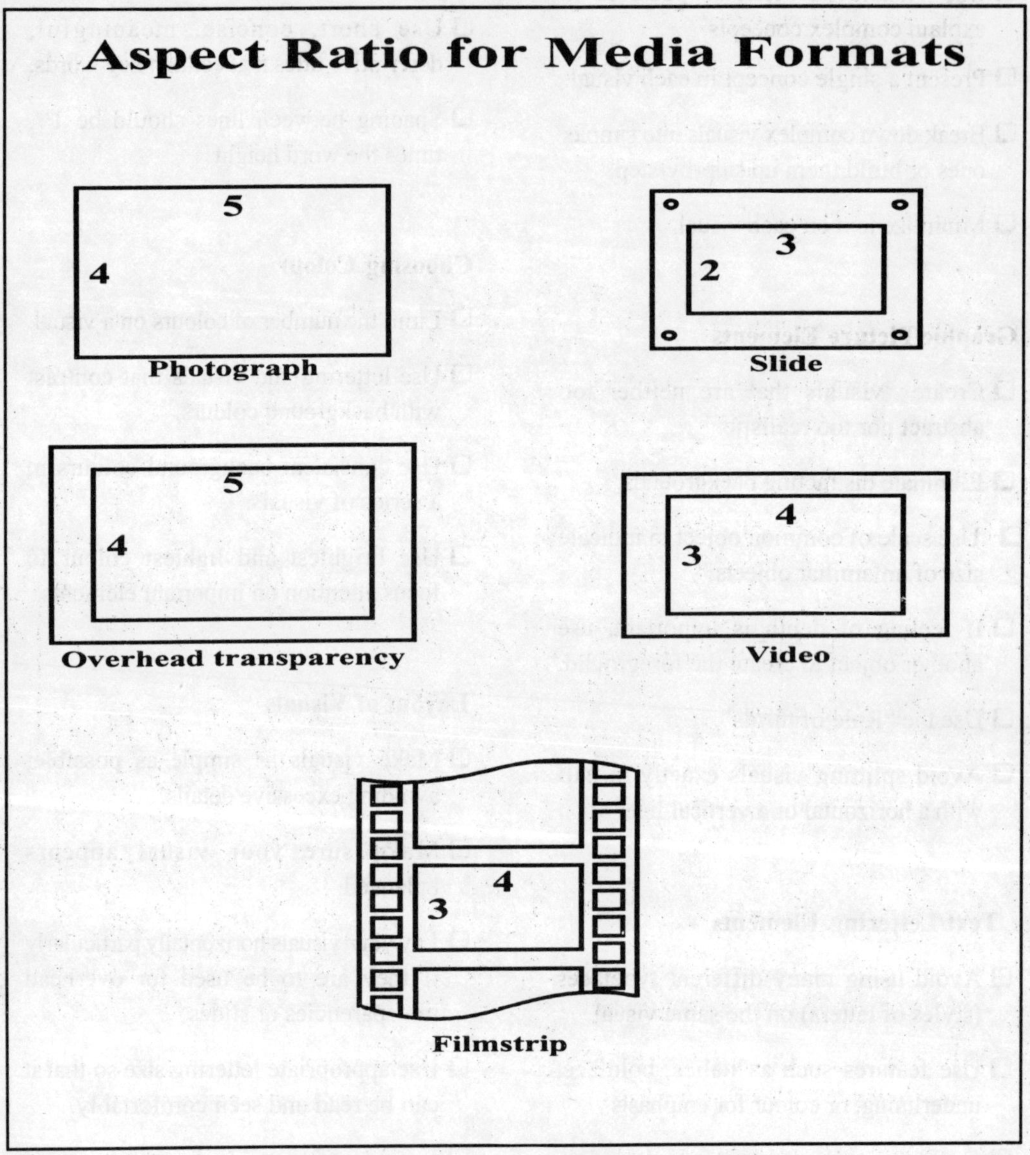

Fig. 4.13 Visual Aspect Ratio for Different Media Options.

5

NON-PROJECTED MEDIA OPTIONS

Types of Nonprojected Media Options

The Chalkboard

Other Writing Surfaces

Still Pictures

Charts and Flat Displays

Maps, Exhibits and Realia

Using Nonprojected Media

NONPROJECTED MEDIA OPTIONS

Nonprojected media options have sustained the teaching profession from the very beginning.

Eventhough advanced technology has somewhat overshadowed this category of media options, their instructional value must never be underestimated. Trends may change, gadgets may come and go but these basic, traditional learning supports are here to stay.

They have several strong points in their favour. They are cheap and easy to obtain; they do not need elaborate infrastructure and can be used without much fuss or pre-arrangements. A teacher can exploit her own creative potential to make innovative and interesting use of these options.

Non-Projected Media options include:

* The Chalkboard
* The Whiteboard
* Cloth boards
* Hook and Loop Board
* Bulletin Boards
* Still pictures
* Flip Charts & Maps
* Exhibits
* Realia
* Models & Mock-ups.

Each one of these support options is used for visual reinforcement. A teacher can use these media aids in many informal, yet dynamic ways. They are particularly suited for a small audience offering the opportunity for individual participation.

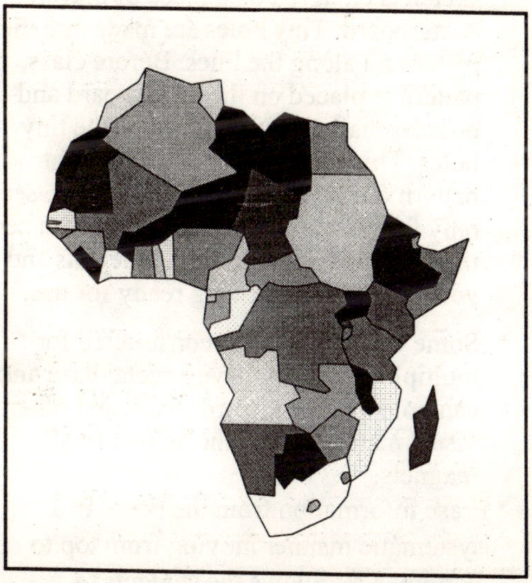

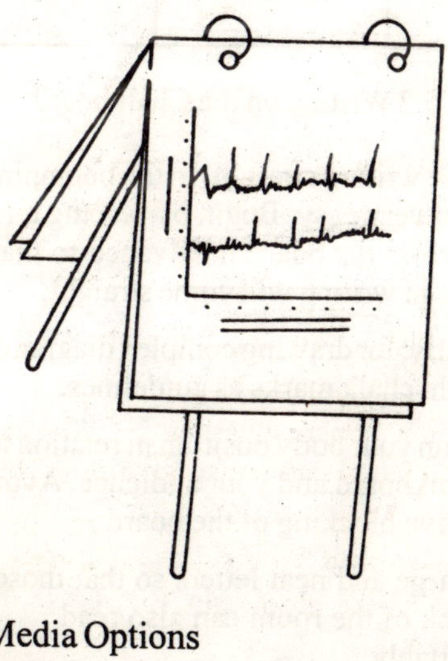

Fig 5.1 Some Nonprojected Media Options

The CHALKBOARD -

A chalkboard is a teacher's best friend, always there, waiting patiently to serve. It is a pity that most teachers and instructors take it for granted and do not use it to its full potential.

With a little pre-planning, the chalkboard can compete with any sophisticated media option. Chalkboards are not only useful as writing surfaces, they can also be used to dispaly materials like maps, posters etc.. For effective use, several things need to be considered - how much to write; where to place a particular information and how and when to erase it.

Using the Chalkboard

Here are some suggestions:

* Envisage the chalkboard as a partitioned surface to be used in a planned, systematic manner. The following divisions may be tried.

Visuals	Main Points	Material to be copied

Fig. 5.2 Writing on the Chalkboard

* Practise writing straight. In the beginning it is not very easy. Begin by placing a few dots across the board in advance so that the line of writing will come straight.
* Similarly, for drawing complex diagrams use light chalk marks as guidelines.
* Work on your body position in relation to the chalkboard and your audience. Avoid excessive blocking of the board.
* Use large and neat letters so that those at the back of the room can also read comfortably.

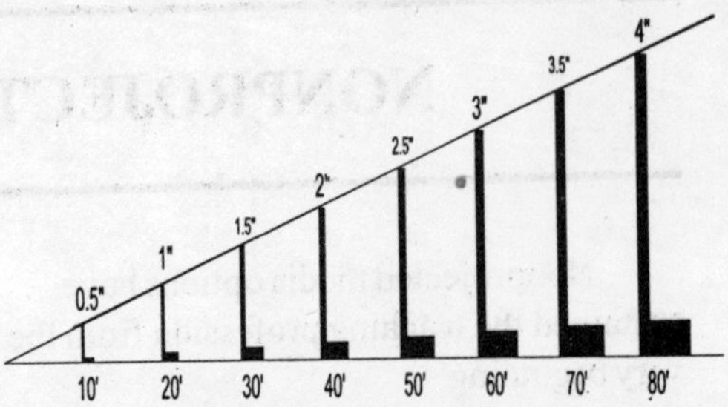

Fig. 5.3 Recommended Lettering Size for Nonprojected Media

* There is a recommended minimum lettering size for nonprojected media which is in relation to the class size. For example, for a classroom which is 10' long, the minimum lettering size should be 1\2".
* Use templates made of plywood or heavy cardboard for tracing frequently used shapes.
* Use coloured chalk to highlight important words or parts of a diagram.
* A major challenge is to make complicated drawings during the class. A commonly used technique called the *Pounce Pattern* may be helpful. The selected drawing or sketch is enlagred on a piece of thin posterboard. Tiny holes are made into this pattern all along the lines. Before class, the pattern is placed on the chalkboard and pounce chalk is dusted through the tiny holes. This method leaves a very light pattern on the chalkboard that can be seen only from a close distance. When you need the drawing, simply connect the dots and you have a neat drawing ready for use.
* Some chalkboards are constructed for multiple use. They have a metal base and can hold pictures, word strips, and other visual materials with the help of small magnets.
* Erase information from the board in a systematic manner moving from top to bottom. This allows the students to complete taking notes and the dust is directed downwards .

THE WHITEBOARD -

Sometimes also called a *markerboard* or a *multipurpose board*, the whiteboard is used with special felt pens and erasers. These boards can be erased just like chalkboards but have the added facility for displaying bright, colourful visuals like maps and charts with the help of small magnets. Whiteboards provide a neat, dust free teaching environment and therefore, are specially useful in computer laboratories, language laboratories and other areas where chalk dust would be a problem.

The latest addition to the family of whiteboards is the *Copyboard* or an *Electonic Board* - a board which offers the magic facility of giving a photocopy of the writing on the board by just pressing a button.

Using Whiteboards -

* Most whiteboards are magnetic and can be used to display bright colourful cut outs and posters with the help of small magnets.
* When writing on a whiteboard, print letters which are large and legible.
* Use colours as an effective communication tool.
* Place the board high enough and in a carefully selected position, so that it is easily seen by all members of the audience.
* Keep your message simple. Limit the information to one concept at a time.

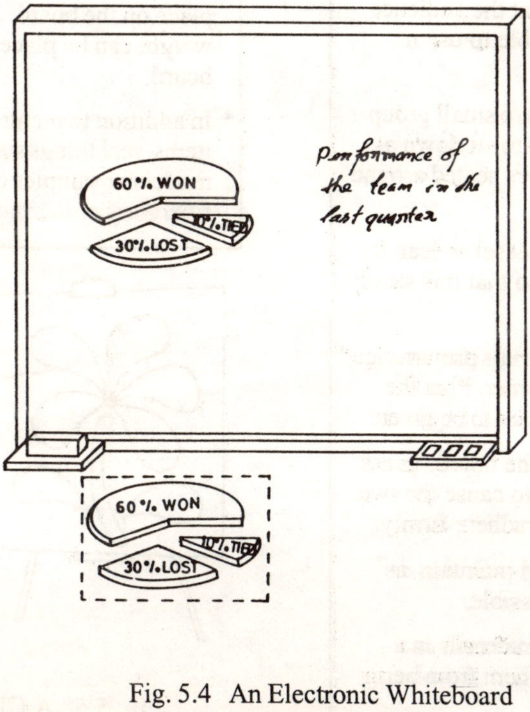

Fig. 5.4 An Electronic Whiteboard

THE CLOTH BOARD

Also known as the *Felt and Flannel Boards*. Here, visual materials are made to adhere to the fuzzy surface of the felt, or flannel board with the help of appropriate backing material. A variety of materials such as sandpaper, felt , styrofoam, blotter paper and yarn can be used as backing material. To provide maximum stability, cover the entire back surface of items to be displayed on the board.

Even though many people think that Clothboards are suitable only for children, they are found to be effective for audiences of any age.The ability to move visual materials around easily on the surface makes this medium very popular for instruction involving sequenced steps.

Using a Cloth board -

* Position the board so that the audience can see it and you are able to use it comfortably.
* Felt and flannel boards are small group media so you may want to sit down as you present, with learners seated around in a semicircle.
* Secure the board on an easel or lean it against a solid surface so that it is steady during the presentation.
* Have your display materials pre-arranged in proper presentation order. Plan the handouts or questionnaires to be given.
* As you place items on the board, press them against the cloth to cause the two surfaces to interact and adhere firmly.
* Talk to the audience and maintain as much eye contact as possible.
* When not in use, store materials in a marked box to prevent them from being damaged.

THE HOOK AND LOOP BOARD -

A Hook and Loop board is used in similar fashion as the felt and flannel boards. The material used is easily available and is called *Velcro* which is generally seen in fasteners on shoes and clothing.

A hook and loop board is covered with velcro and a bit of velcro is adhered to the back of the instructional materials to be displayed on the board. It only takes a small piece of velcro to provide enough holding power to keep heavy materials on the board.

Using Hook and Loop Board -

* The Hook and Loop board can be used exactly like any other dispaly board.
* Velcro is available in rolls with adhesive on the back. It is very easy to cut a small piece, peel off the protective paper and stick it to the back of the item you want to place on the board. Surprising amounts of weight can be placed on a hook and loop board.
* In addition to pictures and posterboard items, real things such as tools, small models or samples cut outs of plyboard, fiberglass or thermocol can be displayed.

Fig. 5.5 A Clothboard

BULLETIN BOARD -

Bulletin boards, though not used directly in teaching are a very important part of the instructional infrastructure and serve as effective supplement aids.

Initially designed to post information and general announcements, the bulletin boards can be used to achieve multiple instructional objectives.

While designing material for the bulletin board, ask yourself :

- Will it attract attention?
- Will it hold attention while the message is being read?
- Will the message be understood in the first reading?

Placement of a bulletin board is critical. An effective location is just opposite the main door to the room where instruction is to be imparted. The best way to catch the eye of the learner is to use good design and appealing graphics.

It is important to change the board as often as possible because it loses its attraction after people become familiar with the display. Sometimes, it is appropriate to leave a board blank for a period of time, so when you do display something effectively, it is really noticed and appeciated.

Using a Bulletin Board-

* Before designing the display on the bulletin board, decide about the actual objective. If it is meant to impart specific information then maximum amount of information should be included without cluttering up the display.
* Some boards are designed to motivate the learner and to provoke desire to seek additional information on a subject. It is a good idea to use a motivational board to create curiosity prior to beginning a new topic
* Production of a bulletin board is time consuming so you should preserve the materials so that they can be used again. Between uses, a good storage and filing system should be devised so that the life of the material is extended.
* Use information provided on visual design, layout provided in the previous chapter to, create high quality displays.
* Select three-dimensional objects or create a three-dimensional appearance from flat pictures by raising them from the surface.
* Engage the attention of the viewer with a question, a guessing game, a contest of skill, or by offering something to be picked up and taken away.
* Use attention-getting devices like an unusual design, striking colour combinations, a startling or unusual leading statement, or moving parts on the board. It is possible to show movement by attaching a motor run on small batteries.
* As far as possible, use visuals in place of words.

STILL PICTURE -

Well-mounted sketches and large still pictures continue to be a popular learning support material, particularly for teaching young children. These are also very useful in non-formal adult education programmes.Still pictures are generally used with small groups of learners.

It is possible to obtain sets of commercially produced still pictures, but these should be carefully evaluated for quality and relevance. Pictures should be chosen to meet specific instructional objectives. Still pictures also serve as great motivational tool and can be used creatively to conduct a quiz or a test.

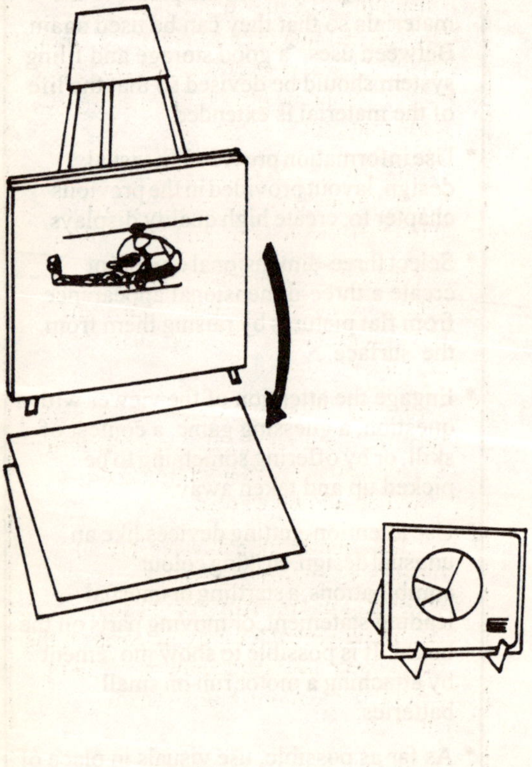

Fig.5.6 Using Still Pictures

Using Still Pictures -

* Ensure that the size of the pictures is large enough for the group viewing them, particularly, if you intend to display them in front of the room.
* Acquire an easel to display the pictures. Free standing or table top easels are available. Ensure that the easel is high enough to allow for unobstructed viewing by the learners.
* If the pictures are small, they may be passed around among the learners for close inspection. However, count for the time delay and potential distraction that this will create.
* A good utilization technique for a series of still pictures is to mount them all on a standard sized poster board. Stack them in correct order and place all of them on an easel. As you finish discussing a picture, simply flip it down onto a table in front of the easel.
* It is a good idea to have your teaching points noted on the back of each picture to serve as cues. While teaching do not hide behind the picture, hold the picture up high, to your side and out in front of you. This technique contributes to a professional presentation and eliminates holding notes or glancing down to see them.

FLIP CHARTS -

Flip Charts comprise a pad of chart size paper fastened together at the top and mounted on the easel. Flip charts are ideal for displaying maps, graphs and charts to a small group. It is possible to use them in combination with slides and transparencies. Flip charts are equally useful for both pre-prepared materials and for spontaneous writing using felt pens.

Like whiteboards, flip charts are very neat and offer a dustfree environment.

Using Flip Charts -

* Stand to the side of the easel facing the audience. If you use it regularly, the flipchart is worth spending the time and effort to practise standing to the side and reaching across so that your body blocks as little of the writing area as possible. Talk to the audience, not to the easel.
* Lettering on flip charts should be large, legible, and kept to a minimum. Printing is preferred to cursive writing.
* Use felt pens with a broad tip to ensure legibility.
* Consider coloured felt pens to design your message so the audience can follow it with ease.
* If cross references need to be made to charts already shown, these may be torn from the pad and taped to the wall at the side of the room.
* Flip charts, prepared in advance and shown as and when required, save time.
* You can put small, lightly penciled cues or notes on the edges of the charts, which can be seen only by you. This frees you from having to hold notes in your hand and allows you to be more mobile.

EXIHIBITS -

Exhibits refer to a display system which incorporates various media formats such as realia, still pictures, models and graphics assembled to form an integral whole. Display materials are attached to a backing surface called the *vehicle* using screws, glue, or nails. The vehicle can be almost anything ranging from plywood, cellotex, formica, rope, fish line, mesh wire to thermocol. Exihibits are generally designed to be taken apart and packed for travelling.

Using Exhibits -

* Exhibits should be considered only in situations where the materials are of continuing value and can be used with different sets of audiences.
* If the exhibit is not a free standing type, it should be attached to the wall at eye level.
* Exhibits are excellent for displaying real objects and specimens.
* Value addition to the exhibits can be made by illuminating the entire exhibit or some selected portions of it.
* Exhibits should be placed strategically to catch maximum attention.
* Exhibits should be displayed in one place for sufficient amount of time to attract widespread attention.
* Slides can be projected along the exhibits.
* If required, sound can be included easily by placing an audiocassette player containing a continuous loop tape which is played by the visitor..

REALIA -

Realia is a term loosely used to cover real object and materials used for instructuional purposes. Historically speaking, they are the original instructional materials. Instructors have always used realia to illustrate and teach. Whether rocks used for teaching geology or a gear assembly used by an auto training instructor, realia remains the best kind of instructional resource a teacher can use.

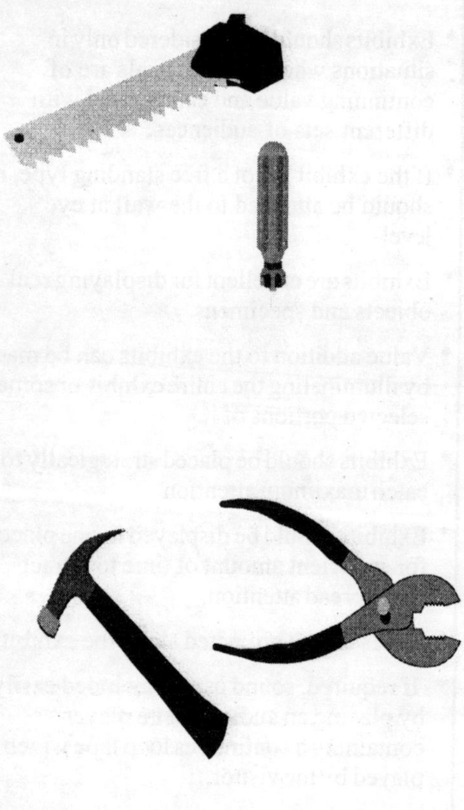

Fig. 5.7 Teaching with Realia

Using Realia

While using realia, ask the following questions:

* Does the real object truly show the concept being taught or would some other form of media be better?
* Is it too heavy and cumbersome to carry and hold?
* What safety precautions are required to secure the object and protect the learner.
* Can the real object be seen clearly by the audience. If the item is too small to be seen can it be passed around?
* Can the object be dispalyed on the board and the coding, labels and arrows be added in view of the class?
* Would it be better to open up the object and show it to the learners. If yes, are necessary arrangement available for doing so?
* Are pictures, handouts, questionnaires required to improve the instructional impact?

MODELS & MOCK-UP -

Models and mock ups are fascinating instructional materials with great teaching potential. With models and mock ups, you can allow the learner to examine things which are difficult to see in the reality.

Models are designed to be an exact replica of the real thing, The size may be smaller or larger depending on the intended use by the teacher i.e whether it is to be displayed from a distance or passed around for closer examination by the learners. Often models are constructed in clear plastic so the learner can see the inner workings of the item being studied.

A **Mock-up**, on the other hand, is designed to exaggerate certain selected aspects of the real object for instructional purposes.

It is generally difficult to create your own models. As models and mock ups need to be highly accurate in technical detail, it is generally better to procure them commercially.

Fig. 5.8 Model of a Piston

Using Models & Mock ups
Some guidelines:

* Because models and mock ups are expensive, care should be taken to store them properly.
* When using them, be sure they are secured to a surface and are placed so they can be seen by the audience. Also, you should be able to show and operate them comfortably.
* Normally, you will need to ask the learners to gather around the model or mock up. Pre-arrange an area for this activity to avoid unnecessary confusion and distractions during the presentation.
* For a very large group, it may be a good idea to use a videocamera to capture close-ups of the model and project them through a television or a monitor.
* If the model or mock-up is a functioning one, allow the learners to handle and operate it. This creates high interest and permits a close observation of the concept being studied.
* After the presentation, it may be appropriate to leave the model or mock up on display for a period of time, allowing learners to independently study it.

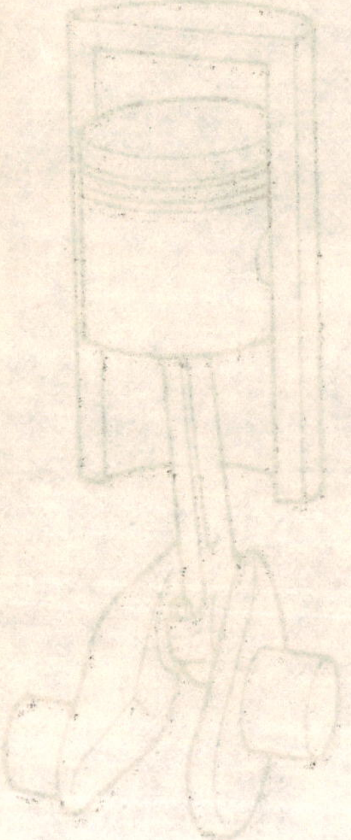

6

THE PRINT MEDIUM

The Print Medium in Instruction

Designing Print materials

Elements of Page Layout

Using Artwork and Photographs

Fundamentals of Desk-top Publishing

Handouts: Types, Design and Use

THE PRINT MEDIUM

No instructor can survive without using some kind of print support material. The volume and the complexity of the printed materials used can vary from a single-sheet handout to a set of notes to a work book. Like other media, the printed materials can be used for instruction, information, or motivation.

The print material may consist entirely of words (*handouts*), illustrations (*guide sheet)*, or live pictures (*picture series*).

Instructional materials in print format may include :

* Guide sheets
* Job aids
* Picture series.
* Handouts
* Worksheets
* Study guides
* Instruction manuals.
* Brochures
* Newslettters
* Reports.

Even though certain elements related to planning and preparation are common to all of them, each of these aids is different in format and is designed to serve a special instructional purpose.

Guide sheets, Job aids, and *Instruction Manuals* are training tools designed to provide step by step instructions for acquiring a skill or performing a task. For example, the objective, may be to provide instructions for assembling and then operating equipment, troubleshooting, maintaining or operating. The information and directions provided must be specific, simple, and clear because most often they are used by a learner, a new employee or a technician who is expected to work independently without supervision.

Handouts, Worksheets, Study Guides, and *Picture series,* on the other hand, are more academic in nature and provide directions, information, and activitities for various instructional purposes.

Whereas a *handout* briefly treats a limited portion of a topic, a *study guide* contains more details. Both are designed to be learner or trainee centred and should contain information about the content as well as the methodologies to use the information provided. Picture series, on the other hand, are often used to focus on the sequence of activities to be performed by the learner.

Designing an effective instructional aid in print form is not as simple as it may appear to be. It is a specialised activity requiring motivation and some training. With the advent of new electronic tools fror printing, it has become equally important for a teacher to have some knowledge about the potential and operation of these tools.

DEVELOPING PRINT MATERIALS

While developing print support materials, the three stages of *planning, preparing* and *using* the media need to be carefully worked out.

Planning Checklist:
When you have decided to develop some form of printed media, begin with this checklist :

* The objective to be served by the proposed materials.
* The nature of the intended audience or learner group who will read or learn from the proposed materials.
* The type of printed media to be designed and produced.
* Funds available for production and duplication of the printed media.
* The time available for preparation of the proposed materials.
* The number of copies required.
* The proposed mode of utilisation.
* The essential information or subject content to be communicated in terms of the objectives.
* The equipment required for the production of mateials.
* The manpower required.

Once these questions have been satisfactorily answered you are ready to begin.

Preparing Materials

Two distinct activities are involoved:
1) Preparation of text, and
2) Production of materials.

Preparing Text

The quality of the final product of printed material will depend, to a large extent, on the care and competence with which the text is written. Professional writing experts recommend the 7 Cs of good writing.

Good writing must be:
- Correct
- Clear
- Concise
- Complete
- Consistent
- Coherent
- Courteous

Effectiveness of writing can also be evaluated in terms of its *readability* and *ease in understanding.*

To test readibility, one can apply the readability formula which is discussed in detail on the next page.

Whatever the topic, the success of writing depends on how easy it is to understand. One must develop the competency to choose the right word. In addition to the normal meaning, words carry strong connotations which must be attended to because they can be easily misinterpreted for intention and attitude.

Words must be chosen for *correctness* and *effectiveness.* On the whole, prefer the familiar word to the unfamiliar one; the shorter word to the longer one and the positive word to the negative one.

The Readability Formula and the Fog Index

Readability depends on word choice, sentence length, sentence strructure, organization and the messages's physical appearance. The most common readability formulas measure the length of words and sentences to give a rough idea of how easy your writing is to read and understand. The formula expresses the difficulty in reading in terms of *Fog Index.*

Edward Fry (1968), one of the well-known reading experts, has worked out the following formula for acertaining the grade level difficulty.

Age	Grade	Sentences per 100 words	Syllables per 100 words
9-10 yrs.	4	7.5	124
12-13 yrs.	7	5.0	138
14-15 yrs	9	4.3	148
16-17 yrs.	11	4.3	154
18 +	12 +	4.0	162

How to calculate readability

Let us work with a sample paragraph:

A thirty-four clause charter explains the principle of equity and mutual benefit in international economic and technological relations and the sovereign right of every State to choose its own economic, political, social and cultural system. The charter stipulates that each State must have the right to regulate and supervise the activities of transnational corporations under pertinent circumstances. The charter emphasises the importance of correcting imbalance between the developed and developing nations. The affluent nations feel that some of the provisions of the charter are premature while others are too sweeping. The developing societies can in their turn complain that the affluent States are the real beneficiaries in the long run.

To calculate the *fog index* of this paragraph follow the given steps.

Step 1 - Calculate the number of words in the sample paragraph = **109** words

Step 2 - Calculate the number of sentences = **5**

Step 3 - Work out the average no. of words per sentence = (35+22+14+19+20) ÷ 5 = **22**

Step 4 - Calculate the percentage of long/difficult words = 14 - 109 = **13%**

Step 5 - Work out the *Fog Index* =

Average no. of words + %age of difficult words X 0.4 = 22 + 13 x 0.4 = **14**

The paragraph has a fog index of 14 which is very high meaning that it is very difficult to read. A fog index of 9 to 10 is considered good. Most international magezines are very particular about this aspect. Magezines such as *The Readers' Digest, The Wall Street Journal* have a fog index of 10. Now some computer software offer the facility to work out the fog index of your writing.

WRITING TEXT FOR INSTRUCTIONAL MATERIALS

While it is hard to become a competent writer by just reading a few instructions, some of the following suggestions may help:

* Develop the habit of using the *Pyramid Technique* which advocates placing the most vital information on top.

* Material should be organised in a logical order with strict control over the flow of information. Procedures, facts, events, ideas, or whatever content is to be treated, should be organized so that there is a continuity of thought. The reader must be able to easily follow each idea in turn, making sense out of what is presented.

* The arrangement of information and instructions should parallel the logical order of understanding an action that the reader will need to perform.

* Select vocabulary and examples keeping the potential reader in mind. It is always very useful to have a good dictionary at hand.

* Use technical terms only when you must. Most of the document should be in simple words that are readily understood. Every time a technical term is used for the first time, it must be explained and illustrated.

* Sentence structure is also very important. Attention should be paid to the construction of sentences with reference to the placement and relationship of the different elements of speech such as subject, verb, modifiers, and so forth.

* Correct use of punctuation, especially commas and semicolons is imperative.

* Decide on a pattern for using uppercase (capital letters) and abbreviated expressions. The entire document should follow the pattern consistently.

* Use short paragraphs because the appearance of lengthy paragaphs often discourage careful reading. Each paragraph should treat only one concept or aspect of a topic. In technical documents it is quite normal to have paragraphs as short as three lines.

* Use headings and sub-headings to identify and separate sections of the writing.

* Regular summarizing of the information is desirable. This repetition increases the reader's understanding of the subject by placing the various elements of the topic in relative perspective.

* For a major publication, develop a table of contents with sufficient detail so that the reader can quickly find the required information.

* Consider the inclusion of a glossary containing definitions of important terms and possibly an index if the publication will be an extensive one.

PLANNING TEXT PRESENTATION

The first decision to be taken is how you wish the text to be presented on the page. One may choose from a full page width or two/three column format. Most typed or word processed materials are of full page width. This arrangement is ideal for materials meant for slow, careful reading. However, this format is rather plain in appearance and does not offer scope for attractive page design.

A two or three column format, generally used for megazines or newsletters is becoming very popular even for text books. This format is very easy and pleasant to read.

Setting the Text

The text may be prepared in final form using an electronic typewriter, a high-quality printer using a wordprocessing software or a typeset machine. The decision depends on the desired level of professional appearance and the availability of time and funds.

A teacher/instructor can set text herself by using a good type-writer, or a computer controlled word processor that prepares a clean, crisp copy on a laser printer. Typesetting is the most expensive method and is suitable only for documents which are highly formal or those required in very large quantities..

If you are using a typewriter, know that a typewriter makes six lines per vertical inch. There are two type sizes **elite** and **pica**. *Elite* prints 12 characters per inch (letters, numbers, symbols, and punctuation marks inclusive); while *Pica* prints 10 characters.

Headings & Sub-headings

The main heading of the document has special importance as it is meant to guide the reader's expectations. Headings should be short and carefully worded. They should be explicit to orient the reader towards the main topic and its scope. By just glancing at the heading and a set of sequential sub-headings, the reader should be able to gain a clear insight into the topic and the treatment of the content.

Each sub-heading should have a clear purpose and should not unnecessarily interrupt the flow of ideas. Sub-headings should be consistent and parallel in structure. Headings and sub-heading are generally designed to be different from the main body of the text. They are designed to attract attention and guide the reader. They should have a distinctly different appearance. They could be be larger or/and bold. There should be consistency in lettering style of the headings and text that follows. Headings can be prepared by typesetting, computer fonts, dry-transfer letters or pressure machine lettering, with excellent results.

Using Pictures & Artwork

Illustrations in the form of diagrams, photographs, cartoons, charts or graphs can add a lot of value to the material. These may be decorative, designed to attract attention to the page, to explain complex concept or to just enhance the reading pleasure. Sketches and artwork illustrate and clarify the content and contribute in enhancing comprehension and retention.

Graphs, tables, and other diagrams should be included to convey large amounts of statistical data. It is easier for a reader to understand complex information when it is represented visually. While using graphics care should be taken to place the visual and its description close together.

decision whether photographs, diagrams, or other illustrations will really enhance the effectiveness and the beauty of the document.

Here, a word of caution is warranted. poorly chosen or designed illustration can have an equally negative effect on the reader.

All sketches should be first drawn on paper and then created either by drawing or generating on the computer screen. Several different arrangements may have to be worked out before all elements are accommodated in the planned space.

DESIGNING PAGE LAYOUT

Several points need to be considered while designing the page layout in printed material. Typically, designing a page involves considerations such as:

* Page size
* Number of columns
* Arrangement of heading and page numbers.
* Width of margins
* Length of lines
* Special emphasising features

Choosing a Typeface

The term *Typeface* refers to the physical look of the words used in the text. A particular typeface involves elements of shape, size, weight, width and scope.

Shape refers to the name of the typeface. A type- face is generally named after its designer or its dominant physical features, or the purpose it was designed to fulfill.
Size refers to vertical measure of the type in *points* i.e. height measured on capital letters.

Weight refers to the visual width of the strokes that build each letter form. These are measured on a scale of blackness or density. Descriptive terms used are *light, medium, bold* or *extra bold.*
Width refers to the horizontal measure of a type character which may be *condensed, normal,* or *expanded* on a visual scale from narrow to wide.
Scope refers to the angle of the axis of a type character. This is either *vertical* or *italic* (Inclined).

Creating Emphasis:

A word, phrase or a sentence may be emphasized by using:

* Quotation marks -	"Highlight"
* Underlining -	Highlight
* Using upper case -	HIGHLIGHT.
* Using boldface -	**Highlight**
* Using italics -	*Highlight*
* Enclosing in a box -	Highlight

Spacing out Text

Three types of spacing is to be considered:

* space between characters in a word;
* space between words within a line; and
* space between lines within the text.

Textistoo closeand crampedto beread	Text is too far apart and a p p e a r s unconnected	Text is legible and very easy to read.

DESKTOP PUBLISHING - SOME FUNDAMENTALS

In the present age and time, it is essential for every teacher to have some idea about **Electronic Desktop Publishing.** When printed material is generated using a personal computer, it falls in the category of electronic publishing. The word *desktop* is used because the required equipment is compact enough to fit on top of a desk and *publishing* because the output closely matches the output generated by a publishing press.

Print material designed with the help of a computer can have several additional features such as different lettering size **(point size)** for headings/sub-headings. Parts of text can be made **bold** or *italicized.* It is also possible to align text either on right, left or both sides. The procedure involves automatically changing the spacing between letters and words so that every line is of the same length. Facilities are also available to check spellings and keep a word count.

It is also very important to have some idea about the **Software** to be used. Three different kinds of software are used -

a) to write out text,

b) develop graphics, and

c) to design pages.

To write out text, **word processing** software is used. The software allows the text to be edited, formatted or reformatted. With a typewriter, every mistakes requires retyping of the entire document.

A great variety of software are available ranging from the very simple to ones offering several special features. Some well-known software for wordprocessing are *Wordstar, Word Perfect, Write or Microsoft Word.* Special programs are available for designing graphics and different types of illustrations. These programs are available in various levels of sophistication. Most of these programmes have a very large variety of shapes and symbols called *Clip Art.* These can be imported directly on to the text. Some of the well known graphic software are *Corel Draw, Harvard Graphics, Photoshop.*

Graphics from the clip art can be adapted, or modified to achieve specific objectives. Graphs and histograms can be instantaneously created with the help of these *tools*. Most software offer the facility for creating your own graphics by using simple sketching tools.

To make the text even more attractive, pictures and photographs can be added. Photographs can be scanned by a special equipment called *scanner* and used directly as graphics to be incorporated in the text.

The material thus entered needs to be combined as finished pages. Software for both formatting and page layout are available. The more popular ones being *Page Maker, Ventura or Publisher*

These software allow you to design pages, including the selection and placement of typeface styles and sizes for headings and text, coloumn design, and other features.

Each page can be *pasted-up* into what the publishers call a *camera-ready* copy. The results can be clear, attractive and very satisfying.

The strongest feature of electronic publishing is the flexibility it offers for experimenting with different arrangements of images. One can arrange, rearrage or modify formats to achieve the desired result.

FEATURES OF PRINTING

Small - Large : Contrast here is the size big to small. M M

Thick -Thin : Contrast here is the weight of the letter: Heavy to Light ; Black to Grey; Strong to Weak. M M

Hard - Soft: Contrast here is in a sense of touch. We "Feel" the shape, edges etc.. M *M*

Narrow - Wide: contrast here is in the horizontal measure of letters. Closed to open. Narrow to wide. Tight to Loose. M M

Vertical - Inclined: Contrast here is like stable to Dynamic; Perpendicular to Angular; Stop to Go. M *M*

Solid - Outline: Contrast here is like Full to Empty, Positive to Negaitve, Off to On, Black to White, Yes to No. M M

Solid - Fragmented: Contrast here is like whole to Parts, Complete to Incomplete, Tranquility to Disruption. P P

Vertical Type : is typeset which is arranged vertically and is often used for headlines, book spines, covers, and signs. It is not a very easy type to read.

T
Y
P
E

Vertical Stack: Uncomfortable to read

TYPE

Bottom to Top: Used for Signs. Less Readable

TYPE

Bookspine: Most Readable

Inclined Type is typeset which is rotated at an angle on its format. Inclined type attracts attention and carries the association of innovative, progressive, leading edge.

Rotated type is typeset which is moved up or down. Text which is rotated up and to the right is more comfortable to read than text which is inclined downwards.

Leave notes that won't get lost in the shuffle

Power-assist front disc brakes Hauls 1,400 pounds of cargo and Billion-mile proved 2-liter overhead Torsion-

Identification : Type is labelled by decribing its visual characteristics for example- New Times Roman

Dd This specimen will be described as - New Times Roman, bold, italic, 40 point (Normal width)

Use of Colour

In print materials colour can be used to seperate elements or to call attention to portions of particular importance. Often, colour is used just to make the document more attractive. Colour reproduction of printed materials is very expensive, therefore, unless the need or advantages are substantial, the cost may not be justified. A simple way of obtaining coloured effect is to use coloured paper. An intelligent choice of paper in terms of its weight, colour and finish can appreciably enhance the appearance of the final output.

DEVELOPING PROFESSIONAL QUALITY DOCUMENTS !

* Choose easy-to-read typeface styles.
* Set type in upper and lowercase letters for ease and speed in reading. Use uppercase words for emphasis and to attract attention.
* Take time to plan and prepare high quality illustrations. You may decide to pick some directly from the available clip art.
* Decide on the indenting pattern to be used.
* Provide space between items for visual separation
* Number each item if the list is sequential. Use bullets or other attention-getting symbols.
* Use lines, tones, and texture patterns to differentiate and emphasize or to create special effects.
* Use colours judiciously for achieving specific objectives.
* Develop tables and graphs in a form that makes their meaning explicit as well as interesting.
* Design an attractive, cover or first page, which is in good taste and has visual appeal.

VALIDATING LAYOUT...

* Is the design attractive enough?
* What are its special novelty features ?
* Does it hold attention?
* Is it formal (or informal) enough?
* Is it easy to read?
* Are the blank spaces properly used and are creating a feeling of openness.
* Are headings/sub-headings clear and appropriately placed?
* Would addition of colour be useful?
* Are the illustrations/graphics clear and well displayed?
* Should the material be presented as a single open sheet or folded into any specific shape?

It is advisable to print a set of pages, for examination and approval before the final run. It is also important to keep a clear record of layout information (margins, point sizes & font for headings etc.) for reference, correction and future use.

Proofreading

Proofreading is very important. It avoids errors which are very annoying and expensive. To proofread properly, one needs to be familiar with the standard symbols used by the printers. Some of the more common symbols along with the corrections they stand for, are given on the next few pages.

COMMON PROOFREADING SYMBOLS

EXAMPLE	SYMBOLS	CORRECTED VERSION
1. The chalkboard should be fixed according to the average height of the users. Technology in education leads to enhanced learning ; technology in training leads to better productivity.	Begin Paragraph ¶	1. The chalkboard should be fixed according to the average height of the users. Technology in education leads to enhanced learning ; technology in training leads to better productivity.
2. Technology in education leads to more effective learning process. Technology in education leads to more effective learning process.	Run on	2. Technology in education leads to more effective learning process. Technology in education leads to more effective learning process.
3. Technology in education leads to more eff ective learning process.	Close up ⊃	3. Technology in education leads to more effective learning process.
4. Technology in education leadsto more effective learning process.	Insert space #	4. Technology in education leads to more effective learning process.
5. Technology in education leads to more effective learning process; technology in training leads to better productivity.	Align *align*	5. Technology in education leads to more effective learning process; technology in training leads to better productivity.
6. Technology in education leads to a effective more learning process.	Move as indicated	6. Technology in education leads to more effective learning process.
7. Educational Technology Technology in education leads to enhanced learning ; technology in training leads to better productivity.	Raise title	7. Educational Technology Technology in education leads to enhanced learning ; technology in training leads to better productivity.
8. Educational Technology Technology in education leads to enhancelearning ; technology in training leads to better productivity.	Lower title	8. Educational Technology Technology in education leads to enhanced learning ; technology in training leads to better productivity.
9. Using slides has 3 imp. advantages. (sp)	Spell out (sp)	9. Using slides has three important advantages.

EXAMPLE	SYMBOLS	CORRECTED VERSION
10. Technology in education leads to enhanced learning technology in training leads to better productivity.	insert comma	10. Technology in education leads to enhanced learning , technology in training leads to better productivity.
11. Educational Technology is technology in education technology of education.	Insert semi-colon	11. Educational Technology is technology in education ; technology of education.
12. Technology in education leads to enhanced learning ; technology in training leads to better productivity	Insert full stop	12. Technology in education leads to enhanced learning ; technology in training leads to better productivity.
13. Before taking pictures ensure the following	Insert colon	13. Before taking pictures ensure the following:
14. Can instructional materials be developed without knowing who is going to use them	Insert question mark	14. Can instructional materials be developed without knowing who is going to use them?
15. A visual is worth a thousand words	Insert exclamation mark	15. A visual is worth a thousand words!
16. For developing videodiscs, one needs state of-the-art technology.	Insert hiphen	16. For developing videodiscs, one needs state-of-the-art technology.
17. You must take students needs into account.	Insert apostrophe	17. You must take students' needs into account.
18. It was Hamlet who said, To be or not to be, is the question	Insert quotation marks	18. It was Hamlet who said, "To be or not to be, is the question."

EXAMPLE	SYMBOLS	CORRECTED VERSION
19. The flow chart figure 24 shows the different media options available with an innovative teacher.	Insert brackets ( )	19. The flow chart (figure 24) shows the different media options available with an innovative teacher.
20. The modern teacher cannot afford to be ignorant about the different Media Options at her disposal.	Put in lower case l.c.	20. The modern teacher cannot afford to be ignorant about the different media options at her disposal.
21.] Educational Technology [	Centre][	21. Educational Technology
22. EDUCATIONAL technology	Capitals caps	22. EDUCATIONAL TECHNOLOGY
23. Have you tried designing transparencies with Power Point?	Italics ital	23. Have you tried designing transparencies with *Power Point*?
24. Have you tried designing transparencies with Power Point?	Bold Bold	24. Have you tried designing transparencies with **Power Point**?
25. Instruction needs to be planned, packaged and delievred carefully. tr	Transpose letters tr	25. Instruction needs to be planned, packaged and delivered carefully.
26. The chalkboard should be fixed according to the ~~average~~ height of the users. stet	Retain word/s stet	26. The chalkboard should be fixed according to the average height of the users.
27. The chalkboard should be fixed accordingly. (?)	Query author (?)	27. The chalkboard should be fixed according to the average height of the user.

ABOUT HANDOUTS . . .

To a teacher, the most valuable tool in the print format is the *handout* which merits a detailed discussion.

To an observant learner, a *handout* is almost a personality document of the instructor which, in a very subtle manner projects the teacher's own interest in the subject and her dedication to the task of teaching. Handouts are very useful for giving selected, pointed information. They are equally effective for instructional as well as motivational purposes.

Functions of handouts ...

A handout helps to :

* Enhance comprehension
* Enhance motivation
* Enhance learner paticipation
* Enhance retention
* Highlight points of interest
* Summarize

Types of Handouts ...

Type	Content
* Notes	Main points, case studies, examples difficult concepts etc.
* Summary Type	Key concepts, definitions, principles, rules and formulae
* Laboratory Reports	Redefining concepts, data, table of analysis, questions, points for discussion
* Exercises	Complete a diagram, fill in the blanks, label parts of a sketch, objective type tests

Designing Handouts ...

While designing handouts, the teacher has to take into account several different parameters. Here are a few suggestions:

* Choose the most suitable type of handout. Innovate and experiment with different types.
* Select contents carefully, focusing on areas of high difficulty.
* Use the simplest possible words.
* Use active voice.
* Use short crisp sentences.
* Highlight key words, concepts or definitions.
* Prepare graphics with care and precision.
* Use colours to emphasise the content and motivate the learner.
* Distribute handouts at a planned point of time during presentation.

7

THE AUDIO MEDIUM

Evolution of the Medium

Special Advantages of the Audio Medium

Some Key Terms

Getting to Know the Equipment

Developing Audio Programmes

Using Audio Laboratories

THE AUDIO MEDIUM

The audio medium, a base resource, is equally powerful by itself and as a life-giver to other media.

In this chapter, effort is made to motivate the teacher to use **other sounds** in addition to her own voice to make instruction more interesting and effective. Generally, we tend to take sounds for granted but the fact is that however sophisticated a visual may be, it is lifeless without its audio component. If perception is an important requisite in the learning process, then sound must be given due respect.

The audio materials are a very valuable resource suitable for almost all different learning environments: classroom - small groups or large groups, individual, distance and open learning and special education. A teacher is most comfortable with this medium and has no hesitation in experimenting with it. In many areas, the audio medium emerges as the prime choice as for example, in the case of language learning.

Over the years, the audio medium has also evolved significantly. In addition to the conventional tape recorder and the compact discs, we now have digital audio tapes and the audio cards. The audio cards, in the form of 1/4" thick magnetic strips are used in language laboratories. Digitized sounds have now become standard accessories for educational software and hypermedia.

•

Special Advantages of the Audio Medium -

- Helps the teacher to bring a touch of the real world into the classroom.
- Highly cost-effective, well within the means of most budgets.
- Hardware and software are easily available. This feature is of great value to systems which cater to learners in remote areas.
- Can be easily duplicated and distributed.
- Can be corrected, modified or even erased.
- The entire equipment is portable and can be operated with batteries.
- The learner can use it conveniently without much ado.
- Important teaching/learning points can be audio-taped for follow up analysis.
- Audio notebooks and audio tutorials can be used with great success.
- Provides the best support for language learning.

SOME KEY TERMS -

Talking about sounds, it is important to begin with understanding the exact meaning of a few familiar terms which we hear often but have seldom bothered to comprehend -

1. Frequency

We are quite familiar with the sounds which the musical instruments or motors make. These sounds are due to the number of *Vibrations per Second* made by a specific machine and vary in quality and strength according to the vibrations produced by the machine or an instrument. Frequecy is measured in units(cycles per second) called Hertz, named after the scientist who worked in this area. The human ear is very sensitive to sound frequency and has the capacity to receive frequencies ranging between 50 hz to 1500 hz.

2. Fidelity

Refers to the authenticity of a sound: closer the recorded sound resembles the real sound, higher is its FIDELITY. High fidelity implies that the reproduced sound is hard to distinguish from the original sound. To obtain high fidelity, recordings must be carried out with good equipment and in ideal conditions.

3. Dolby

A process to eliminate the hissing sound of the tape.

4. Analog & Digital Sounds

Analog sound forms a wave structure by which audio signals are stored and transmitted. When sound or music is produced, a sinelike wave is created.

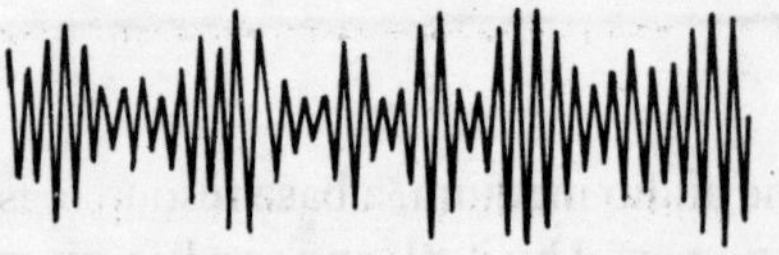

Fig. 7.1 Analog Sound Pattern

This causes compression and expansion of the air resulting in changes in air pressure and vibrations. Sounds recorded with the analog system are of fairly high quality but the quality deteriorates when copies are made.

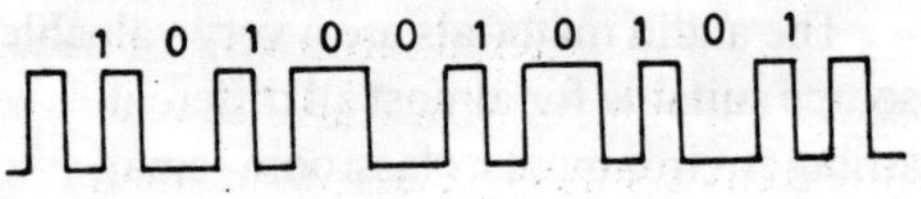

Fig. 7.2 Digital Sound Pattern

In a Digital system, the analog audio waves are converted to binary signals. Here, the signals are identified as zeros and ones. These are recorded on tape as digital data in the form of voltage-level pulses of specific length having 'on' and 'off' components. When the recording is played back, the process is reversed and the audio signals are converted back to analog waves. Digital system gives the same quality copies generation after generation.

Monoaural & Sterophonic Sounds

The quality of the recorded sound also depends on whether the sound has been recorded using one microphone or two microphones. The quality is different because the sound reception in each ear is slightly different. The two sounds are processed in the brain to provide a sort of 3D effect. When the sound is recorded by using one microphone and played back through one speaker, it is said to be monoaural.

The streophonic sound, on the other hand, is the sound that is recorded using two microphones and played back through two speakers. This sound, obviously is of higher quality and is closer to the original sound.

Note that the quality of the recorded sounds depends on the recording system used. If a sound has been recorded on mono, its quality will not improve even when it is played back on a stereo system.

Transducers

Transducers are devices that change energy from one form to another. Transducers are a very essential part of the electronic world. It is important to know that the signals that we receive are not the same in reality. TV pictures, for example, are actually a pattern of tiny cluster of dots in three primary colours of red, green and blue. We see movement which is actually just a series of still images moving at a specific speed.

Transducers convert the sound waves into electrical energy with the help of a microphone and the electrical energy is converted back to sound waves by using a speaker. The efficiency of a microphone and that of a speaker depends on the transducers used. The better the transducer, the more complete is the transfer of energy without any loss of frequency.

Once the signals have been transduced, they can be stored in a variety of ways. They can be turned into patterns which represent music, human voice or other sounds which were origanally transduced.

Computer Synthesized Speech

With the help of digital sound, a computer can produce words. A very important application of this concept is to develop materials for the blind and physically handicapped. Here, the computer can speak out words from a printed text.

Voice Compression & Expansion

Special cassette players have a built-in microprocessor for the purpose of increasing and decreasing the rate of speech without any distortion to the quality of speech.

GETTING FAMILIAR WITH THE EQUIPMENT

Preparation of audio resources requires:

- Recording equipment
- Play-back equipment
- Microphones
- Audio mixers
- Audio tapes
- Compact discs

Recording Equipment requires the use of a *TAPE RECORDER* and *MICROPHONE.* In case a number of sounds from different sources are required to be recorded, special types of microphones may be required and the outputs are combined or edited with the help of a *MIXER.* The recorded sound can be played back using either a cassette player, a reel-to reel tape recorder or a compact disc player. In most cases audio tapes are used to record and play-back. The entry of compact discs has given the audio medium a significant boost.

A. The Tape Recorder

Two common types of tape recorders are used -

- *Open reel recoder,* a reel-to reel tape recorder,and
- *Cassette recorder*

For professional recording, an open reel recorder is preferred. It provides the facility of being operated at faster speed of 3.75", 7.5" & 15" per second for recoding high fedility sounds.

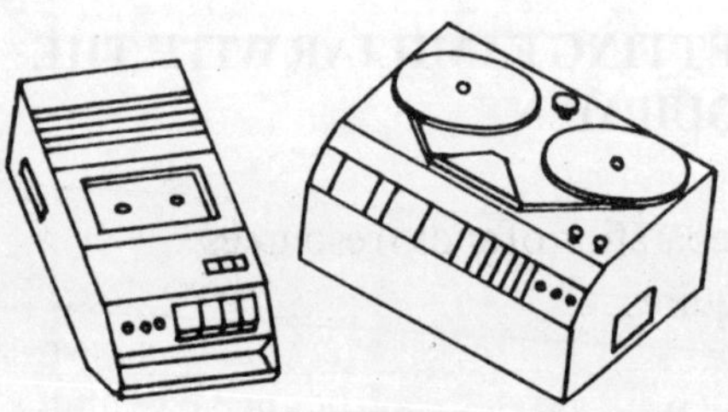

Fig. 7.3 Open-reel & Cassette recorder

The Cassette Player

The cassette recoder, on the other hand, permits a speed of only 1.9" per second. Even when the tape needs to be edited, it is better to use a reel-to-reel recorder.

Although the shape, size and operation of these two recorders differ a great deal, the fundamental working principle of recording and playback remain the same.

HOW IS SOUND RECORDED?

When sound is recorded, electrical signals from the microphone or other source/s are received by the tape recorder. They are amplified to the requisit level. Then they pass through the recording head which is an elctromagnet. During the passage of the tape over the head, magnetic patterns are recorded based on variation and the intensity of signals. When the tape is played back, the magnetic particles resulting from the recording create small electrical currents through the playback head. These also vary in frequency and intensity and when these are amplified, the recorded sound becomes audible. There is also the erase head which demagnetises any patterns of signals that may be present on the tape.

Tracks or Channel Arrangement

Both the cassette player and the reel-to-reel recorders have *Channels* or *Tracks* which allow mixing of different types of sounds to create special sound effects:

Two types of arrangements are commonly found on the audio cassette players -

* *The MONOPHONIC*

* *THE FOUR TRACK STEREOPHONIC*

The Monophonic format is found on most commonly available audio recorders. A single track is recorded on one half of the tape and as the cassette is turned over, a second track is recorded on the other half. Each track can be played back seperately.

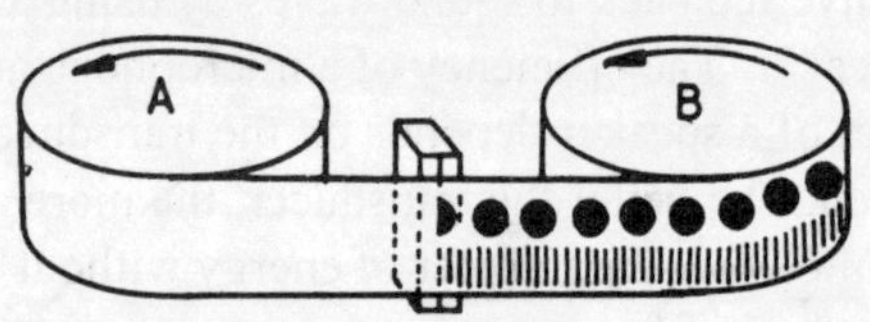

Fig. 7.4 Two Track Recording on Side A of the Tape

In the four track stereophonic format two seperate tracks are recorded simultaneously side by side (A &B). When the tape is turned over, two new tracks (C & D) are recorded similarly on the other side of the tape. Thus, two sets of sterophonic tracks are recorded and are also played back in pairs as they have been recorded.

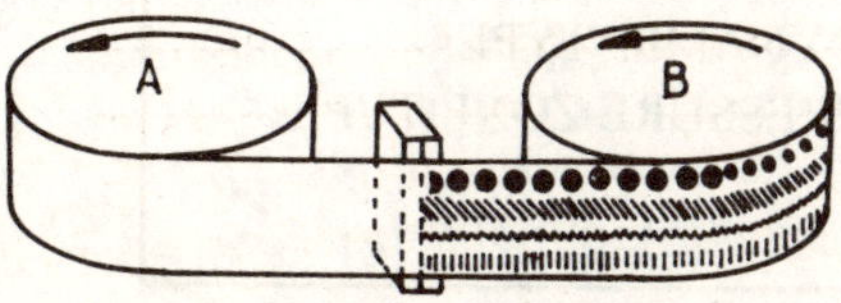

Fig. 7.5 Four Track Recording

In reel-to-reel tape recorders several different possibilities are available -
TWO TRACK MONOPHONIC
TWO TRACK STEROPHONIC
FOUR TRACK STEREOPHONIC
MULTITRACK STEROPHONIC

The basic principle remains the same. Multitrack sterophonic recorders permit 4,8,16 track recording and are mostly used for professional recording. Here each channel is used for a different type of sound i.e. music, commentary, special sound effects etc. Each track can be played back seperately or with others in any chosen combination. This system is highly flexible and offers a vast number of possibilities in preparing high quality audio materials.

The Playback Systems

The playback equipment is the same as the one used for recording. However, the system itself is independent and the audio material prepared on a stereophonic tape-recorder can be played back on monophonic player. In this case all tracks are being picked up simultaneously. However, it is better to prepare the original recording on a sterophonic recorder, preferably on high quality quarter inch tape using a multichannel reel-to-reel tape recorder.

The small cassette player does not offer the same production quality. If a small cassette player is to be used for playback, it is advisable to add a large speaker.

The Compact Disc Player

A very common piece of equipment now freely available, uses sound which has been recorded digitally using a laser beam. The principal advantage of this mode is the large storage capacity on a very small surface. Moreover, the sound quality is consistently high.

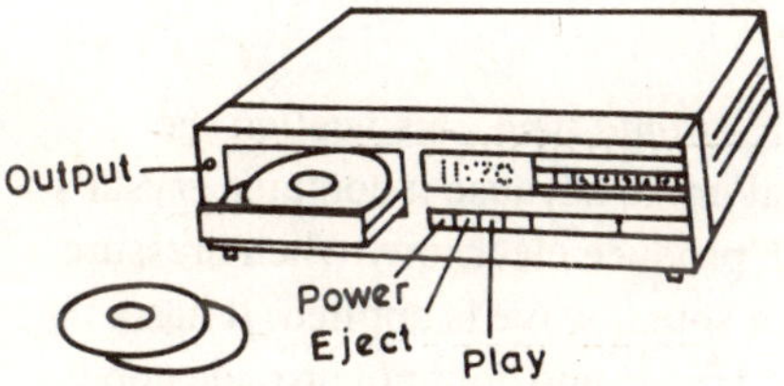

Fig. 7.8 Compact Disc Player

Maintenance of Tape Recorders

To obtain good results in continous recording it is important to keep the tape-recorder clean. Two types of 'dirt' need attention - first, the iron oxide particles that come off the tape as it rolls over the head and other rollers. The second type of dust is the accumulated magnetism from the heads. The first can be removed by using a cotton swab dipped in alcohol and the second by using a head-cleaning cassette or moving an electronic demagnetiser across the heads without touching the heads. This cleaning operation must be done after every 20 hours of use.

C. The Microphone

Most cassette players have built-in microphones which adjust automatically to the volume of the sound received but these are not very powerful and all other ambient noise also gets picked up.

For high quality recording, it is essential to use a separate microphone with manual volume control.

Microphones are of different types, the most common types are -

* CEREMIC TYPE
* CONDENSER TYPE
* DYNAMIC TYPE
* PRESSURE ZONE TYPE

Ceramic type - also called the crystal mike because it contains crystals which produce electricity when pressure from a sound wave is applied. It has a limited range and does not provide good fidelity. This is the microphone that is fitted in most of the cassette players.

Condenser type - here the sound received makes a plate vibrate which causes variations in current carried on a neighbouring plate. It has a wide range and provides high fidelity sound. It is very small and can be clipped on the person/source. This microphone is used in recording studios.

Dynamic type - here a diaphram is attached to a wire placed within the magnetic field. When the coil vibrates, it picks up a wide range of sounds and provides fairly high fidelity.

Pressure zone type - here a special electronic capsule is used to capture sound waves. It is powerful and can pick up low level sounds from over 25 feet. This type of microphone is generally used for outdoor recording.

RANGE OF DIFFERENT TYPES OF MICROPHONES

Cardioid - used for a single narrator or performer. It has a narrow range so as to minimise the ambient noise.

Nondirectional - used for a group of people, panel discussions etc. as it can pick up sound coming from all directions.

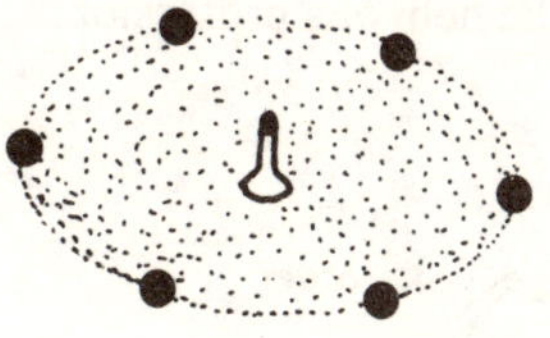

Unidirectional - used for picking up sound from a distance. Also called the 'shotgun' microphone. As it receives sounds from a very narrow angle, it needs to be pointed in the exact direction. The advantage is that it picks up no sound from behind.

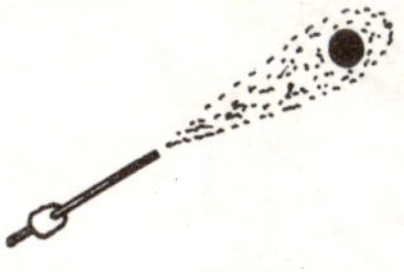

Bidirectional - used for capturing sound from two sides. Ideal for interviews etc.

Using a Microphone

For ideal use, the microphone should be placed at 6" (15cm) from the presenter's mouth. Generally, the tendency is to speak into the microphone at a higher volume. The microphone placed close to the mouth picks up 'breath noise'. It is better to place the microphone just below the mouth rather than hold it at perpendicular in front of the mouth. Where the microphone is hand held it should be held at 45° angle. The presenter should speak in normal conversational volume without any strain to the vocal chords.

The Audio Mixer

This piece of equipment helps in mixing sounds received from different sources. Supposing we have two people participating in a discussion. If they are using different microphones, the sounds need to be 'mixed' for placing on a single track. The 'audio mixer' allows the possibility of balancing volume, adjusting tones etc. Mixing is a highly specialised activity and it is advisable to take the help of a professional for doing it well.

Fig. 7.7 The Audio Mixer

E. The Audio Tape

The audiotape that is commonly in use consists of a plastic base coated on one side with microscopic magnetic particles which are dispersed evenly using a binding agent. These particles form magnetic patterns during the recording.

The same tape can be used for *mono* or *stereo* recordings. The quality of reproduction depends on the type of tape being utilised.

Types of Audio Tapes

Type I - the base material is mostly plastic or polyester which has Iron oxide coating on it. This type of cassette is inexpensive but gives medium quality reproduction of music and voice.

Type II - with ferrochrome coating, a mixture of iron and chromium oxide, it is more expensive but gives recordings of a higher quality.

Type III - with Chromme dioxide coating is even more expensive but allows even a higher quality recording in terms of lower tape noise, greater range of sound reproduction and higher sound output.

Type IV - is the 'metal tape'. It is the most exepensive but the high quality reproduction justifies it.

The upper range of cassette players offer settings for playing different types of tapes.

Duration of the tape - depends on the length of tape. Audiotapes are available in different lengths translated as different playing time.

The most common types are -

C-30, C-45, C-60, C-90, C120.

The number indicates the minutes of the total playing duration on both sides of the tape combined. The running time of the tape has a bearing on the thickness of the tape.

AUDIO DELIVERY FORMATS

FORMAT	SPECIAL FEATURES	LIMITATIONS
DISC RECORD 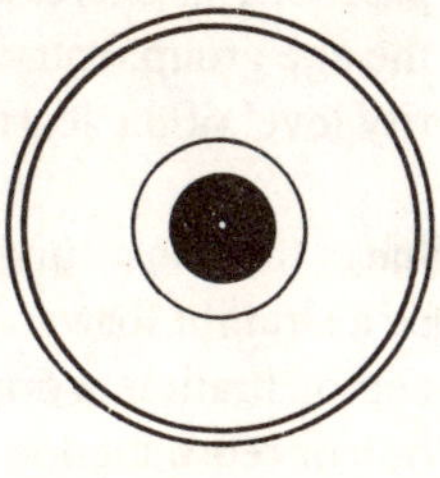 Diameters: 7, 10, 12 in.	Excellent frequency Selective Listening Inexpensive	Difficult to prepare Easily scratched Difficult to Store
AUDIO CASSETTEE 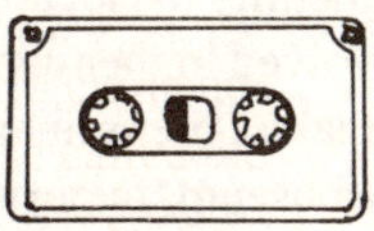 $2\frac{1}{2}$" x 4" x $\frac{1}{2}$" Tape $\frac{1}{8}$ in. wide	- Very portable - Durable - Easy to use - Protection against erasing - Little storage space	Easily distorted Noise and hiss Mediocre fidelity Difficult to edit
MICROCASSETTEE  $1\frac{5}{16}$" x $1\frac{3}{32}$" x $1\frac{1}{2}$" Tape $\frac{1}{8}$ in. wide	- Very compact - Portable - Selective Listening	Lack of compatibility Poor fidelity
COMPACT DISC 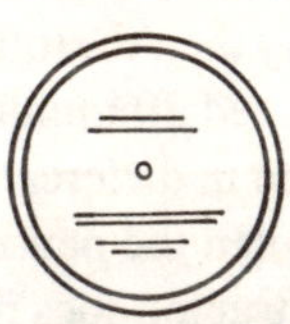 4.72"	Very durable High fidelity Random search	Only playback facility Difficult to prepare Initial expense v. high
AUDIO CARD 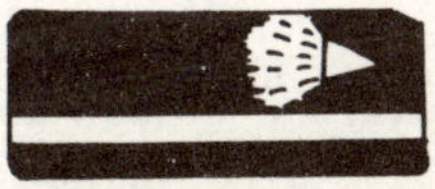 $3\frac{1}{2}$" x 9" or $5\frac{1}{2}$" x 11"	Sound with visual Designed for individual use Interactive;	Very limited capacity less than 15 seconds Time-consuming Difficult to prepare

The base thickness varies between 0.5,1.0,1.5 mil (1/1000th of an inch). As a rule, thinner the tape, longer the running time because a larger amount of tape can be put on the reel. **For recording purposes, best results are obtained by using a tape of 1.5 mil thickness.**

The mono or streo reproduction depends on the machine and not on the tape. Therefore choose the machine according to the desired reproduction quality.

Digital Audiotape -

A fairly new addition to the audio family, a digital audiotape can reproduce sound which is even better than that of the CD. The tape is run on a special equipment containing a microprocessor chip. The same equipment can be used for playing, mixing or editing. Digital audio cards are used to capture audio component in a multimedia workstation and language laboratories.

Developing Audio-based Resource Materials -

It is very easy to develop one's own audio resources. The experience can be very rewarding professionally but also very gratifying creatively. For best results the work should be completed in three phases -

A. Planning

B. Preparing, and

C. Packaging the product.

The following sequence of activities is suggested -

A. Planning -

1. Identify the teaching-learning point for which the audio resource is to be developed. Mark out the concepts/points to be highlighted. Be clear about the specific contribution being made by the audio medium.

2. Write down a line about the audience profile. This exercise will help you define the age group, entry level and the maturity level of the learners.

3. Select the most suitable format - should it be a straight forward explanation, a demonstration, a drama-based presentation or reproduction of real sounds. Is the recording accompanied by slides or is to be used only as audio medium?

4. Identify the locations/people to be involved in the recording. One may need to make a preliminary visit to the location (museum, factory, garden etc.). It is always very useful to meet the people involved in the recording and explain to them the objective of the activity.

5. Make a list of special effects required: real sounds, background sounds, interviews of people etc.

6. Estimate recording time. This will depend on the intended use. Supposing you want to use the material in one class lecture only then the total duration should not exceed 30 minutes. If the material is to be used in different sessions then you need to plan the pauses and breaks so that the instructor does not have to be running the tape randomly to find where it was stopped in the previous session.

7. Select the music. A portion from a ready piece of music may be chosen (permission may have to be obtained) or original music may be recorded for the purpose. Here, talent of local artists/ students may be explored or special pieces composed by professionals. Vocal music is seldom used for resource production, soft instrumental music is generally most suitable. Make sure that the beat of the selected music matches the overall mood of the programme.

B. Preparation -

Work on the following guidelines:

1. Prepare an outline or a detailed script. The detail to which the script is to be written out is variable and dependent on the chosen treatment.

   If just an explanation/discussion is to be recorded then a mere outline of points to be covered would not only be sufficient but also desirable. This leaves ample room for sponteneity of the presenter and the participants.

   If drama format is to be used then a detailed script along with cues will have to be prepared.

2. Select the narrator. A decision may have to be taken whether a male or a female voice would be more suitable (depending on the nature of the topic & pitch requirement)

3. Rehearse the script with the narrator giving her/him the objectives of the programme, marking out areas where specific pitch changes are desired.

4. If the recording is not being done in a professional audio studio, make the rooom as sound proof as possible :

   * Use heavy curtains.
   * Operate in a small portion of the room.
   * Simulate a cabin by putting chairs and draping blankets over them.
   * Make sure to switch off the fan, tubelights etc. as the microphone can pick up the hiss produced by these apparatus.For the same reason the narrator should avoid using sheafs of loose papers.

5. Set up the recording equipment. Determine the best distance to place the microphone. 10" -12" is a good option and generally the microphone should be below the mouth level. This helps the narrator to speak across the microphone rather than speaking into it. If a condenser type microphone is to be used, clip it about 10" below the mouth for attaining the best results.

6. Make a volume check. This should be done for each individual voice if more than one voice is being used. It is advisable to select a moderately high volume setting, but one below the distortion level. This reduces the background noise & tape hiss. It also provides much greater flexibility while playback.

7. Ensure that the narrator is physically comfortable. Have a glass of water (preferebly hot water) readily available.

8. Always do a test run before doing the final recording.

9. If editing of the tape is envisaged for incorporating other sound effects or music, mark the pauses carefully and leave sufficient tape for editing.

C. Packaging Audio Materials -

Some points to be kept in mind at this stage are -

* Choose a title for each programme. Effort should be made to choose a title which is self-explanatory. It should be concise and attractive.
* Design the cover/labels. You will need a cover to go into the transparent plastic cover and two labels for side 1 and 2 respectively. It is very easy to design these.

Fig.7.8 Designing Packaging for User

A simple approach is to take an existing cover of a commercial audiocassette, cut out a piece of the same size from thick paper (bond 150 gms).

Mark the three portions into which this piece is to be folded. Once again be guided by the ready cover. Give the piece borders according to the folds required.

Frame the exact text that has to go on to the three parts. As the exact space available is now visible, lay out the text creatively. Here again, clarity and the comfort of the reader is more important than the aesthetic considerations. The cover should include as much information about the programme as would be required by the user. The back portion is generally used for this purpose.

Along with the cover, you may need to prepare a brief documentation about the the programme:

* Plan to provide a brief description of the programme - the objectives, target audience and outline of content and any special features. This brief can go into the packaging or may be included in the accompanying notebook or other print support material.
* If the design requires, 'index' the tape. This means information about the content available at different segments of the tape is provided. An effective way to do this would be -

Topic	Available at
1. Definition of pollution	1., 000 - 097
2. Types of pollution	1., 099 - 207

* Thought may have to be given to the final container, pouch or paper envelop in which the cassettes have to be mailed.
* Finally, you will have to think about the need of protecting your material with a *copyright*.

DUPLICATING AUDIO RESOURCES

The greatest advantage of the audio medium is its ease of duplication. Once the *master tape* has been prepared after editing etc., it is copied to create *sub-masters* which are then used for mass duplication. It is essential to store the master carefully in a cool, dry place. Steel almirahs/cabinets are not good because they disturb the magnetic field on the tape. High speed equipment is available for making multiple copies. If a very large number of duplicated copies are required, then it better to use commercial tape duplication services.

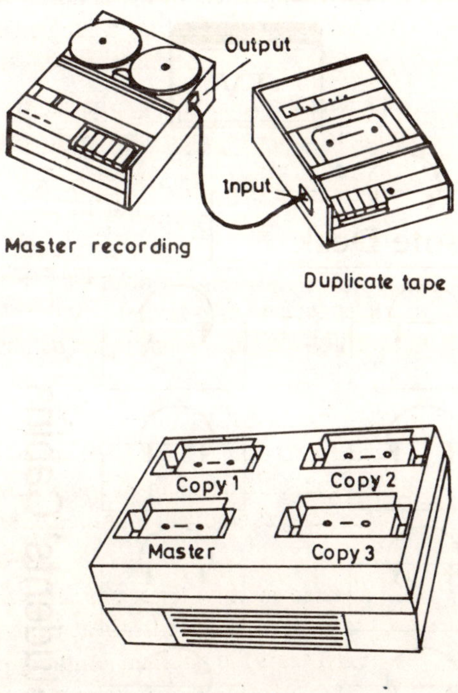

Fig. 7.9 : Duplicating Audio Tapes

USING AUDIO RESOURCES

It will not be wrong to say that media entered the world of education through 'Audio". It was the potential and availability of audio channel in the form of radio that the birth of ' Open University' could be realised. The radio popularised learning through direct lessons, talks, discussion forums and quiz sessions.

This is one medium which is equally effective for individual learner or small, medium or large groups. It is equally valuable for physical as well as mentally handicapped learners

In a recent research project the high potential of audio medium for the use of Educable Mentally Handicapped children has been established.

Audio resources can be used by a teacher to bring in 'live' sound effects into classrooms. One of the earliest uses of the audio medium designed by BBC is the concept of ***Audio-vision*** where the audio clippings are accompanied by a series of still pictures. A popular adoption of this concept is used in India for training programmes in rural development where audio commentaries or dramatized episodes are accompanied by 'Flash Cards'.

Audio resources can be used very effectively as 'Manuals" be it for teaching simple to complex operations or conducting experiments in the open/distance learning mode.

Audio-notebooks are another very effective teaching/learning aids. An audio notebook consists of an audio-recording of selected portions involving procedures and activities accompanied with a 'study guide' and/or a 'workbook'. When such material is used for student-based activities or practical work, it is called audio-tutorial.

THE LANGUAGE LABORATORY

The language laboratory is perhaps the best example of active use of the audio medium in learning. The equipment designed on the principle of controlled repetition and feedback, is very effective in exposing the learner to sounds, rhythm and intonation of the target language.

A typical language laboratory houses a console unit placed on a large table used by the teacher, while the learners use individual cabins. Earlier models were limited to listening to the master voice and repeating aloud. Now, most language laboratories provide the facility for recording the learner's response so that she could play back and listen to her own response in comparison with that of the master.

Today, fully computerized laboratories exist whereby students can work as a group or enter into conversation with one chosen student, a set of students or the teacher. The teacher also has the possibility of dividing the learners into small groups which could be discussing different topics. The teacher can listen and interrupt any speaker.

More sophisticated laboratories have video monitors linked with a central console equipped with a LCD panel. Provision is also available for a mobile camera and the teacher can capture pictures, slides or faces of students by just pointing it towards them.

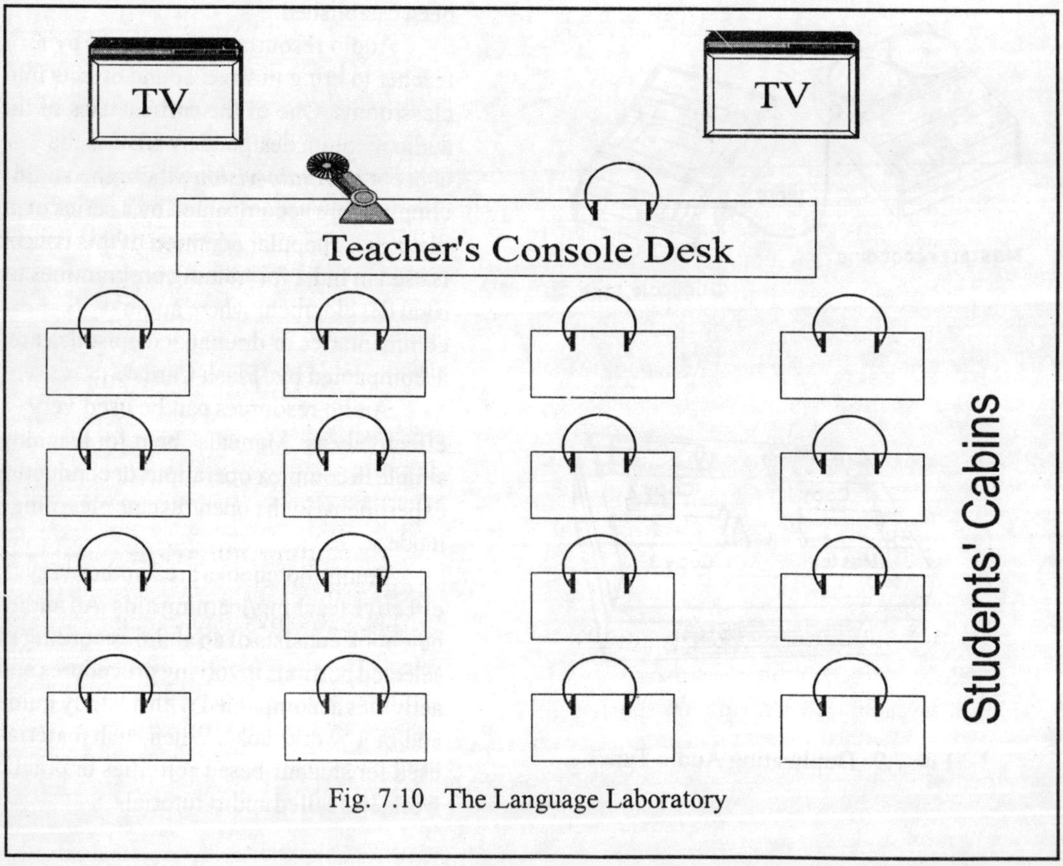

Fig. 7.10 The Language Laboratory

AUDIO CONFERENCE

Audio conference is nothing more than an extended telephone communication. Growth in telephone technology has made it possible for small groups of people in different locations to communicate with each other, discuss & learn. The system can be used for larger groups by using an amplifier at the receivers' end.

Audioconferencing using telephone lines or satellite, works through a *bridge* which is an electronic system that joins the calls from all participating locations and equilizes the sound levels. The *bridge* can be obtained either from the telephone company on permanent basis or rented from a commercial company.

For good results, the coordinator needs to do a good deal of preparation and ensure that all background materials and handouts required during the audio conferencing are already with the participants. The system is very practical and cost effective in the long run. Each participant is able to participate actively.

The main limitation of the system is the lack of visual dimension. Of course, some orientation may be required to overcome the hesitation one experiences in conversing with recorded voices as is generally found in the use of answering machines.

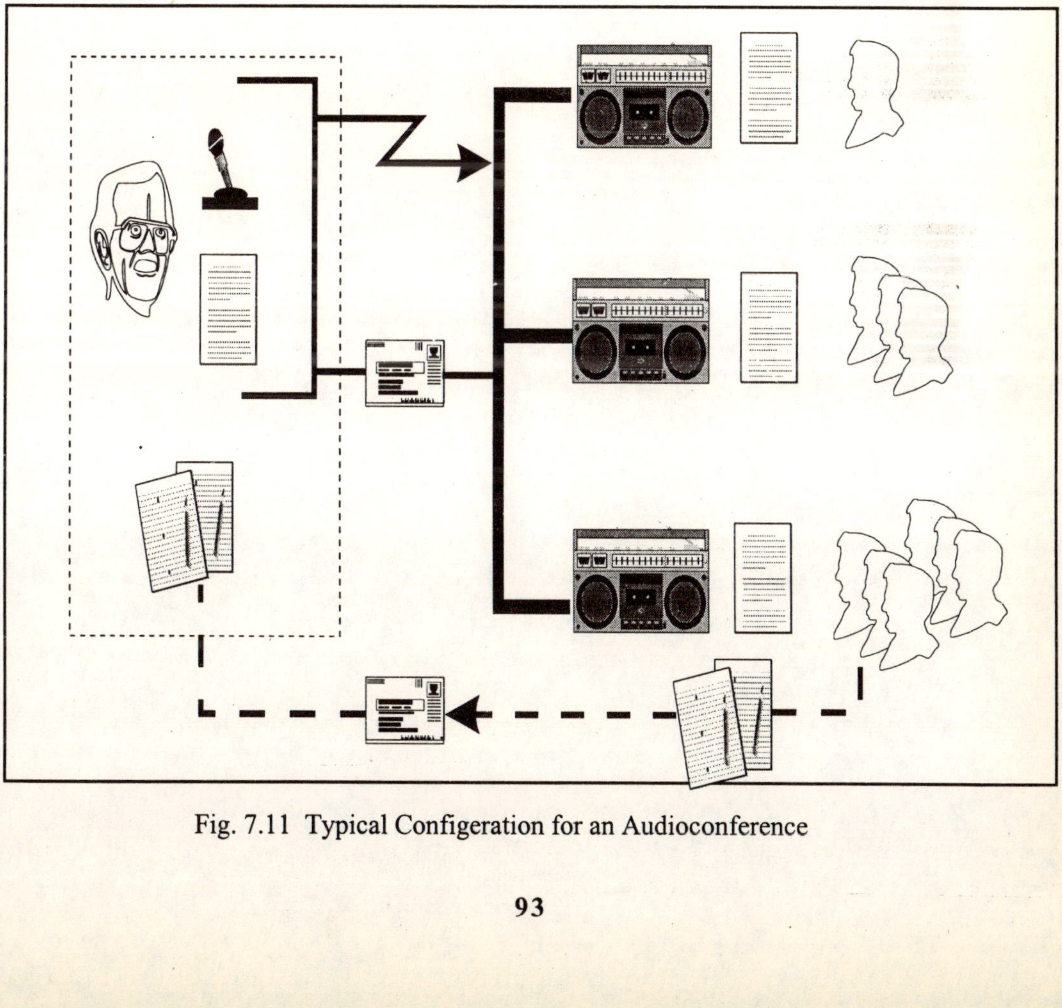

Fig. 7.11 Typical Configeration for an Audioconference

8

OVERHEAD PROJECTION

Special Advantages of Overhead Projection

The Overhead Projector & the Screens

Use & Maintenance of Overhead Projector

Types of Transparencies

Design & Development of Transparencies

Special displays with Transparencies

OVERHEAD PROJECTION

Perhaps the simplest and the most popular of all media options is the Overhead Projection.Overhead projection comes under the category of direct projection systems. The light which comes from the lamp of the projector is transmitted through the transparency to a mirror and finally to the projection area. Overhead projection displays specially designed transparencies . Transparencies project large, bright pictures which a teacher can use for visual presentation of concepts, processes, data, facts, highlights and summaries.

The most interesting feature, however, is its ability to cope with different sized learner groups as it is equally effective with small groups (3-8); medium groups (8-20) or large groups (+20). As a large amount of information/sketches can be pre-prepared, it helps the instructor to save time during the lecture/presentation. Today, overhead projection has become an integral part of classroom/laboratory instruction and whatever technological advancements may come, overhead projection, like the blackboard, is here to stay.

More sophisticated models of overhead projectors are also available which give very high quality projection . A fairly popular model generally used by teachers, instructors and executives is the one that can be neatly folded into a briefcase.

Special Advantages of Overhead Projection:

- Easily available.
- Inexpensive.
- Fairly hardy on wear.
- Allows the instructor to face the class/audience.
- Room does not need to be darkened.
- Saves time as complex drawings can be prepared beforehand.
- Motivates active student participation.
- Offers possibility of using real materials for demonstration.
- Can be used for solving problems step by step.
- Can be used to show animation.
- Can be used to show chemical reactions.
- Can be used for class tests/quizes.
- Can be used to show models, parts of a machine etc.
- Facilitates summarizing ideas or steps in a process.
- Blends well with other media to be used simultaneously.

GETTING TO KNOW THE HARDWARE

In order to use any piece of equipment well, the instructor must know about the hardware: the principle on which it works, its major components, its effective use, care and storage.

A. THE OVERHEAD PROJECTOR

The overhead projector is one of the simplest pieces of media equipment. It comes in the category of *direct projection system.* The light which comes from the lamp inside the projector is transmitted through the transparency to a mirror, then through the lens to the projection area.

It is important for an instructor to get familiar with the different components of the projector. Let us go through them-

1. on/off switch
2. focusing knob
3. lamp
4. reflector
5. the glass plateform
6. special lens (Fresnel lens) below the platform
7. fan to keep the lamp cool
8. head assembly with
   a) mirror
   b) projection lens

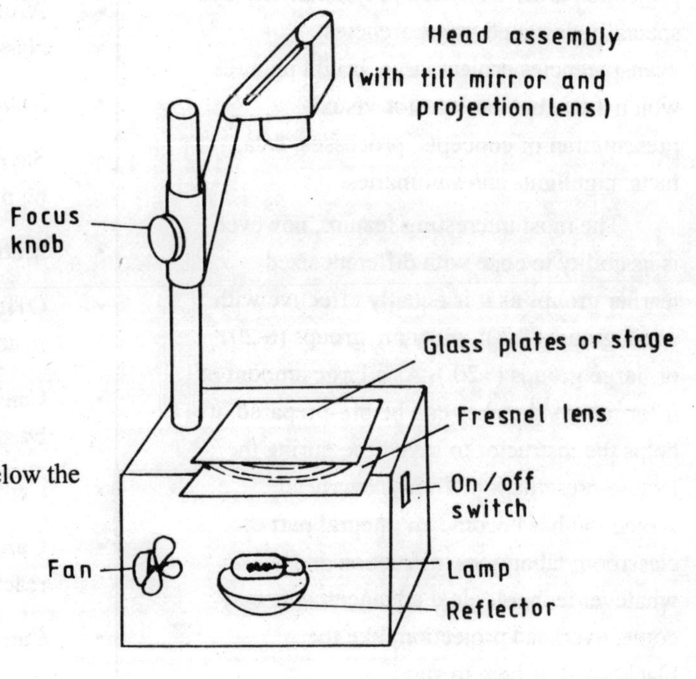

Fig. 8.1 The Overhead Projector

SOME MORE MODELS OF OVERHEAD PROJECTORS

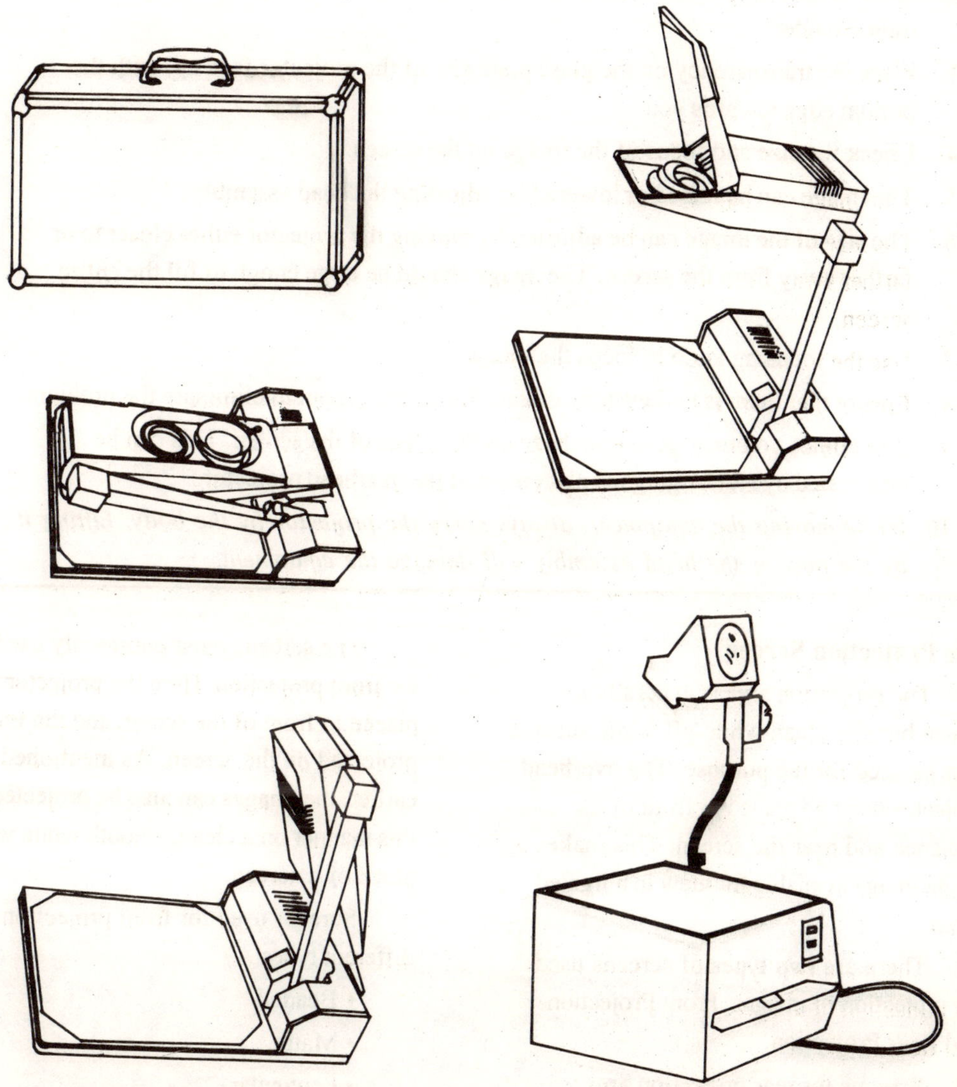

Fig. 8.2 Folding Overhead Projector

Operating the Overhead Projector

1. Connect to power.
2. Stand behind the projector, usually on the left side, with the light crossing over your right shoulder.
3. Place the transparency on the glass platform of the projector face up, with the bottom edge towards you.
4. Check the size and focus of the image on the screen.
5. The image can be raised or lowered by adjusting the head assembly.
6. The size of the image can be adjusted by moving the projector either closer to or farther away from the screen. The image should be large enogh to fill the entire screen.
7. Use the focusing knob to focus the image.
8. Ensure that there is no keystone effect. Adjust the screen to eliminate the problem.
9. Sometimes you may get a blue haze on the edges of the screen. This can be eliminated by rearranging the placement of the overhead projector.
10. *While moving the equipment, always carry the projector by the body. Lifting it by the post or the head assembly will damage the equipment.*

The Projection Screen

The projection area is generally a screen but any clean white/off white surface may be used for the purpose. The overhead projector must be placed in front of the audience and near the screen. This makes a bright image available for view in a lighted room.

There are two types of screens used for projection of images: Front Projection and Rear Projection.

Screens for rear projection are translucent and the projector is placed behind the screen. In this case, the image is projected *through* the screen. This system is generally used in large/special auditoria or lecture halls.

The screens most commonly used are for front projection. Here the projector is placed in front of the screen and the image is projected *on* the screen. As mentioned earlier, the images can also be projected in this manner on a clean, smooth white wall in place of a screen.

Screens used for front projection are of different types:

- Beaded
- Matte
- Lenticular

The beaded screens are most suitable for rooms which are long and narrow; the matte screens are best suited for rooms which are wide but shallow. Both beaded and matte screens are white while the lenticular screen is silver grey and suitable for display of more sophisticated and multicoloured visuals/graphics etc.

Screens may be *Wall Mounted* or *Free Standing*. Both are equally popular. While the former are good for permanent installation, the latter are used for portable systems. In most cases, the projection screens in a classroom/seminar room are fixed on the wooden frame of the blackboard. All three types of screens (beaded, matte and lenticular) are available in both these formats.

It is also possible to get screens which can be set up on a table. This screen comes packed in a box. The screen can be pulled out and made to stand with the help of a support rod which is hinged on to the box.

The great advantage of wall-screens is that they are always available to the user. These are generally kept rolled up for protection. A wall screen may be lowered manually or electrically. A wall mounted screen is generally mounted high enough to permit clear viewing by a large audience.

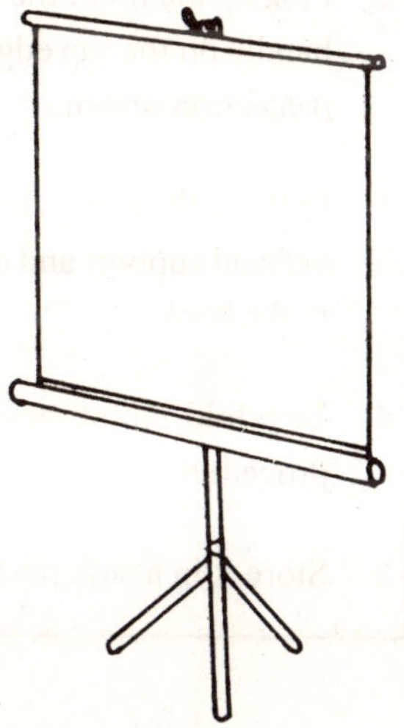

Fig. 8.3a Free Standing Screen

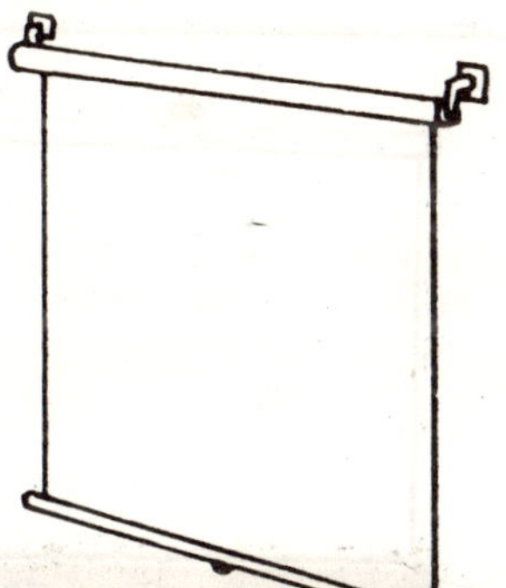

Fig. 8.3b Wall Mounted Screen

Setting Up a Free standing Screen

1. Hold the screen in a vertical position. Release the leg lock with your foot.
2. Extend the legs to their maximum distance to give stable support to the screen.
3. Now pull out the upper extension rod that is inserted into the end of the metal case.
4. Rotate the metal case from a vertical to a horizontal position.
5. Shift the keystone correction bar into place if required.
6. Hold the handle on the edge of the screen and pull the screen up. Hook the handle into the extension bar or keystone correction bar.
7. Raise the extension rod to desired height to pull the screen out of the metal box.
8. To fold the screen, reverse the procedure.

Table Top Screens

It is also possible to get screens which can be set-up on a table. These screens come packed in a box. The screen can be pulled out and made to stand with the help of a support rod which is hinged on to the box.

Setting Up a Table-top Screen

1. Raise the support to its vertical position and hook it in place.
2. Pick up the lid of the box and hold the handle on the top edge of the projection screen.
3. Pull out the screen to the top of the vertical support and attache the handle to the hook.
4. To refold, simply reverse the procedure.
5. Store it in a safe place.

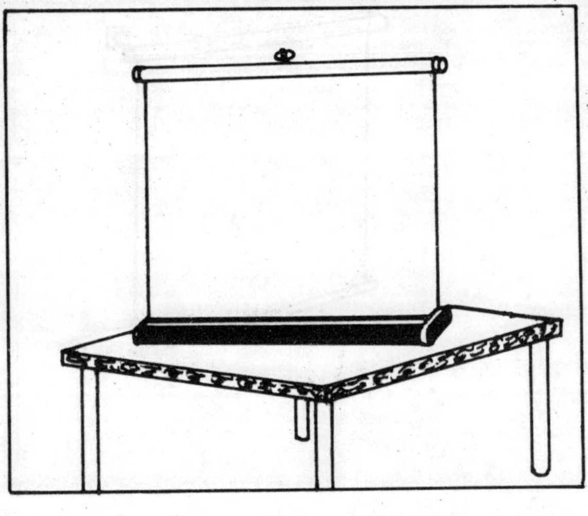

Fig. 8.3c A Table-top Screen

Placement of screens

Decisions regarding the placement and the type of surface required have to be taken on the basis of the size and shape of the room and the angle at which the audience will be viewing the projected images. The ideal locations are right in the centre of the area facing the audience or in one corner in front of the audience.

To resolve issues of placement, it is best to follow the 2-8 rule.

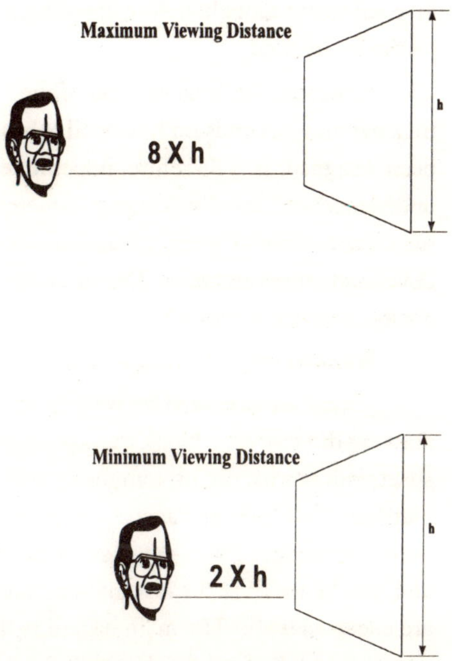

Fig. 8.4 Minimum Viewing Distance

This ensures that the nearest viewer is at least two widths of the screen away from the screen and the farthest viewer is no more than eight widths away.

A common problem faced in setting up screens is the *keystone effect*. The term comes from architecture referring to the shape of the central stone in an arch. Invariably, the image on the screen adopts the *keystone shape* which is rather disturbing to the viewers.

To cure keystone effect, place the screen so that it is perpendicular to the centre of the projected image.

While this is quite easy to implement in a Free Standing screen, for a Wall Mounted screen, the hooks need to be extended so that the screen is permanently inclined to counter the keystone effect.

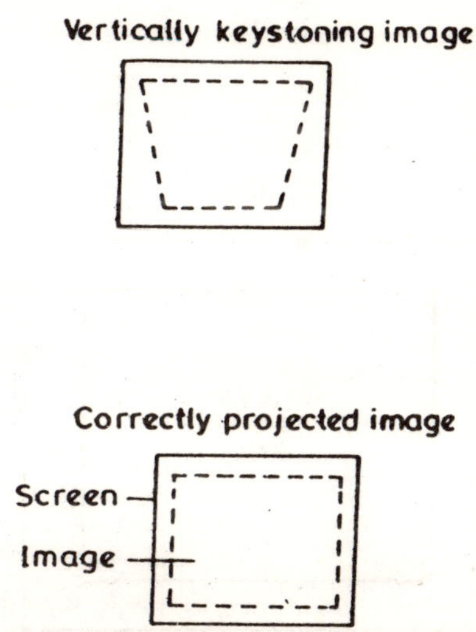

Fig. 8.5 Correcting Keystone Effect.

OVERHEAD TRANSPARENCIES

The commonly used transparency is a transparent sheet made out of acetate. In fact, any transparent sheet strong enough to withstand the heat of the projector can be used for the purpose. The range may cover transparencies made out of PVC to ordinary thin cellophane sheet used to wrap gifts etc.

A standard transparency is cut to A4 size (21cm x 29.7cm) and can be designed to be used either vertically or horizontally.

Although the glass platform for projecting transparencies is square (25cm x 25cm), the transparencies are designed in a rectangular format so that they can be used in any direction.

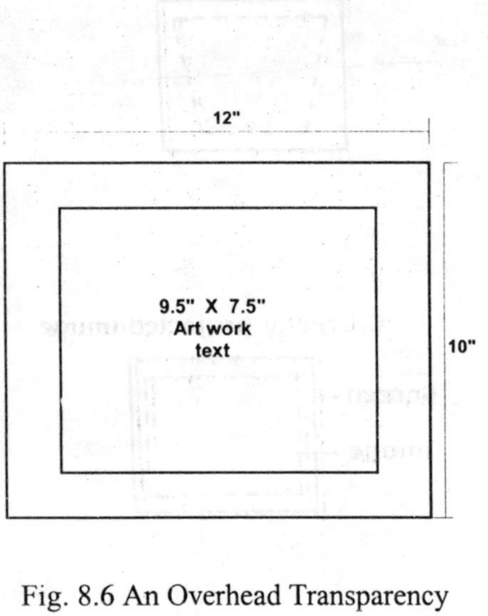

Fig. 8.6 An Overhead Transparency

TYPES OF TRANSPARENCIES

There are several different methods of preparing transparencies such as:

- Writing by hand
- Using a photocopier
- Using a thermocopier.
- Using a computer.
- Using the Diazo film process.
- Using the screen-printing process.

Each of these methods has its own merits and demerits and the teacher should give sufficient thought before choosing a particular method.

However, the final success of the transparency depends on how well it has been designed. It is therefore, imperative to understand and use the design parameters which are constant to any method of developing transparencies. Design must always precede method !

Handwritten Transparencies:

These are prepared by writing or drawing directly on a blank transparency sheet with permanent or temporary felt markers. This type of transparencies have a lot of advantages : they are easy to make and can be made at the last minute; they are cheap as well. The main hazard is the neatness and the final finish which should not look like scribbling. You have to be very careful about the lettering size and the colours to be used. To ensure neat writing of large, well-formed letters of equal size, use a grid. The grid should be placed under the transparency. Always place the material on a hard surface while writing.

To prepare this type of transparencies you need appropriate pens. Pens/markers used for writing/drawing on transparencies are available in variable tips – fine-tipped for writing out text and sketching the outline of visuals; the broad-tipped ones for filling in colour etc. The pens come as *washable* or *permanent* markers. The former can be erased by a damp cloth while the latter can be erased only by using acetone or other special solvents.

Some attention needs to be paid to the choice of colours to be used. Although a variety of colours are included in the pack of pens not all of them are effective communicators on screen. This is hard to judge because all the colours look very attractive on paper. While black, blue, purple and magenta come out very bright, one can be disappointed by results obtained by green and orange. As far as possible use real colours to depict products, circuits etc. As colours are very potent communicators, the viewer tends to look for a code in colours.Therefore, plan to use different colours in an organised manner. At times the user is tempted to write each line in a different colour, this is not a good policy, it is better to choose colour combinations for titles, headings, subheadings etc. You can also use dry-transfer letters or coloured tapes available in different widths and colours. This gives a professional look to the transparency.

Thermal Transparencies: These are prepared using a special equipment - the thermofax providing heat from an *infrared light source* which is made to pass through

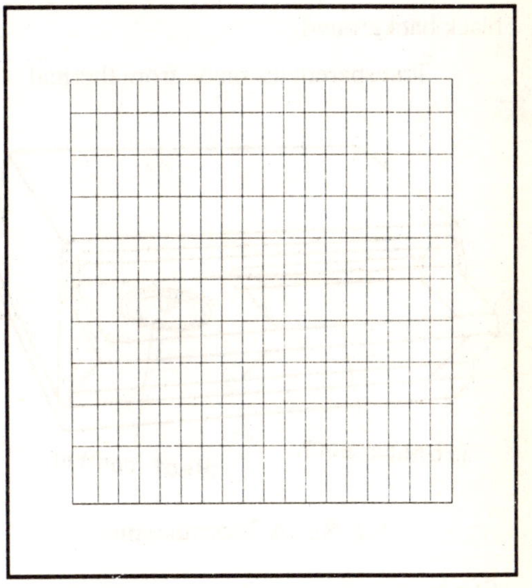

Fig. 8.7 Grid for Designing Transparencies

the film to the master. The master and the film are placed together and passed on a belt or between the rollers around the infrared light source. It sometimes takes a little time to arrive at the optimum speed providing the ideal exposure time. To get the best results, the machine must operate at a speed which in turn controls the exposure time. If the speed is too slow, the transparencies will get over-exposed and if the speed is fast, they will be underexposed.

Care must also be taken to ensure that the belt and the glass surface of the thermocopier are kept clean.

Thermal film is usable for positive or negative transparencies and is available in a variety of colours. The very latest addition to the spectrum of pink, blue, purple and green is the reverse negative. Here, the film over the text or the graphic is actually eaten up by heat and the output is bright white on a jet black background.

Transparencies made from thermal

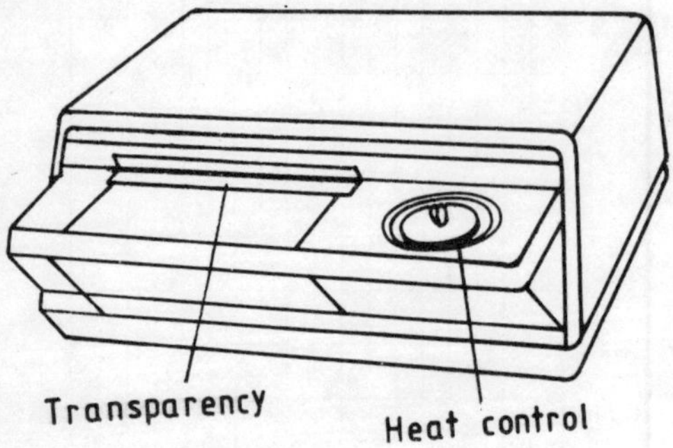

Fig. 8.8 A Thermocopier

film are expensive and require special equipment. They are best suited when high quality transparencies are required and the facts/data being depicted is of somewhat permanent value. The negative transparencies are very easy on the eye and are valuable when the presentation demands that the visuals are left projected for a long duration.

Transparencies Developed Using a Photocopier:

(a) Transparencies can also be made with the help of a photocopier using the original typewritten or printed masters. It is essential to procure transparency sheets which are at least 100 micron thick to ensure that no damage is caused by the heat of the drum of the photocopier.

(b) Coloured photographs can be transferred on to transparencies for display to a large gathering with the help of a coloured photocopier. However, these transparencies are extremely delicate and get distorted very easily with small patches of colour coming off the acetate.

(c) Using material/graphics taken from printed material appears to be a very convenient option, but it is not a very effective one. The text/graphics lifted from a book or other print material by directly photocopying it on the transparency sheet is much too small for the purpose. Even though one may not be constrained by the copyright issue, the printed material on a standard page is far too much for a single transparency. Moreover, the printed materials are not meant to be projected, they are designed to be viewed from a distance no more than 12"-14". If the material *must* be lifted from the printed text, it should be considered only when the graphic is of a rare or very complicated nature. In this case, the transparency has to be almost engineered completely. Some suggestions –

- Study the graphic carefully. See if it can be divided into sections or segments which can be projected on different transparencies. Cut the portion which is most relevant. Photocopy it by enlarging it 200%.

- Paste this on a fresh page in the most suitable direction – vertical or horizontal.

- Add fresh captions, either by hand or using a computer.

Computer-generated Graphics: A variety of options are available. Beautiful and neat transparencies, in full colour can be generated by using any graphic software.

Of course, most printers these days offer the facility of taking a direct printout on the transparency.

Display systems have also been evolving and now it is possible to directly display material from the computer screen designed in the transparency format by using an LCD unit. This display system which looks like a glass window the size of an overhead transparency, is hooked onto the computer monitor output and placed on the glass platform of the overhead projector. When an image is called up it passes through the window and is instantly projected onto the screen. The special advantage here is that the teacher/presenter can explain by working on the graphic in view.

Hard copies containing text and graphics can be generated on computer using any software which allows options in size and font. It is possible to use a font which is hollow and is to be later filled with colours. Coloured adhesive tapes which come in different widths and colours can be used. To do this stick the coloured piece over one line of the visual and ease into place smoothening it by hand so that no air bubble remains to create wrinkles. A double line using two different colours is very effective for creating emphasis.

Transparencies Developed Using Diazo Films: Diazo films give beautiful, brilliant coloured transparencies. Here, diazo salts along with colour couplers are coated on acetate. When the coating is exposed to ultraviolet light, it is chemically changed so that no image appears. But if the coating is not exposed to ultraviolet light and is developed in an alkaline medium like fumes of commercial aqueous ammonia (ammonia hydroxide), the diazo salts combine with the colour coupler in the film to form a coloured image. By using different colour couplers during manufacturing process, desired colours can be coated on acetate.

Diazo transparencies are not very popular these days as the process is long and requires an ultraviolet light printer. In view of the several easier options being available, this type of equipment and even the films have become hard to locate.

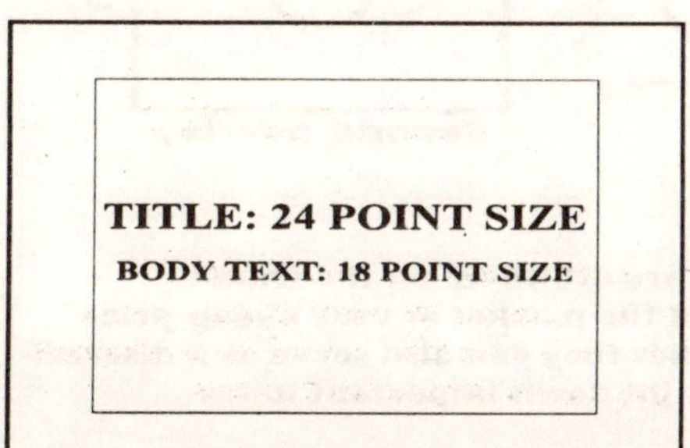

Fig. 8.9 Appropriate Lettering Size

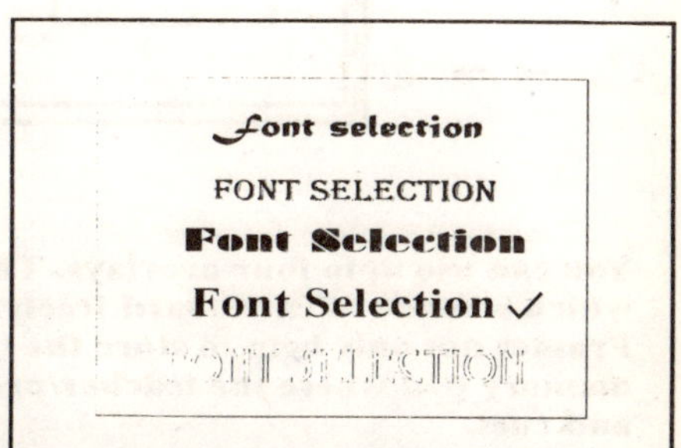

Fig. 8.10 Appropriate Font

Screen printed Transparencies: Here, the transparencies are generated through the process of screen printing. This type of transparencies are very beautiful with striking colours. However, the process is very expensive and is viable only in situations where the colour resolution is very important (as for example in textile designing/printing etc) or when a number of copies of the same transparency are required for mass distribution.

Transparencies with Overlays: One of the most powerful and effective types of transparencies is the transparency with overlays. Here the graphic is broken up into parts which need to be shown successively to build up an idea, concept or model. To make a transparency with overlays use the steps depicted below.

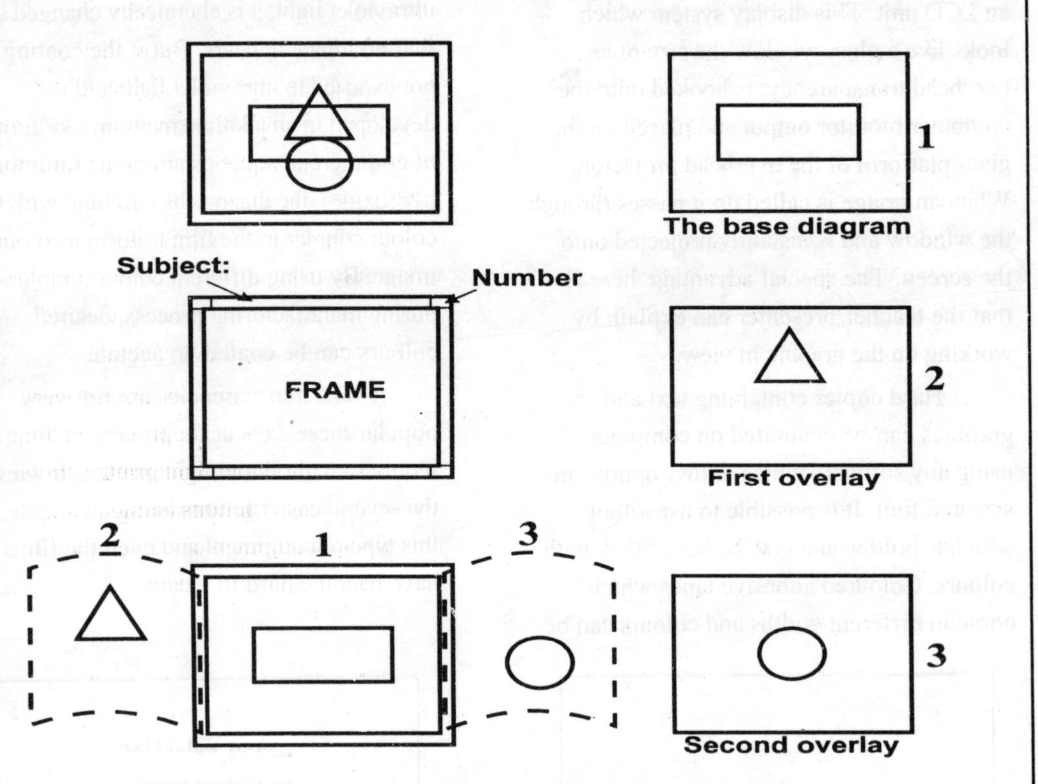

You can use upto four overlays. The overlays are attached on the frame which is made of cardboard freely available in the market at very cheap price. Frames not only help to store the transparencies they can also serve as a discreet memory pad where the teacher/presenter can jot down important notes and cues.

Fig. 8.11 Process of Designing Transparencies with Overlays

Designing Transparencies

- Keep the learning objectives in mind.
- Keep the audience profile in mind.
- Keep to one idea per transparency.
- Keep the transparency uncluttered with sufficient margin on all four sides. Remember your work area is only 7.5" x 9.5".
- To get straight lines and words of the same size use a grid (see fig. 8.7).
- Whatever the size of the text or graphic always maintain the aspect ratio of 4:5 (h:w).
- Remember the dictum: *text is not visual*. Use the shortest phrases that you can construct, if possible use only cue words.
- Limit to writing 6-8 lines per transparency
- Limit to 6-8 words per line
- Respect the minimum lettering size of 6 mm. To ensure the legibility of your writing on a projected transparency, hold the hard copy at a distance of 1 meter and if you can read it comfortably, the lettering size is adequate.
- For computer generated transparencies, consideration has to be given to the choice of ***fonts***. Not all fonts are suitable for projection. All fancy fonts should be avoided. It is better to stick to a few standard fonts which are solid rather than hollow.
- The size of graphic is important. Place it right in the centre of the transparency.
- While transparencies can be designed in vertical or horizontal format, it is better to stick to one format for one lesson/ presentation – either vertical or horizontal.

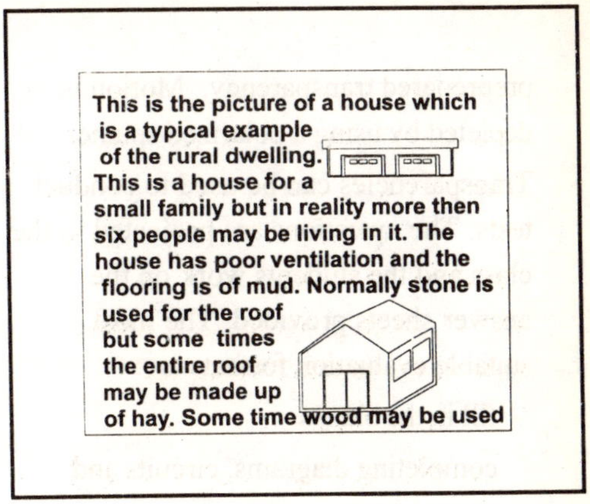

Fig. 8.12 What Not to Do.

- If you are sure that you need to mount the transparency on a frame, avoid borders or corner decorations/logos.

Special Displays on Transparencies

- Use opaque real objects (such as small models, metal parts, match sticks, small coins) to suggest silhouettes which provide very pleasant learning experience.
- Use cutout from coloured acetate sheets or any other transparent materials.
- An ordinary A4 size paper with letters cut can give the same effect as a negative reverse transparency
- Chemical actions can be shown through formation of coloured solutions or precipitates.
- Animation can be shown by using polarized plastic to rotate on a

preprepared transparency. Motion is depicted by using a polarized spinner.

- Transparencies can be used to conduct tests. The questions are projected to the class and the students work on the answer sheets provided. The most suitable evaluation formats are:
  - fill in the blanks
  - completing diagrams, circuits and statements
  - labelling a blank diagram

The teacher can then make on the spot corrections. This is very effective and pleasant for the learner with ample scope for interaction.

- Biologists can make effective use of the overhead projection to show small skeletons or parts of a flower/plant encased in plastic.
- Try to innovate new ways of creating interactivity and interest by putting the overhead projection to new uses and you will discover that this is a very flexible medium limited only by your own imagination.

Maintaining Overhead Projection Equipment

The following points may be noted carefully:

1. The most delicate part of the equipment is the ***lamp***. All care should be taken to protect it from getting burnt due to overheating. That is why a fan has been provided which makes its presence felt with a soft humming sound. To avoid overheating dim the light while changing transparencies and in case you are going to take sometime to explain a point, switch off the projector. This does not cause any inconvenience because the projector (unlike say the photocopying machine) does not need any warming up. When switched on, it is instantly available for use.

Also, when the presentation is over, do not move the OHP immediately as the lamp is still hot and very vulnerable. Allow a few minutes for the lamp to cool down before shifting the projector.

2. Like all equipment, the overhead projector tends to accumulate dust, particularly chalk dust. The OHP is generally placed near the blackboard and most instructors like to use both simultaneously. When you see dust on the lens, mirror or glass surface, avoid the temptation of cleaning with hand. The oil from the skin transferred on to the surface will gather more dust. Use a clean, soft, lint-free cloth or a soft brush kept exclusively for this purpose. Occasionally, you need to open and clean the inside of the projector. While doing so make sure that the projector is unplugged from the source.

TEACHING WITH OVERHEAD TRANSPARENCIES

When You Teach with an Overhead Projection System, remember to ...

- Place the transparency on the projector before turning on the projector. Bright light on a blank screen can be very unpleasant for the audience. This has to be avoided even during the presentation.
- Steady your hand on the platform of the projector, and use a pencil to point to information. Small, nervous movements are magnified on the screen.
- Look at your audience, keeping a discreet eye on the screen to check from time to time that the image is straight and visible.
- Point at the different components of the transparency from the platform. Do not point from the screen. This requires you to turn your back on the audience and look at the screen.
- Reveal one point at a time, sliding a piece of paper down the transparency. If you use a computer-based presentation system, "build" the sequence of ideas by having the computer "grey out" the previous point as the next one comes up.
- Do not darken the room, it is better to leave room lights on.

9

FUNDAMENTALS OF PHOTOGRAPHY

Photography and the Projected Media

Types of Cameras and Lenses

About Films and their Use

Composing Good Photographs

Using Photographs for Instruction

FUNDAMENTALS OF PHOTOGRAPHY

To a teacher, photographs can serve as an important instructional resource. In any case, a teacher who is interested in developing media-based instructional materials, must have basic knowledge regarding photography because it forms the basis of all projected media formats. Now-a-days, advances in photographic equipment allow you to compose and produce high quality pictures not only without much ado but with a sense of pleasure and satisfaction.

GETTING TO KNOW THE EQUIPMENT

Photography requires knowledge about -

- Cameras
- Lenses, and
- Films

1. The Camera

Although cameras can be classified into groups according to film size or operating characteristics, its basic concept remains the same and most cameras include seven essential parts:

The body enclosure
The lens
Lens diaphragm
The shutter
The viewfinder
Film-support channel
Film-advance and rewind knobs

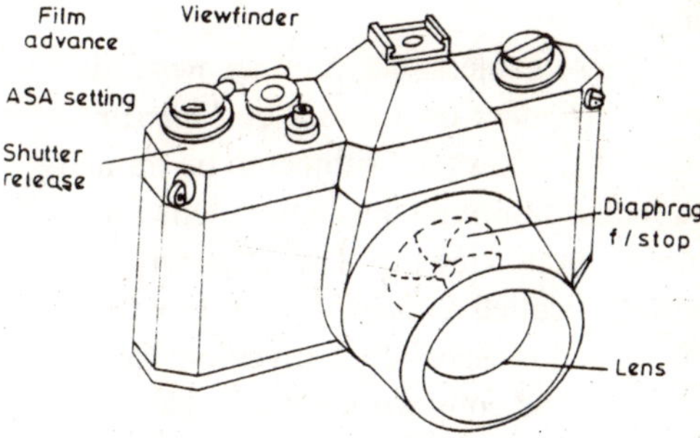

Fig. 9.1 The 35 mm Camera

Most cameras offer the possibility of changing lens-diaphragm openings, shutter speeds, and focus. Additional refined features are available in more sophisticated and expensive kinds. Cameras come with a wide variety of lenses and the price of a camera depends on the type of lens it contains. Lenses and shutters of high-priced cameras can be adjusted over a wide range of settings, which broadens the possibilities for taking pictures under varying light conditions.

TYPES OF CAMERAS

Cameras come in different formats. Most commonly used camera are :

a) the small format camera
b) the medium format camera
c) the large format camera

d) the polaroid camera
e) the digital still camera, and
f) the videocamera

a) Small Format Cameras (35 mm)

This is the most commonly used type of camera for preparing visual materials, particularly slides. Any 35 mm film can be used to obtain colour or black-and-white prints.

These cameras have either *window-type viewfinders* or a *prism and mirror system* that allows the subject to be framed and focused through the camera lens for more accurate viewing. The latter type of camera is called a ***single lens reflex*** **(SLR)** camera and is especially convenient for close-ups and copy work which means taking photographs from charts, pictures and other flat displays. This is the type of camera most commonly used for preparing instructional media.

Some models of single-lens reflex cameras have automated features, controlled by a microchip, which allows quick adjustments of exposure and focus settings with precision. Models of window-type viewfinder cameras are also available in very compact sizes - which are small enough to fit into a pocket.

b) Medium Format Cameras

These cameras use a film size (generally 120) to provide 2.25" x 2.25" inch or 2.25" x 2.75" inch slides.

Coloured or black-and-white negatives can be obtained. The larger size is generally preferable when oversized enlargements and exceptionally sharp images are required. However, this type of slides are expensive and need special projection facilities.

One advantage of these cameras is that the camera back, which serves as a film cartridge, can be easily removed and interchanged. This allows the use of different types of films (black-and-white, colour reversal or instant Polaroid) without unloading the roll being used in the camera.

Another type of medium format is a *twin-lens camera.* Here, the lower lens is used for taking pictures, while the upper one carries light rays to the ground glass. With the twin lens camera the subject can be viewed even as the shutter is released during exposure.

c) Large Format Cameras

These cameras, available in many sizes, use cut sheets of film rather than rolls, thus permitting single pictures to be processed. The larger negatives can be easily retouched and allow large size enlargements.

These types of cameras are used in a studio or copy room. Precision graphic processing is also done with these cameras. They are bulky and the film required is expensive. Their main use is for preparing large-size negatives from paste-ups and other art work for offset printing.

d) POLAROID Self-Processing Film Cameras

The Polaroid camera (named after the manufacturing firm) is unique because here the film is developed automatically into a print in the camera, thus eliminating the need for darkroom work. The results of the pictures taken are seen almost immediately. Prints and slides in both black-and-white and colour can be produced in one minute.

The film consists of light sensitive negative material and a nonsensitive positive stock (paper or film). The latter is fixed with sealed pods, one for each picture, which contain developing chemicals. After a picture is taken, a motorised movement advances the film, rollers squeeze the developer from a pod, allowing gelatin like material to spread between the negative and positive stock. Development takes place quickly. The result is a print or slide ready for use.

An added advantage of this system is that pictures can also be developed with a regular 35 mm camera using a reversal colour film (ISO 40), which is also available from Polaroid. These can be immediately processed in an *autoprocess* unit. The advantage being that the slides can be shot and the results seen in a few minutes. Continuous-tone black-and-white and high-contrast 35 mm films are also available in this process.

e) Digital Still Cameras

Recent developments in video imaging and computer technology have created a new photographic medium - the hand-held, still-picture digital camera. Subjects and scenes, recorded as video signals, become binary patterns on a disc in an accompanying recorder. Images are seen through a videoplayer; then with a videoprinter full-colour paper copies can be obtained.

The signals can be transmitted via telephone lines to any location. The visual information can be copied, re-arranged, and enhanced in many ways. This type of camera gives very high quality pictures.

f) Videocameras

Videocameras have almost completely replaced both 16 mm and Super 8 mm motion-picture cameras for producing instructional materials. The special features and functioning of videocameras will be discussed in greater detailed in the chapter on the Video Medium.

2. Camera Lenses

The most precious component in a camera is its *lens*. The cost of a camera is dependent upon the type of lens it contains. In inexpensive still-picture cameras, a standard lens is used. But expensive cameras are equipped with additional lenses for special purposes. There are advantages in using different lenses to capture different subjects under different conditions.

The major feature of a lens is its ***focal length***. This term refers to the distance measured from the center of the camera lens to the film plane within the camera when a subject at a far distance (infinity) is in focus. Lenses of different focal lengths form different-size images on a film even though the camera is used from the same position. When a camera with a longer focal length is used, a larger image is projected on to the film.

The focal length of a lens is measured in millimeters (mm). A normal focal length has been established for various cameras. For the 35 mm camera the normal focal length is 50 mm. A lens with a larger or longer focal-length number (135 mm) than that of the normal lens is called a ***telephoto lens***. A lens with a focal-length number smaller or shorter (28 mm) than the normal lens is called a ***wide-angle lens***.

A ***zoom lens,*** which in effect is a series of lenses within one housing, allows one to rapidly change the focal length along a predetermined range. Such a lens may be marked 35-70mm, 75-200 mm, and so forth.

In using this lens, you choose your subject by zooming in or out without moving the camera with respect to the subject. With this lens on a video or motion-picture camera, it is possible to continuously change the size of a subject by zooming in or zooming out.

Dramatic effects can be obtained by using a slow zoom for establishing relationships between elements of a scene. However, there is generally a tendency to overuse the zooming feature, which can be distracting to the viewer.

To obtain multiple effects, professionals work with several different cameras at a time. For example, a *wide-angle lens* is useful when you cannot move far enough away from a subject to shoot with a normal lens. When you cannot get close to a subject or do not want to, a *telephoto lens* may be more helpful.

Special lenses, called ***macro lenses,*** are available for close up and copy work. They are designed to reproduce details more sharply.

Camera Settings

We are now in an age of automatic cameras. However, for taking high-quality pictures, it is essential to know about the settings. While composing a picture, one has to take care of three essential settings:

* lens diaphragm,
* shutter speed, and
* the focus

The amount of light that enters a camera is controlled by the lens diaphragm and the shutter, working together. The lens diaphragm controls the amount of light that can reach the film while the shutter controls the length of time the light will take to reach the film.

Lens Diaphragm

The lens diaphragm acts somewhat like the iris of an eye. It is always open, but its size can be changed to control the intensity of light passing through the lens.

Lens-diaphragm settings are indicated by a series of numbers - 4, 5, 6, 8, 11, 16,... - called f/numbers or f/stops. The larger the f/number the smaller the opening. An f/number expresses the relationship between the focal length and the diameter of the lens's aperture.

Thus, for f/11 the opening has a diameter which is equal to one-eleventh of the lens's focal length. In commonly used terminology, a lens with a low f/number (f/2 or f/1.4) is considered a "fast" lens. This means that the camera equipped with such a lens is capable of taking picture under poor light conditions.

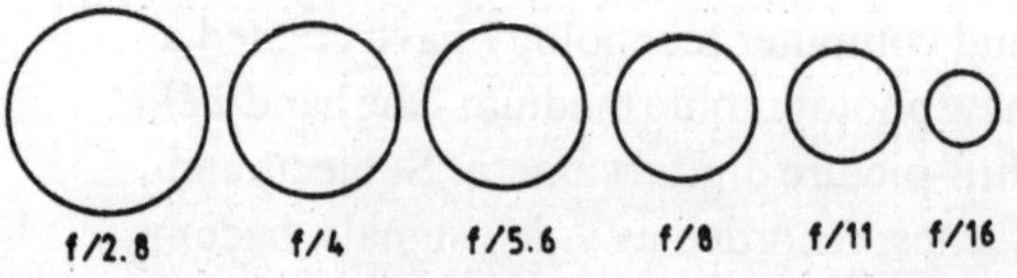

Fig. 9.2 Relative Aperture Sizes

Shutter Speed

The camera shutter is similar to the eyelid as it closes and reopens rapidly. In the camera, the shutter remains closed until opened to permit the lens to *see*. The most common type of shutter is placed between the elements of the lens and consists of thin pieces of metal that can be moved to allow light to pass for various lengths of time.

Generally, shutter speeds are measured in fractions of a second: 1/2, 1/3, 1/8, 1/15, 1/30, 1/60, 1/125, and so on. On the camera, the shutter speed is indicated as whole numbers instead of fractions, the number shown being the denominator of the fraction. A shutter speed of 1/60 second is slower than a speed of 1/125 second, admitting light for twice as long a time.

On your camera you may have many speeds from which to select. For general scenes, a shutter speed of 1/60 or 1/125 is suggested. But when a moving subject is to be filmed, the choice of a shutter speed becomes important and depends on factors such as - the speed of movement, the distance from camera to the subject, and the direction in which the object is moving in relation to the camera.

Focus

Different cameras have different arrangements for adjusting focus. Some cameras may be able to focus the image on the ground glass, others may have a built-in rangefinder coupled to the lens which automatically sets the lens for the correct subject-to-camera distance.

Many cameras now include an *automatic focusing* feature. When the focus is adjusted, an electronic pulse, like a small sonar beam, is emitted from the camera. It strikes the subject towards which the camera is pointed. The time for the pulse to reach and then reflect from the subject is measured. This period of time is translated into a distance (feet or meters), and the camera lens is focused automatically.

Depth-of-Field

Depth of field refers to the distance within a scene from the point closest to the camera in focus to the farthest point in focus. Just as appropriate coordination is required between the lens-diaphragm opening and shutter speed to admit various amounts of light into the camera, coordination between lens-diaphragm openings and distance settings is required to obtain high quality, sharp pictures.

Two points must be noted here. First whatever the lens setting, it provides greater depth-of-field at far distances than at near distances. Second, whatever the distance, it provides greater depth-of-field at higher-numbered lens settings than at lower-numbered ones.

The Film

The quality of the picture produced also depends on the film chosen for the purpose. One must have some basic knowledge about films and their special features to be able to make an intelligent choice. Here is a checklist.

Criteria for choosing a film :

1. The subject	- an object, a scene, a person, a group
2. The objective	- display, enlargement, slides, transparencies multimedia.
3. Type of Shot	- close up, long shot, portrait, landscape, suggestion shot.
4. Light Conditions	- day light, falling light, flood lights, flash light
5. Colour Resolution Required	

Black and White Film

Black and white films are inexpensive and simple to process and print. Their primary use is in making enlargements mostly for overhead projection. Black and white films are available in both high-contrast and continuous tone emulsions. The former is used for photographing black line material on a white background, while the latter is useful for reproducing subjects in all tones of grey as well as in black and white.

Colour Negative Film

Colour negative film is very versatile and is equally useful as negative for colour prints, for black-and-white prints, and for positive colour slides.

Colour Reversal Film

Once exposed and processed, the colour reversal films become positive in the form of slides, filmstrips, or motion pictures. In processing, the image on the film is reversed to make a positive picture.

Colour reversal films are available for 35 mm and other standard-size roll-film cameras. They come in different speeds and for different light conditions - daylight or artificial light (tungsten) etc..

Correct Exposure

The term *exposure* refers to the correct camera settings for a given film in relation to the light conditions under which it is to be used. Your camera may have a built-in exposure meter and semi or completely automatic features for determining the exposure.

For obtaining correct information regarding exposure, it is best to refer to the data sheet packaged with the film. A table gives general guidelines for proper exposure.

For general pictures to be taken under bright sunlight, you can use the f/16 rule. Set the lens at f/16 and the shutter speed at (or close to) the ASA/ISO rating of the film. For example, if you are using Ektachrome, 200, the correct exposure would be f/16 at 1/250 second.

Select camera settings of f/11 or f/16, which utilize the sharpest focus characteristics of the lens, and which ensure adequate depth-of-field.

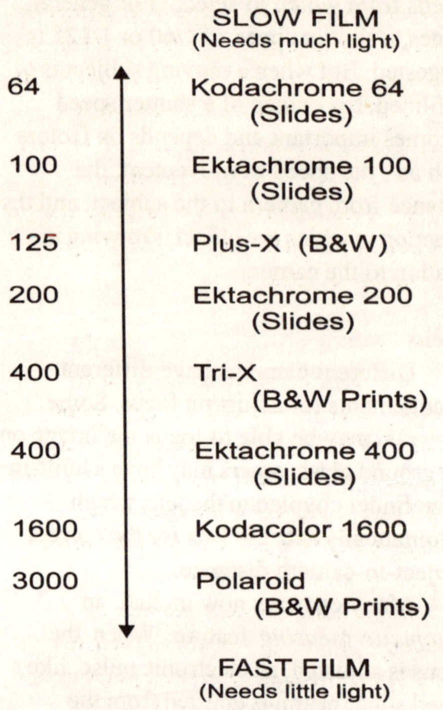

Fig. 9.3 Choosing a Film

Storing Films

All film packages are stamped with an expiration date. For best results, the film should be used before this date. The film can deteriorate by the effect of high temperature and high humidity. Therefore, unopened films to be stored for a long period of time, must be kept under refrigeration (50°F or lower). To avoid damage from moisture that may condense on cold film, it is advisable to allow the package to warm up for a few hours (to room temperature) before being opened. Similarly, the exposed film should be processed as soon as possible to avoid deterioration of the latent image on the film.

COMPOSING GOOD PICTURES

Composing good photographs is an art. It is a highly subjective activity and personal choice in framing and arranging a picture becomes very important. A number of composition principles based on the studies in perception and artistic designing can be used as guidelines.

Good composition implies that the contents of the picture are clearly recognizable, easily understood and convey the intended mood. One can begin by asking why the pictures are being taken and what specific purpose are they supposed to fulfill. Identify the objects or areas which need to be highlighted. Study the subject from different positions. Take at least three times the number of shots required so that you have ample choice for final selection. As each situation is different, it is hard to lay down standard rules as such. On the spot decisions have to be taken, therefore, only a few suggestions can be given :

* Study the scence carefully to decide which fomat - vertical or horizontal - is more suitable. Generally, it is noticed that most visual materials appear good in horizontal format and the additional benefit is that this format can be easily adapted for video or film media. As far as possible, one should try to keep consistency in format for one set or series of photographs.

* Keep only one major subject as the centre of interest in each photograph. It is not good to clutter a photograph with too many elements..

* If it is difficult to convey the correct size of the object under study, it is better to include some familiar object for comparison and to give the viewer an idea of the size.

* To centre attention on the object, it is important to keep the background simple. If required use a screen to hide the disturbing background items.

* While the focus of the picture is on the identified object/s, avoid placing them right in the centre of the picture. By making the composition somewhat asymmetrical, it is possible to create a dynamic and more interesting arrangement.

* Study the object to be photographed from different angles and choose the most flattering one. If a series of photographs have to be taken of the same object, try different camera positions to provide variety and dynamic impression.

* To convey *depth* in a photograph, study the foregound and include some details from it. Foregounds add interest and help to balance the picture, particularly if it is a long-shot exterior scene.

* If you need to capture an object in motion, then compose the shot carefully, allowing more space in the direction of the movement. This makes the pictue more dynamic.

10

TEACHING WITH SLIDES

Special Advantages of Using 35mm Slides

Getting to Know the Equipment

Types of 35mm Slides

Designing and Developing Slides

Teaching with Slides

Slide-tape Programmes

TEACHING WITH SLIDES

Slide series offer an important media option for instructors. Slides are small transparent negatives of the pictures taken with a special film meant for slides. Prepared slides are projected with the help of a slide projector.

35mm Slides offer special advantages, they

- Can portray real life events, objects, products or processes
- Can give rich colourful representation.
- Are easy to make
- Are comparatively inexpensive.
- Are small in size, and can be taken around
- Can be used in different sequences for different presentations
- Can be combined with other media, specially the audio medium to make, Slide-Tape programmes.
- Equally effective for different modes of presentations (lectures, tutorials, practicals etc.)

GETTING TO KNOW THE EQUIPMENT

Equipment required to develop photographs has already been discussed in the previous chapter. For slides, the same procedure is followed except for the film which is special for slides.

The main equipment required to project slides is the *slide projector.*

THE SLIDE PROJECTOR -

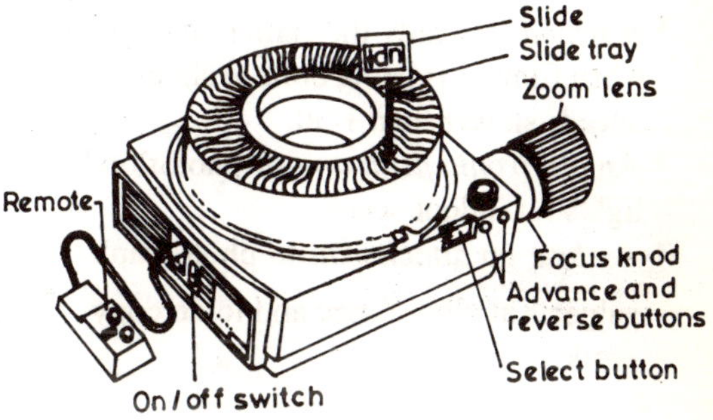

Fig. 9.1 The Slide Projector

The key component in a slide projector is a quartz halogen lamp. The light from the lamp is reflected with the help of a reflector through a filter and a set of condenser lenses on to the slide. The reflected light which passes through the slide, projects an image which is laterally inverted. This is done by an objective lens placed between the slide and the screen.

The filter, which is a thermo-crystal, absorbs most of the heat generated by the lamp and a fan is provided to ensure cooling of the filter and other components. It is therefore, advisable to switch on the fan before switching on the projector.

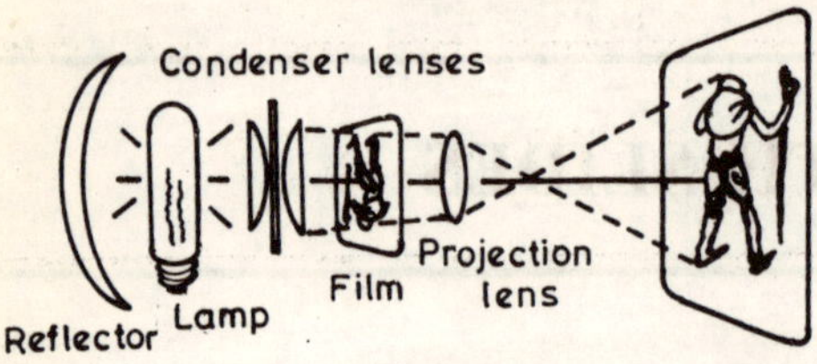

Fig. 9.2 The Principle of Slide Projection

To take high quality pictures, you may require some additional equipment such as -

* A *photographic light meter* to determine exposure accurately.
* A *tripod* to steady the camera particularly when filming is being done at shutter speeds slower than 1/30.
* An *electronic flash unit* or photoflood lights for indoor scenes.
* A *close-up attachment* to photograph subjects at close range and to do copy work.

THE SLIDES

Although a slide looks square in shape with the outer dimension of 50mm x 50mm, the actual visual area is rectangular in outline with the dimensions 24mm x 36mm.

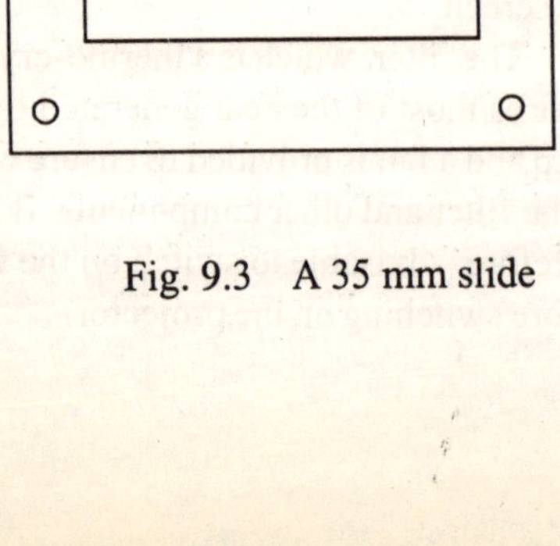

Fig. 9.3 A 35 mm slide

The pictures or graphics to be captured in the slide therefore should be in the aspect ratio of 2h:3w.

The Slide Tray

For projection, slides need to be loaded in special slide trays. These come in two very different formats. When you plan to use slides, you would like to have the tray loaded in advance. Therefore, it is vey important to find out what type of tray will be used

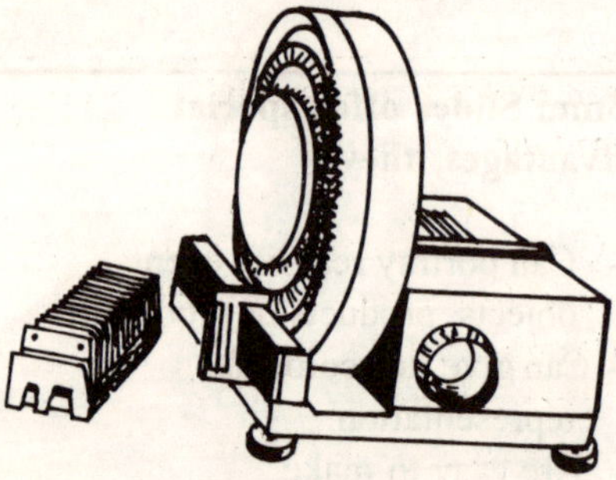

Fig. 9.4 Two Common Types of Trays to Use Slides

Different Methods for Preparing Slides

35 mm slides can be prepared by using any of the four different methodologies:

a) the subject is photographed live
b) the subject/graphic is photographed from a specially designed master. A special equipment called the *copy stand* is used.
c) the master (graphics and/or text) is generated by using a computer and captured from the screen.
d) the material generated on the computer is captured directly from within with the help of a special equipment.

Whatever the type, the basic steps

remain the same. Production of good slides involves methodical planning of different activities.

Preparing slides involves:

1. Taking pictures
2. Preparing art work and the title slide
3. Processing film
4. Mounting slides
5. Editing & sequencing slides
6. Loading slides,
7. Filing slides, and
8. Preparing the printed support materials.

Taking Pictures for Slides

The first step to peparing slides is taking pictures. Although any camera can be used for taking pictures, high quality slide series are mainly made with 35 mm cameras particularly, when close up and copy work is involved.. The 35 mm SLR cameras with adjustable lens settings (f/numbers), shutter speeds, and attachments for focusing are especially useful to photograph various subjects under almost any light conditions. These are particularly suitable for taking pictures in which involve close-up and copy work.

Before taking pictures, one should carefully study the three settings that need adjustment: the lens diaphragm, the shutter speed and the focus.

Selecting the right film

Different options are available and a decision regarding the choice of film will depend on several factors already discussed in the previous chapter.

If only one or a few copies are needed, one could select a reversal film to prepare slides. If many copies will be required, a colour negative film may be used so that inexpensive positive slides can be made by contact printing.

If, for some reason, the slides are required to be seen immediately, consider using the Polaroid's 35 mm Instant Slide System. It consists of colour or black and white film which can be used with any 35 mm camera. The film is developed in a manually operated processor for immediate viewing.

Some recommendations for composing good pictures have already been made (page 121). Same hold good for preparing photographs for slides. It is very helpful if some sort of sequence is planned out in advance. This will help you to identify and prepare material in a very organised manner saving a great deal of time and energy.

Keeping in mind the instructional objective for which the slide series is being prepared, one should compose pictures which are both beautiful and effective for the intended objective.

Designing Illustrations and Graphics:

Slides are not only made with photographs, very often slides are made with the specially designed graphics, diagrams prepared at work. You may even select a ready picture, a map or an illustration to be made into a slide. The following points should be kept in mind while preparing artwork to be used for slides:

1. Plan the art work in terms of the slide proportions.
2. Select suitable backgrounds.

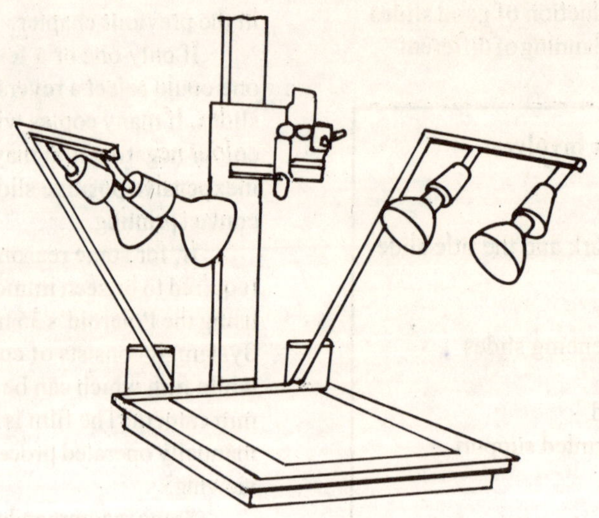

Fig. 9.5 The Copy Stand

3. Use appropriate illustrating, drawing, and colouring techniques.
4. Prepare the titles and captions carefully.

Copy Work for Camera Slides

Close up and copy techniques are used for preparing coloured or black and white slides from ready graphics or masters in the form of flat displays, maps, pictures, or diagrams.

A ***Copy Stand*** offers a stable arrangement for holding the camera on an adjustable arm. A lamp on either side allows you to play around with light to get the desired effect.

To get the best results, **masks** can be used to block off the unwanted areas. A wide variety of paper, cardboard, or plastic masks are available in the maket. These can also be easily designed and produced in-house.

Masks can hide the unwanted areas of film, change proportions of a slide, create unusual outlines for the projected images, or allow more than a single image to be put on one slide.

While using a copy stand, titles have to be taken first. If a mask is used to frame the original art work, make sure that the camera is aligned to take in the open area of the mask. Remove the mask. Then proceed with routine copying of materials made to the required size and format.

If a mask is not used, adjust picture size by raising or lowering the camera. Special attention must be paid to the recommended legibility limits of printed materials. When printed matter is copied into slide format, lettering is at times too small to be readable. Please note that acceptable legibility requires ***lettering size to be a minimum of one-fiftieth the height of the projected area.***

Composing Titles & Captions for Slides

Two different activities are involved. First, the titles and captions have to be composed and written out and then these have to be photographed and displayed on the slides. While composing the titles and captions, make sure that -

1. Each title is worded to be crisp, brief and communicative
2. Font and lettering size is appropriate for the objectives
3. Lettering and art work is designed as per slide aspect ratio
4. Titles/captions are composed neatly by using tools such as stencils, transfer letters etc.

Once the titles are composed, they can be captured for display in a variety of ways. Any one of the following formats may be chosen:

1. Clear letters on black background
2. Coloured letters on black background
3. Clear letters over subject
4. Black letters on clear background

Titles can be shown using *scrolling or revelation technique* whereby titles appear one after the other in a series, one at a time, but in cumulative order.

The easiest way to achieve this is to prepare the total list on a white paper, then use the negative slide method for preparing the titles. Frame the entire list in the camera, then cover all items but the first one with a sheet of white paper. Film the first item. For the second picture, uncover the second item and film the two that are exposed. Repeat the process. The result will be a series of slides, each one revealing an additional title or item on the list.

A variation of the above procedure is to shoot the required number of negatives, each one showing the total list of items. Then block out the unwanted items on each negative by brushing on any opaque material.

Computer Generated Slides

Here, the text and/or graphics are generated in full colour with the help of a computer and then captured by the camera from the screen.

First, the graphics should be developed and approved. To develop computer graphics, special software is required. A number of powerful software such as *Power Point, Coral Draw, Haward Graphics* etc. are available for generating high quality graphics.

The simplest way is to generate the complete visual and then photograph it directly from the computer screen with a regular 35 mm SLR camera equipped with a close up lens.

Fig. 9.6 Capturing Images Directly from the Computer Screen

The camera lens is masked to eliminate reflections of the camera parts on the computer screen. Evidently, this is not the perfect way to capture graphics. Some loss in image resolution and sharpness, colour reproduction, and distortion due to curvature of the cathode ray tube, are to be expected.

Better results are obtained when slides are prepared by using a special equipment which is specially adapted to receive impulses directly from the digital data stored or created in the computer. The camera is loaded at the back of the equipment which is attached to the computer. Here, you need to prepare the slide as they are to be finally seen by the viewers. The visuals are then downloaded and clicked automatically.

This process gives very high quality slides without any surprises in colour combinations etc..

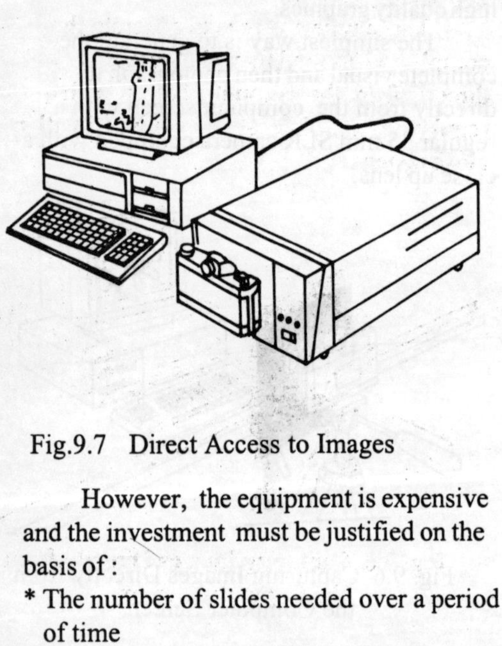

Fig.9.7 Direct Access to Images

However, the equipment is expensive and the investment must be justified on the basis of :

* The number of slides needed over a period of time
* How quickly the slides are needed
* The level of slide quality required in terms of resolution, colour selection etc.

Mounting Slides

Once the slides are developed, they must be mounted before they can be used in the slide projector. Different types of mounts or frames are available -

a) ***Cardboard Frames*** - These are the frames in which slides come mounted from the processing laboratory. These are fairly cheap. The main advantage here is that the presenter can number them and also mark cue words etc. with a felt pen. However, these frames donot last very well. They often open up with heat and dampness and bend easily causing jamming up in the projector.

b)***Plastic Frames*** - These are stronger than the ones in cardboard, they do not bend or fray. Mounting of film is easy and quick. But they are more expensive.

c) ***Glass Frames*** - These frames ensure best protection for the slide. Comparatively very expensive, they are more useful for slides meant to be used over a long period. The disadvantage can be that they are heavy and liable to break. Also, glass mounts do not fit into all trays.

Loading Slides

Once slides are mounted, they are ready to be used. It is impotant to learn the correct way to load them into trays.

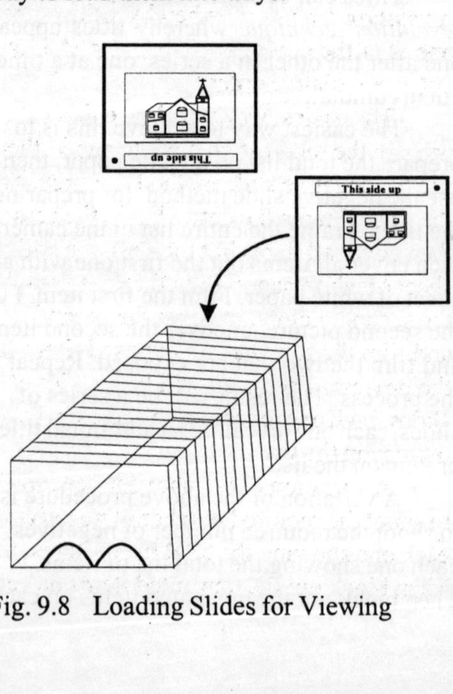

Fig. 9.8 Loading Slides for Viewing

Slides are notorious for getting loaded the wrong way. Every user has to practise loading slides in a tray.

One way to ensure correct loading is to place a dot with a felt pen in the lower left corner of the frame when the slide is viewed correctly by the naked eye. *When placed in a tray for projection, the mark will be in the upper right corner.*

You may have to try this several time before acquiring full control over the loading process.

Filing Slides

As the number of slides accumulates, some type of filing system becomes essential so that individual slides can be located easily. Develop a numercial or colour-coded filing system.

Slides can be stored in specially designed plastic covers with small pockets to hold each slide seperately. The advantage here is that you can recognize the slides with the naked eye, select and use them.

If you depend heavily on slides and serious filing effort is called for, a very effective, though somewhat labour intensive method is to create reprographic prints for visual reference. To do this, classify slides according to topics. Place numbered groups of slides on a light box and photograph them using a black and white film. Develop large size prints (minimum 8" x10"). This sheet, with its numbered slide pictures, can be referred to when slides are being selected for a presentation.

An easier way is to use a computer filing (database) system to maintain information on the slide file. It is also a good idea to maintain other information about each slide set. Information regarding each slide set including the date of preparation, names and addresses of the subject experts, location, photographer, film type used etc. can be very useful for future reference. This information can be either pasted inside the file or put on small printed labels which can be pasted on to sets of slides.

The Slide-tape Programme

The slide-tape programme comprising slides accompanied by recorded commentary, is a very popular media option used in different instructional environments.

A Slide-tape Programme offers several advantages -

* It is easy to prepare.
* It is cost effective.
* It offers real sound effects.
* It can capture real life events.
* It can capture activities in stages.
* It can explain, demonstrate a process in steps.
* It has strong dramatic appeal.
* It can be used by different instructors in different learning situations.
* It is equally effective as an instructional and motivational tool.

Preparing a Slide-Tape Programme

While preparing a slide-tape programme, all the basic considerations of designing instructional media have to be applied. You need to be sure about the exact learning outcome and the special suitability of this particular medium.

A very important step is preparing the *script.* A script helps in clarifying ideas, selecting the best sequences and planning special visual or audio effects. A well worked out script can save a lot of time and effort. A script also becomes absolutely necessary if the programme is to be developed by someone else.

SCRIPT FOR A SLIDE-TAPE PROGRAMME

Please note that the visuals have to be designed in the propotion of 3:4:

No.	Visual on the Slide	Spoken Words/Sounds

Fig. 9.9 Format for Writing Scripts for Slide-tape Programmes

Preparing a Slide-tape Programme?
A checklist :

* Why is a slide-tape programme more suitable?
* How will it ensure the specific learning outcome?
* Who is going to view the programme?
  - their age,
  - academic background
  - cultutral background
  - language competency
* Will the programme benefit from a male or a female voice?
* How can the viewers be involved ?
* Is any printed support material required.

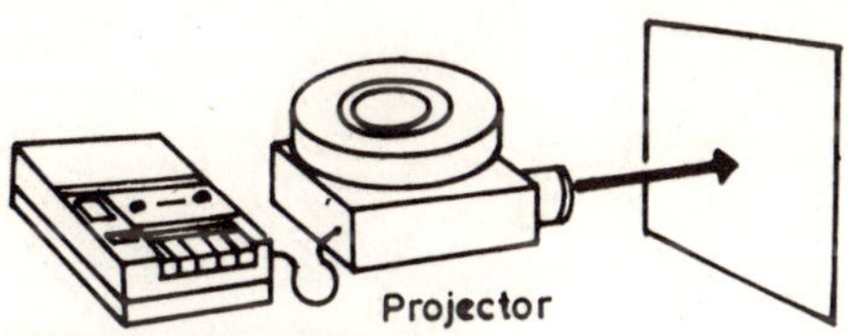

Fig. 9.10 A Slide-tape Programme

Using the Slide-tape programme

When your slides is ready to be used, a number of final details need to be attended to.To begin with, it is important that you view the entire programme in the sequence in which you plan to use it. Identify points where you would like to pause for related activities. These should be points of high interest or high difficulty for the learners. Always have a duplicate copy of the audiotape handy.

Two Projector Presentation

Very interesting and impressive presentations can be made by using two projectors. Here, two sets of slides forming one presentation are prepared and projected by two projectors giving an impression of movement and vitality.

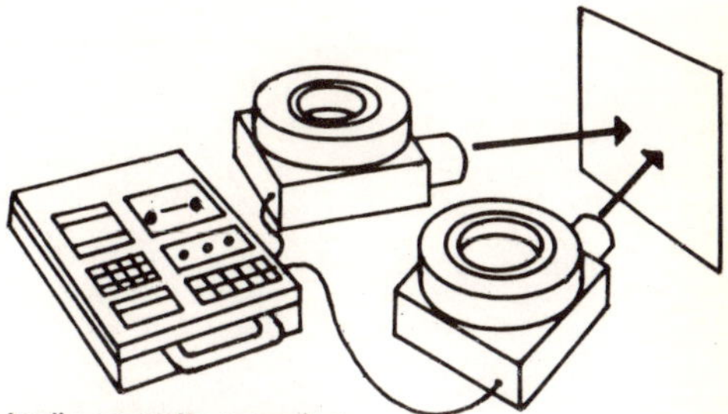

Fig. 9.11 Two Projection Presentation

This type of presentation requires a person to manage the slide projection. With the help of preplanned sequence, slides from the two projectors are called with one image fading out on the screen and the next one slowly taking its place, thus creating an effective impression of gradual change and transformation as images blend into each other.

To project slides in this fashion, a *dissolve* unit is required. The simplest type of dissolve units have one or a few fixed dissolve rates for controlling two projectors. Some sophisticated units can be programmed to create numerous screen effects by controlling the on-off rates of projectors.

More sophisticated dissolve units permit special effects such as flashing, superimposing, pop-ons, pop-offs, forward-reverse-hold and simulated animation.

11

THE VIDEO MEDIUM

Special Advantages of the Video Medium

Films versus the Video Medium

Getting to Know the Equipment

Steps to Video Production

Writing Scripts and Commentaries

Interactive Video

Fundamentals of Video Conferencing

THE VIDEO MEDIUM

Like films, the video medium incorporates images, sounds and movement. Although relatively a young member in the instructional media family, the video medium has become the most popular media option with instructors. The medium has somewhat revolutionised instruction and has made significant contribution in the area of open and distance learning.

Videotape recording and motion picture films share a close relationship in that each can present information, describe a process, clarify complex concepts, teach a skill, condense and expand time, and affect an attitude.

Yet, eversince the arrival of the video medium, the film medium has occupied the back seat. There are several reasons for this. The main reason is the ease with which everyone can use it. The popularity of the video medium is going to increase even further as the technology is improving and becoming more cost-effective.

Special Advantages of the Video Medium

* Video equipment is easy to operate.
* Videotape is not sensitive to light and loading and unloading tape in the recorder is easy and quick.
* Videotape does not have to be developed and can be viewed right after recording, allowing for immediate evaluation of results.
* Videotape is economical and can be reused many times.
* Sound and picture are more easily recorded together (in synchronization).
* Special effects in the form of sophisticated graphics and animation can be produced easily.
* Duplication of programmes is easy and inexpensive.
* Packaging, transportation and handling is easy.
* Other resources like photographs, sounds, slides etc. can be incorporated in a video programme.
* The format is compatible with the computer. The graphics generated on the computer screen can be recorded directly.
* It can reach the most inaccessible locales - on the mountains, in deep seas, and even the sky is not the limit.

GETTING TO KNOW THE EQUIPMENT

As in the case of the audio medium, the video medium requires equipment for recording and for playing back the video programme.

For recording the essential components are:

* The Videocamera
* The Microphone,
* The Videotape recorder, and
* The Videotapes

It is becoming increasingly common to have equipment that combines all these (except the tape) into a single, compact unit called a **Camcorder.**

A. The Videocamera

.Most videocameras in use today transmit images in colour. Visual images are received through the lens and are focused on a light-sensitive surface within the camera. Cameras with the microchip are very stable, rugged, and can be used even in extremely feeble light conditions.

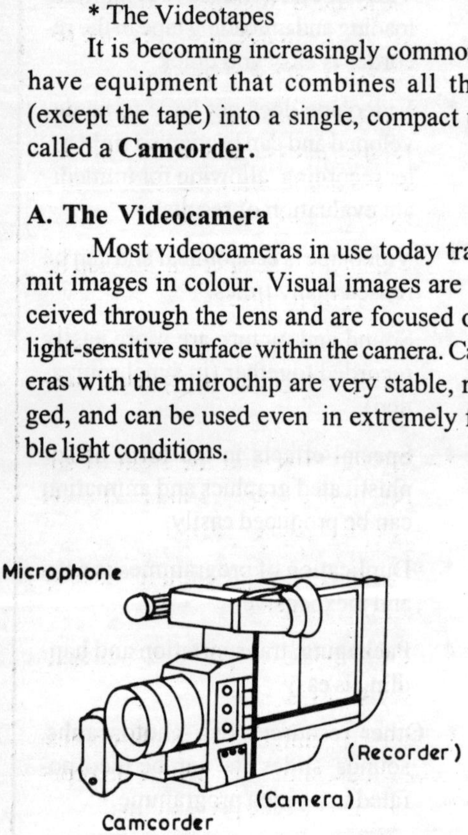

Fig.11.1 The Videocamera

The videocamera has a viewfinder through which the camera operator composes and then observes the scene being shot. The image received in the viewfinder is commonly black and white, if colour representation is important, then it is necessary to attach a colour monitor to the video recorder.

In a television studio, large videocameras are mounted on pedestals or heavy duty tripods. But for most shooting, small, compact portable cameras are used. Their relative light weight and flexibility allow recordings to be made at almost any location under normal or low light conditions.

Most videocameras are equipped with a zoom lens. The zoom lens allows the picture to be captured from a range of magnifications without having to move the camera closer to or farther from the subject. Ideally, the lens should have a zoom ratio of at least 10 to 1, should be motorized, and include automatic setting. It is possible to have *auto focus* lenses which can be activated to focus automatically when the camera is aimed at a subject.

Light is an important factor for video recording. A videocamera reacts to the colour temperature of different light sources. Therefore, it is necessary to adjust it for the quality of incoming light since shooting may take place under different light sources or combinations of sunlight, fluorescent lights, and floodlights. In addition, before recording, a *white balance* setting must be made which fine tunes the camera for the particular lighting conditions under which the scene will be recorded.

On newer, portable videocameras, the indoor/outdoor filter setting and the white balance are adjusted automatically by moving one switch. Some videocameras have built-in titlers too. They permit to compose titles or words to be used as sub-titles.

The Microphone receives the sound waves and converts them into electrical impulses that are also sent through a cable to the videotape recorder.

The Videotape recorder (VTR) is the key equipment. It converts electrical impulses into a magnetic force of varying frequency and intensity, resulting in a precise magnetic pattern representing picture and sound on the tape surface. Picture and sound signals, generated at the camera and the microphone, are received by the videotape recorder through its recording heads. The electrical impulses are converted into precise magnetic patterns.

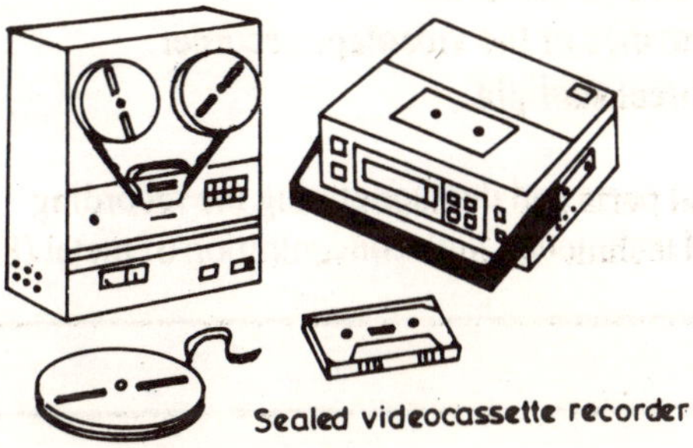

Fig. 11.2 TheVideo Recording Equipment

Videotape width is one factor that detemines the format of a videotape recorder to be used. Widths are available in 2 inches, 1 3/4 inch, 1/2 inch, and 1/4 inch or 8 mm. For low budget educational and training programmes 1/2 inch and 8 mm sizes are the most widely used. Commercial broadcasts and high-quality professional recordings require the wider tapes.

Another important feature found on many VCRs is the flying erase head. While in operation, it permits you to record sequential scenes, or edit adjacent scenes, with a "clean cut" between each scene. Without a flying erase head, a visual discontinuity (called a glitch) appears on the tape when the camera is stopped and then started again.

All models of VCRs can be operated both on electricity and batteries. For location shooting, battery packs are used. The battery pack generally permits 30 minutes or more of recording and playback time.

* **Video monitor** is used to review what has been recorded. With portable, battery-operated equipment, the black-and white camera viewfinder serves as the picture monitor and the sound is heard through an earphone. It may be better to use a colour video monitor or television receiver for viewing scenes after they are shot.

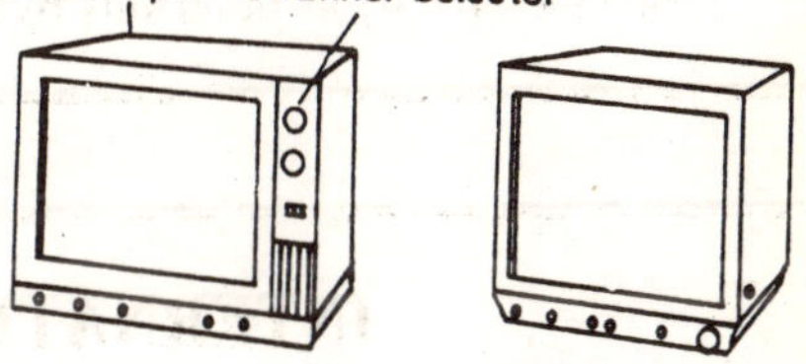

11.3 The TV and the Monitor

There is a difference in the technology used in a video monitor and a TV receiver. Of the two, a monitor is electronically simpler and offers a superior picture. A television receiver, which is used at home, receives television signals through an antenna or cable connection. The electronic signals are converted into video and audio impulses through a process called "demodulation" to become the visible picture with sound. In a monitor, the audio and video outputs come directly from within the circuit of the monitor.

* **Tripod or cart** : For steadiness during use, a camera should be attached to a sturdy support.
* **Lights** : Floodlights are required to illuminate indoor scenes. Quartz halogen lamps mounted on heavy-duty stands are preferred. The lights may be used to supplement available light or to provide the main illumination for recording.

Maintenance of Video Recording Equipment

In order to ensure satisfactory performance from your equipment, particularly, the camera, regular maintenance is necessary.

* Do not aim the camera at the sun or other bright light since this can damage the videotube.
* Turn the camera OFF when it will not be used for a period of time.
* Cap the lens when the camera is not in use.
* Keep the lens clean by dusting with a soft camel's hair brush.
* Use high-quality tape to increase the performance of the videotape recorder.
* Protect the VTR from dirt, dampness, and direct sunlight.
* Periodically clean the magnetic heads.
* In case of a problem, the cleaning of internal parts and demagnetizing the recording heads should only be done only by a qualified technician. high concentration of metal (8mm

INTERNATIONAL VIDEO SYSTEMS

Electronic standards established for video equipment are different in different countries. Variations exist in electrical power requirements, number of scan lines on a frame, frames per second projected to the screen, and the method of encoding colour. There are three main systems.

	NTSC	PAL	SECAM
FORMAT	Developed by National Television System Committee 60 cycles 525 scan lines per frame, 30 frames per second	Phase Alternate by Line. 50 cycles of electricity, 625 scan lines per frame 25 frames per second	Sequential with Memory. 50 cycles of electricity 625 scan lines per frame 25 frames per second
USER COUNTRIES	USA, Japan and South America	England, India, West Germany, Africa and Australia	France, Russia, East and North Africa

About Videotapes ...

The videotape consists of a magnetic oxide coating on a polyester base. For many years, iron oxide had been the standard material. Now, chromium dioxide and other substances, with a tape), are used as the coating for high quality tape. These materials offer better picture and sound quality and improved image sharpness.

When selecting a video tape, make two important decisions. First, identify the format of the recorder. Second, choose a suitable tape recording time. Playing times may vary from about 30 minutes to 8 hours. Playing time is based on both the amount of tape in the cassette and the speed of tape movement in the recorder. For highest quality picture and sound, recording should be done at the fastest speed.

If small black or white horizontal flashes are visible on the monitor when a tape is played back, it is because there has been momentary loss of contact between the head and the tape. Such imperfections are called *dropouts*. There could be many reasons for these dropouts. They could be caused by dust or dirt on the tape, flaking of magnetic oxide because of tape wear, a tape manufacturing defect, or dirty/worn heads in the recorder.

To a great extent, the technical quality of a recording depends on the quality of the videotape used. A poor-quality or a worn tape may produce a distorted picture. A wrinkled tape can damage recording and playback heads in the recorder. To ensure proper tape quality, keep these facts in mind while choosing and using a videotape :

* Select a well-know brand of tape for use. Cheaper bargains may be manufacturer's seconds or slightly damaged tapes.
* Before using a new videotape, fast forward the tape to the end, and fully rewind it without stopping. This adjusts the tape tension to the recorder and reduces sticking between the layers.
* Keep the tape in its original case and store it placed in a vertical position. The pressure on the edges keeps the of tape from curling which often distorts both picture and sound.
* Protect the tape from dust, high humidity (40 to 60 percent preferred), or temperature extremes (60° to 70°F preferred).
* Store tapes away from TV receivers or other equipment that could generate a magnetic field. This can cause erasure of recorded signals on a videotape.
* Consider the effect of carrying videotape recordings (also audiotape recordings and undeveloped films) through an X-ray inspection station at an airport. A single passage may not be harmful, but repeated exposure to the X-ray can disturb electronically created images. Either request hand inspection or place the cassette in a special leadfoil container.
* After recording on a videocassette, remove the cut out tab from the back so the recording cannot be erased accidentlly. If the programme to be recorded is a long one, have on hand sufficient number of videocassettes so you can shoot segments of the program on separate cassettes. This procedure will save time at the editing stage as the scenes can be easily located.

VIDEO FORMATS

FORMAT	SPECIAL FEATURES	LIMITATIONS
VIDEOCASSETTE VHS 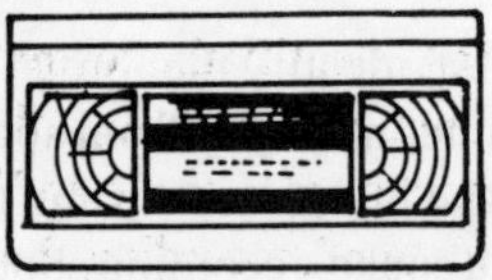 (120 min at standard speed) Tape width: 1/2 in.	Self-contained and self-threading More compact than U-matic Abundant software available Easy local production	Video quality low; not broadcast quality. Quality deteriorates with use
VIDEOCASSETTE (U-matic)  (10-60 min.) Tape width : 3/4 in.	Used as master cassette Superior video quality Studio production,	Mostly used for transmission & field recording, not used in education not distributed
VIDEOCASSETTE (HI 8)  (120 min at standard speed) Tape width :8 mm about 1/4 in.)	Most compact format Full compatibility with all makes and models Easy local production	Video quality lower Limited acceptance in education; Little software available
COMPACT DISC (CDI and DVI)  Variable high speed Diameter : 4.72 in.	Easy to use Low-cost hardware and software Worldwide standard Self-contained hardware	Limited educational software Hardware difficult to install & match Does not show full-motion video
VIDEODISC  30 min. per side Diameter: 12 in.	Flexible storage capacity : can hold 54,000 images, still or motion, or audio Fast random access to specific frames Highly durable Inexpensive when mass-produced	Not for local production Originals expensive to produce

Developing Video Programmes

The Following flow Chart depicts the essential steps in the process -

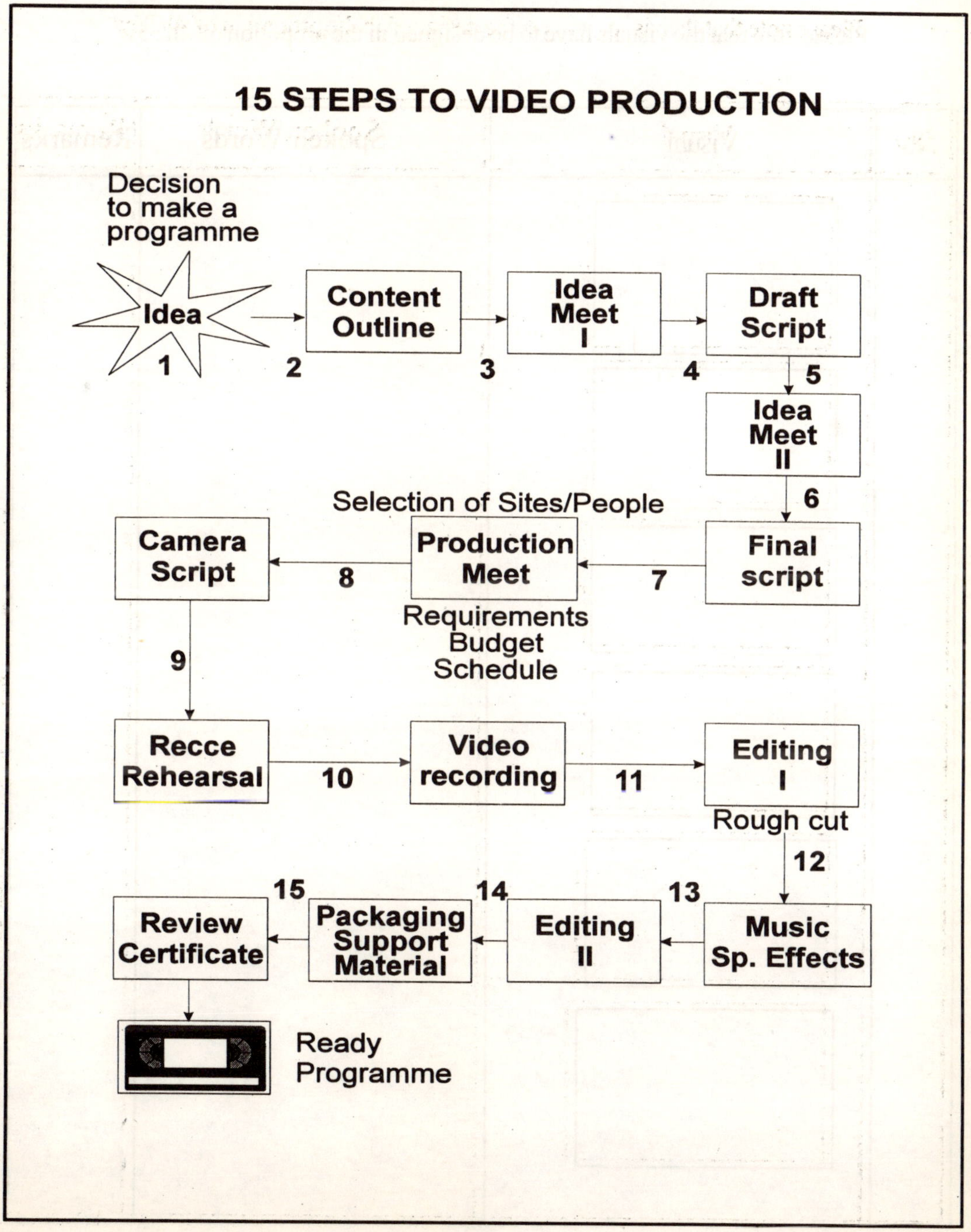

Writing Scripts for Video Programmes

Please note that the visuals have to be designed in the propotion of 4h : 5w

No	Visual	Spoken Words	Remarks

SOME TYPICAL SHOTS USED IN VIDEO RECORDING

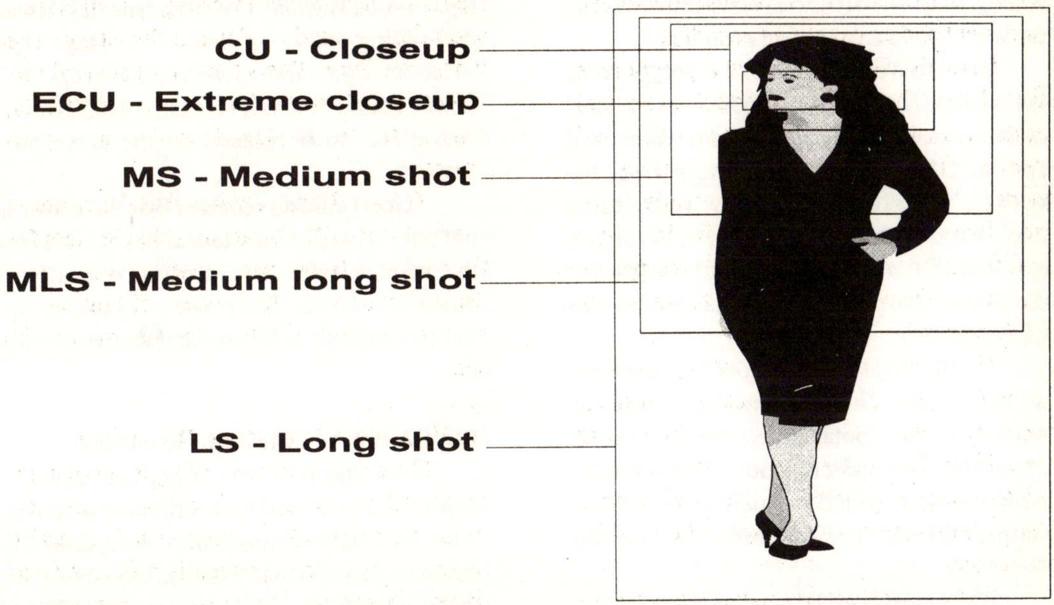

2 Sht - Two shot

3 Sht - Three shot

WS - Wide shot

C Sht - Crowd shot

OSS - Over the shoulder shot

Editing

There are various levels of videotape editing. Each one of them involves professional equipment and an exacting procedure.

It is at the editing stage that a programme takes shape. The resulting product is the final master videotape with all scenes, titles, and special effects arranged in the correct sequence. The progamme is now ready to be used. Even though editing must be done by a qualified *Editor* it is essential for the person developing the programme to have some idea of the process.

The original camera recording is termed as the *footage*. The edited master recording, made from the footage, becomes the *master copy*. From the master, another copy the *sub-master* is made which is usually used to make further duplicate copies meant to be used by consumers.

Editing involves taking decisions concerning content, pace or flow, and ensuring continuity. This requires sequencing scenes; selecting takes; determining scene length or the usable portion of a scene; mixing narration, lip synchronization, and other sound effects; and reviewing the need for the placement of titles, captions, and special effects like animation etc..

We know that while developing a video programme, scenes can be shot in any order. The producer keeps a record of these shots on the tapes from which the final selection will be made. Normally, six to eight times of *footage* is recorded. That implies that for a ten minute programme, raw shots of at least one hour are available for the editor to select from. To begin with the shots are *logged* i.e. a detailed list of shots is prepared so that the editor can locate them.

Two VCRs are used. Shots are selected with the help of a computer are placed on the tape using a *switcher*. Inserting special effects and adding sound is done at this stage. The video medium allows the use of several different sound tracks (voices, sound effects, music etc) to be placed on the same programme.

Good editing requires that the editor is not only visually literate and has the feel for the medium, but is also creative with a great deal of patience. The process of editing involves constant selection and decision making.

Duplicating a Videotape Recording

Once the master recording is completed, copies will be needed for distribution purposes. Also, the playback machines used generally require a tape format which is different from that of the master. Most masters are prepared in U-matic or Beta format whereas copies are made in the VHS format. In either case, duplication of the video programme becomes an important activity.

Duplicating, like editing, requires two VCRs one to play the master tape and the other to record the duplicated tape. If a format change is required the recording unit should match the appropriate format. The unit with the master videotape is set in the playback mode and connected to the unit with duplicate-tape unit, set in the recording mode. If proper care is given to audio and video level settings and machine alignment, a good-quality recording can be obtained.

More than one sub-masters may be prepared. But with each successive generation, there is a slight reduction in image quality. This is particularly true when 1/2 inch or 8 mm format copies are used to prepare further copies.

Tips for Composing Commentaries

* Words must not repeat the visuals but explain and enliven them.
* Select words, terms, expressions and examples from audience's experience range.
* Use the active rather than the passive voice.
* Choose words judiciously because each one of them is time bound.
* Cultivate conciseness by eliminating superfluous words and inadvertent repetitions.
* Make the statements short and potent by reducing wherever possible a clause to a phrase, and a phrase to a single word.
* Make generous use of the rhetorical question.
* Avoid odd, foreign, formal, stilted, literary usages and cliches.
* Do not begin with a negative construction.
* Avoid long-winded, highbrow sentences with multiple clauses.
* Bring life to narration by exploiting variety in sentence structure : by varying their type, length and opening.

STUDIO TALK !!

* ***ZO*** - Zoom out
* ***ZI*** - Zoom in
* ***PL*** - Pan Left (cover left side)
* ***PR*** - Pan Right (cover right side)
* ***Crab L*** - Shift the camera towards left
* ***Crab R*** - Shift the camera towards right
* ***Fade out*** - Get out of the shot
* ***Fade in*** - Get into the shot
* ***Tilt up*** - Tilt the camera upwards
* ***Tilt down*** - Tilt the camera downwards
* ***Track in*** - Bring the camera forward
* ***Track out*** - Take the camera back
* **Recce** - visit to location
* **Q** - cue to start
* ***Roll VTR*** - start taping
* ***AB*** - as before
* ***Action*** - start action
* ***Cut*** - interrupt recording
* ***Dissolve*** - merge shots
* ***Wipe*** - wipe to next shot
* ***V/O*** - voice over
* ***SFX*** - special effects
* ***FX*** - sound effects
* ***Run through***

Using Your Videotape Recording

As with any type of media, the care you give to the preparation for using the materials is important to their ultimate success.

This means that the teacher should plan all the various activities involved in using a video programme in class. She must arrange for the basic equipment i.e. the videocassette player and one or seveal monitors depending on the number of viewers. She has to have the monitors placed appropriately so that the room light does not disturb the viewers. The instructor also has to plan how she wishes to introduce the programme and integerate it with other related activities to be conducted before and after the programme.

A video programme is best utilised if it is paused every now and then to ask questions and to generate discussion.

Appropriate handouts and supplements should be prepared in advance to invite viewer participation. After use, it is essential to take feedback regarding the instructional and enjoyment value of the programme.

VIDEODISCS

A new, more effective and inexpensive option for using the video medium is now available in the form of *video discs*. Preparation of a videodisc requires application of optical disc technology. This refers to the use of a laser beam to transfer images and sound from a videotape recording to a master videodisc, (also called a laser disc) from which duplicate copies are made. The procedure is almost similar to the one used for making audio compact discs (CD).

Information in visual form that has been recorded on videotape can be transferred to a master videodisc for inexpensive multiple-copy preparation.

The most widely used method for producing a videodisc is to start with a videotape recording and from it have a commercial laboratory produce a master videodisc from which duplicate copies are obtained. As professional equipment and skill is requires, it is best to get this done by a reliable qualified agency.

Special Advantages Of Videodiscs :

* Large storage capacity. Very large amounts of information, in any media form, can be put on a videodisc. Typically, on one side of a 12 inch videodisc, between 30 minutes and 1 hour of moving pictures with two sound tracks or 54,000 individual frames of still pictures, text, or combinations of motion and still images can be stored

* Pictures and sound reproduction are of a very high quality. Sharp, crisp images with excellent colour can be shown on a large screen, along with high fidelity sound.

* Pictures do not degenerate with time or use.

* Information can be easily and quickly located. It is convenient to move almost instantaneously from one spot on a videodisc to another for locating a segment or individual frame.

VIDEO TELECONFERENCE

The concept involves an alive, two-way communication arrangement connecting groups of learners located at remote locations. The communication involves the use of satellite and telephone lines. Voice is transmitted both ways and video distribution may be one-way (a) or two-way (b).

(a) One-way video option

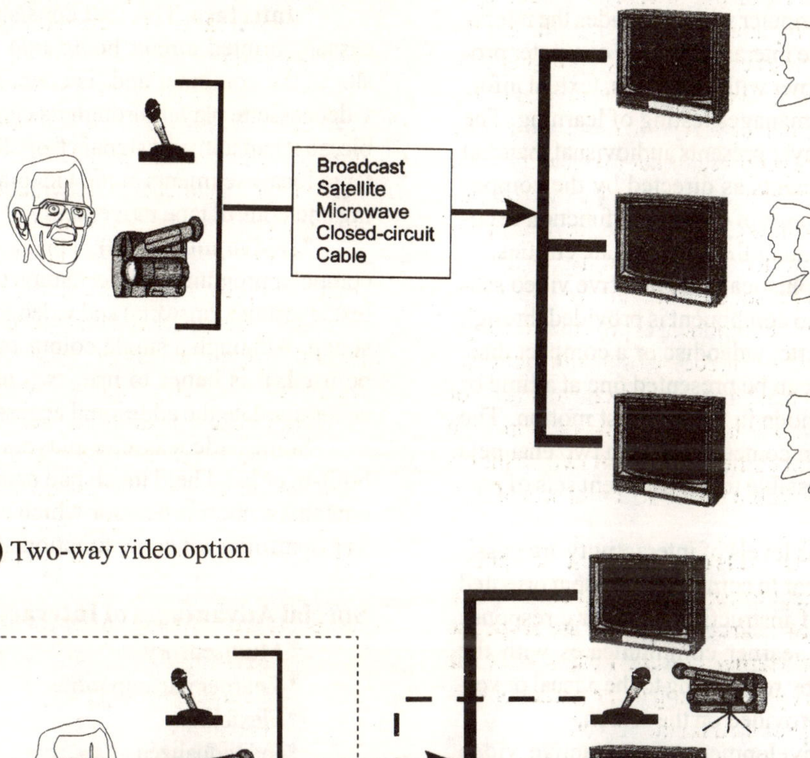

(b) Two-way video option

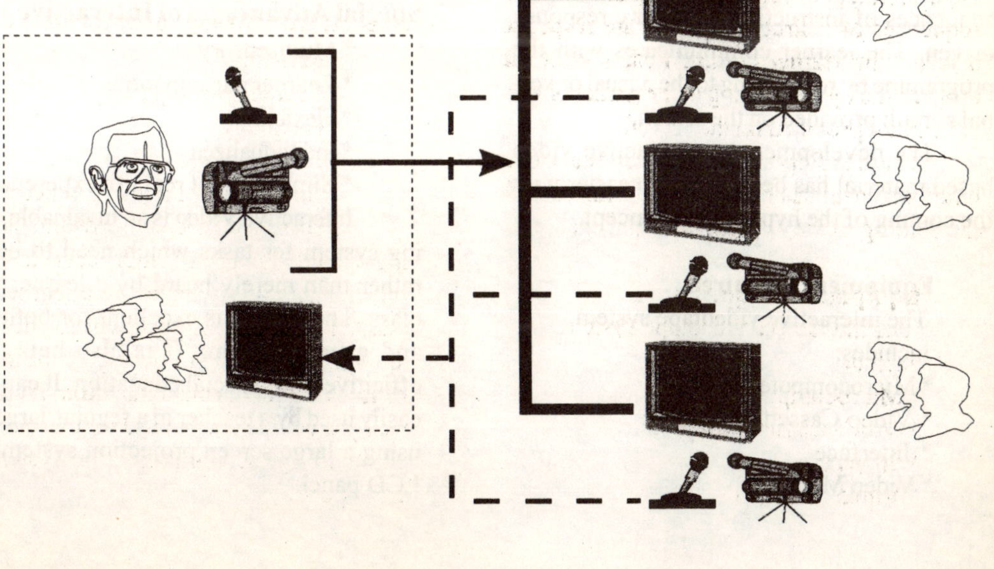

INTERACTIVE VIDEO

It is a delivery system where recorded video material is presented under the control of a computer. The system integerates the powerful features of both the video and the computer assisted Instruction. The learner not only sees, hears and learns but can also respond.

The heart of the interactive video system is the computer which provides the intelligence, and the interactivity. The computer provides the learner with directions, textual information, and manages testing of learning. The videotape player presents audiovisual material in short segments as directed by the computer. The two units of equipment function in coordination, rather than as separate entities.

In a sophisticated interactive video system, the video component is provided through a videocassette, videodisc or a compact disc. The images can be presented one at a time or in running mode in slow or fast motion. The audio portion comes in through two channels making it possible to use different sets of narrations.

Various levels of interactivity are possible from linear to completely student oriented sequences of instruction which are response driven. The learner communicates with the programme by responding to the visual or verbal stimuli provided on the screen.

The development of interactive video based material has become much easier with the coming of the hypermedia concept.

Equipment Required

The interactive videotape system includes:

* Microcomputer
* Video Cassette Player
* Interface
* Video Monitors

* **Microcomputer**. The microcomputer serves as the controlling component of the system. It receives input from the learner, processes the information, and outputs a display on the screen. It also directs which video segment is to be shown.

* **Videocassette player**. This is the unit on which the subject recording is played and controlled by the computer programme.

* **Interface**. This unit consists of an accessory printed circuit board that fits into a slot in the computer and is connected to the videocassette player through its electronic cable, so it can transmit signals from the computer to locate segments of the videotape recording and control tape movement.

* **Video monitor(s)**. This unit displays computer programme information (directions, text, questions, answers) and video images with sound. Although a single colour monitor can be used, it is better to use two monitors to accommodate the additional accessory items.

Some videocassette players include a built-in or hand held touch pad accessory that contains a microprocessor which can be used as a controller for some functions.

Special Advantages of Interactive Video

* Multisensory
* Learner participation
* Flexibility
* Individualized
* Simulation of real life experences

Interactive Video is an invaluable learning system for tasks which need to be *seen* rather than merely heard by a learner in the class. The system is excellent for both weak and gifted learners. It is also being used efficitively for special education. It can be easily used by a teacher in a regular/large class using a large screen projection system or an LCD panel.

Developing an Interactive Video Programme

Planning an interactive videotape recording requires the same procedures used to design a conventional videotape recording. Consider this checklist :

* Have you stated the objectives to be served by your production ?
* Have you considered the audience that will use the material ?
* Have you expressed your ideas clearly and delimited the topic ?
* Have you prepared a content outline?
* Have you considered whether a computer/videotape is an appropriate medium for accomplishing the objectives and handling the content ?
* Have you written a treatment to help organize the handling of the content ?
* Have you prepared a scene-by-scene script as a guide for your shooting ?
* Have you, if necessary, selected your team to assist with the production and testing etc.?
* Have you considered the specifications necessary for your production ?

You may find that a videotape recording already exists that contains most, if not all, of the content you plan to treat. If such a recording is available, you can start with it and avoid much of the production phase. The procedure of using existing video material and adapating it for interactive learning is called *repurposing a videotape recording.*

Using Interactive Video

Effective use of the interactive video demands certain maturity and clear thinking on the part of the learner. The reason is that the learner needs to take a number of decision independently regarding the content and the sequence of learning.

The main difference between conventional video and interactive video is that with the latter, the visual sequences do not have to be viewed in linear order. The teacher/instructor can shuffle the order and choose from several optional paths, depending on the objectives, learner's need and learner's ability.

For most effective use, it is important for the teacher to analyze each instructional segment of the content.

Following questions can help :

* Can points be identified at which choices or decisions need to be made, or at which a test question should be asked ?
* What options should be available to the learner at these decision points ?
* What form should a test question take ?
* Need there be provision for review or rectification ?
* What information should appear on the computer screen ?
* What material should be treated in the videotape recording ?
* What support material or additional exercises should be available on paper ?

The best way to find answers to these questions and to design the various aspects of an instructional segment, is to construct a detailed flow chart. Here, the flow chart acts like a storyboard. The flow chart can illustrate the various instructional events that will occur, the decision points, the alternative paths available to a learner. The flow chart also establishes the relation between different resources: the computer programme, the video segment and the printed materials. Some input regarding flow charts is provided on page166.

12

COMPUTERS IN INSTRUCTION

Computer as an Instructional Tool

How Computers Work

The Computer and the Teacher

Designing Computer -based Support Material

About Multimedia and Hypermedia

Introduction to the Internet

COMPUTERS IN INSTRUCTION

Amongst all technological options available to a teacher, none commands more awe and respect than a computer. However, with every new release of hardware or software, the perplexity increases. Many of us are even reluctant to discuss computers in education, let alone use them. But, the fact is that to harness the vast potential of this technological genie, a teacher needs to have at least selective information on the subject and that is the precise objective of this chapter.

What is required is more a change in attitude rather than expertise of a high order. An attitude of acceptance of computers as a valuable tool for teaching.

Computers are as useful for a teacher as for a learner. Computers can record, store, analyse and communicate words and figures with equal dexterity.

A number of accusations are levied against computers: They are known to be expensive; they generate high expectations but are able to achieve only selected learning objectives; they operate in a highly controlled environment and do not pemit social interaction

In spite of all these limitations, computers have really arrived in the world of instruction and are here to stay.

Special Advantages of Computers in Instruction

* Store large quantities of data.
* Offer flexibility of pace, time & place.
* Offer flexibility to retrieve the precise information without having to go through any prescribed system.
* Are compact and light in weight and do not require much space. Portable versions are very popular.
* Offer interactivity with the learner.
* Are precise and error free.
* Provide immediate feedback.
* Can be integrated with other media.
* Can simulate real life/laboratory objects, operations and situations.
* Allow individualized and private working.
* Can be linked to other learners/users around the world.
* Deliver information in a reliable and consistent, standard form.
* Can be used for any discipline, for any desired tasks

The greatest strength of computers is their compatibility with other media formats. Computers have the capability to utilize the power of different media options to create new, more powerful modes of communication. The graphic below attempts to illustrate the great potential of this wonder medium for absorbing text, sounds, still pictures and moving images.

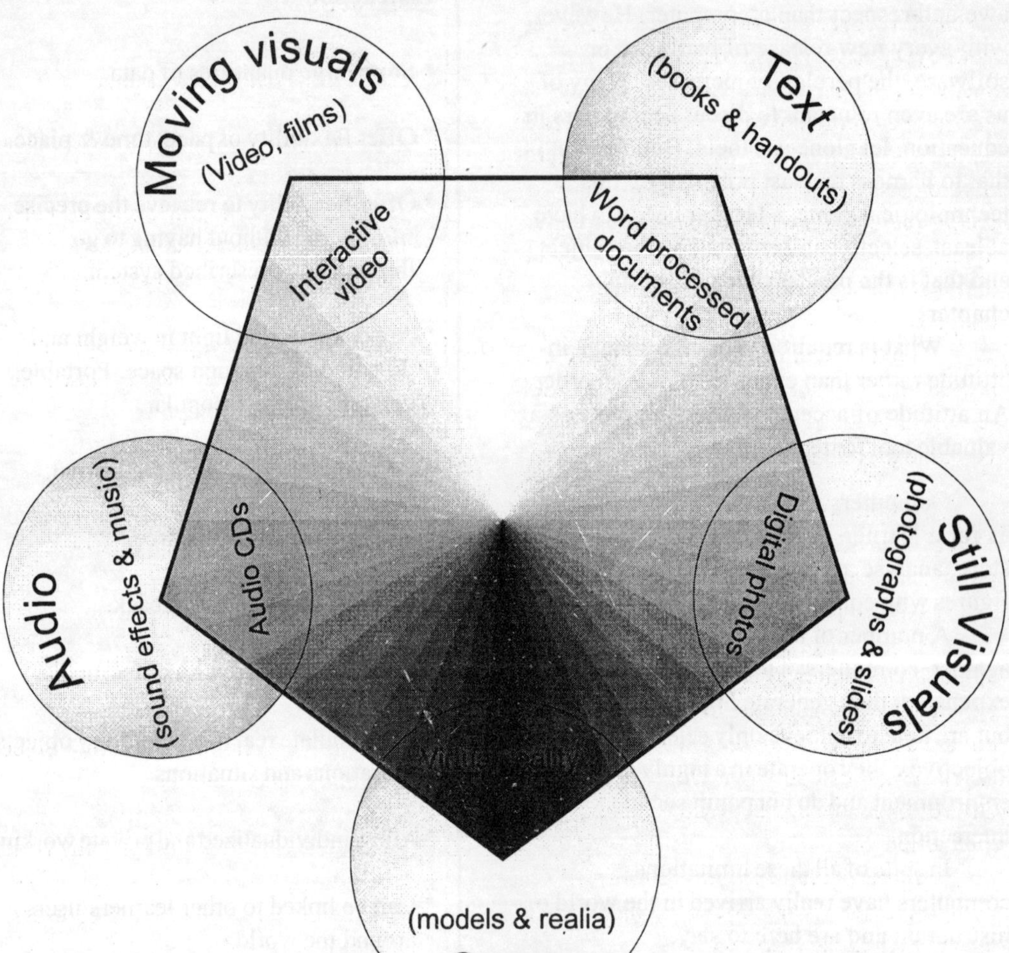

Fig.12.1 The Potential of Computers

HOW COMPUTERS WORK ?

In the simplest of terms, a computer is a combination of four devices

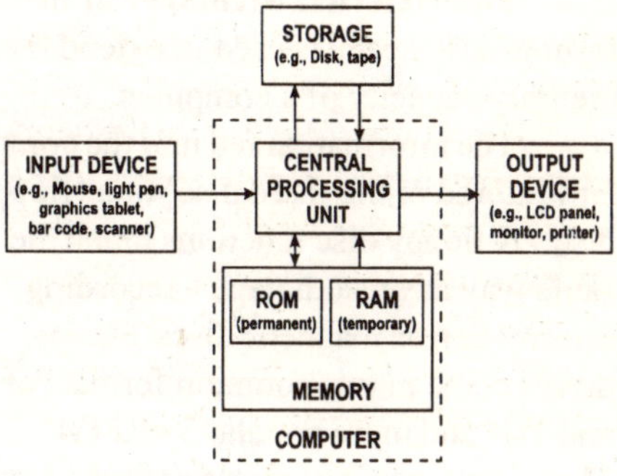

fig. 12.2 The Fundamental Concept

INPUT DEVICES

We know that the computer works on information stored in it by the operator/ expert. Input devices feed the information to the Central Processing Unit (CPU) of the computer. Inputs from audio, video, scanner etc. are converted from analog to digital format. Points at which these additional input devices can be attached are called input ports. Most input devices are manually operated -

* *The Keyboard* is used for typing in or punching in information. It looks exactly like the key board of a typewriter but has several additional features.

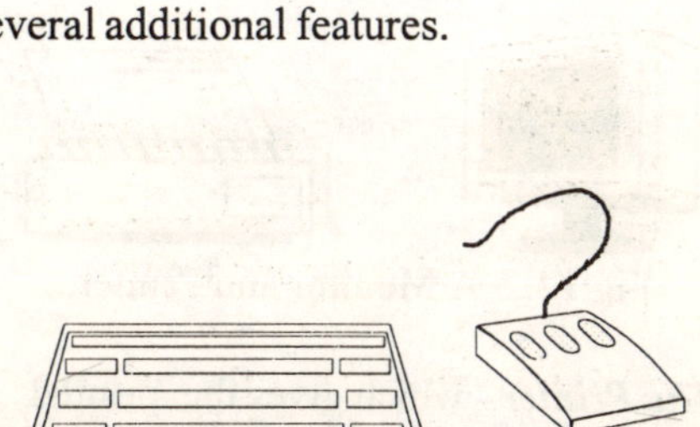

Fig. 12.3 A Keyboard with a Mouse

* ***The Mouse*** - is a device which is designed to operate directly from the screen. It comes in many shapes but is extremely easy to use.

****Joy Stick*** - used for computer games, allows the user to manipulate objects on the screen.

****Barcode reader-*** As barcodes are becoming common to identify location of different pictures, shots and clips stored on the disk, a barcode reader is required to pass this information to the computer.

****The Scanner*** is designed to read the printed information or pictures into the computer system for storage or processing.

****Touch screen/light pens*** - Whereas a computer screen is mostly regarded as an output device, some screens offer the option of feeding information by touching the screen with a finger or a light pen.

Other input devices include voice-recognition unit, microphones, optical character reader and graphics reader.

CENTRAL PROCESSING UNIT (CPU) performs the actual work of the computer system. It is generally built on what is known as the 'Mother Board' which carries different integrated circuits (ICs).

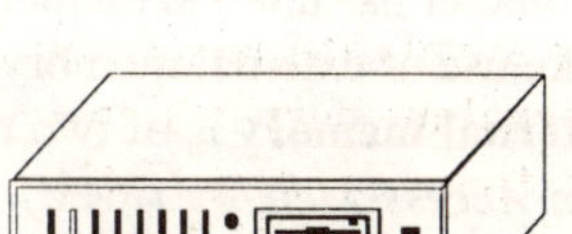

Fig. 12.4 The Central Processing Unit

The CPU is actually made up of two different units : the Control Unit and the Arithmetic/Logic Unit.
The Control Unit- directs all parts of the computer system to work in complete coordination and harmony.
The CPU completes hundreds of transactions fed into the computer. Thousands of bits per second are processed. With every new upgraded version, computers can function at greater speeds.
The Arthmetic/logic unit- controls the basic arthmetic operations: adding, subtracting,multiplying and dividing. This unit also looks after the sorting out and comparing bits of infromation.

MEMORY - The CPU also houses the components where the information fed into the computer is stored and can be retrieved. The information is stored in a systematical manner, in files and directories so that it can be accessed easily.

The higher the memory capacity of a computer, the more expensive it gets. The memory is measured in Kilobytes (K in short) meaning thousands of bytes. A computer with 512K memory for example, can store upto 512,000 bytes of information. One Megabyte memory means the computer can store one million bytes and one Gigabyte memory means one billion bytes.
The computer has internal memory and also can make use of external memory.
The internal memory is of two types;
Random Access Memory (RAM) - serves as temporary storage. Unless saved, RAM gets erased if the electricity goes off accidently.
Read Only memeory (ROM)- is a kind of memory which hold information permanently. As indicated by the name, the user cannot erase or change the information provided. The operating systems are stored in this manner and everytime the computer is switched on, the software stored in ROM starts up.

The External Memory- in the form of disk space is used to extend the memory capacity of a computer.

The information fed into the computer is stored in the 'hard disc' or a 'floppy disc'. A floppy disc functions much the same way as an audiotape - recording information on magnetic discs. Floppy drives come in two common formats of 5 and 1\4" and more popular 3 and 1\4". These disks come as single density, double density or high density formats depending on their capacity to store information.

An increasingly common and useful form of external storage is the optical disk drive employing the CD-ROM (Compact Disk Read Only Memory). New versions of CD ROMs are available which allow the user to even write on them.

OUTPUT DEVICES - Devices which help the user to get back information or responses processed by the computer are called output devices. These include -
The screen - individual or several screens linked together to form a network.

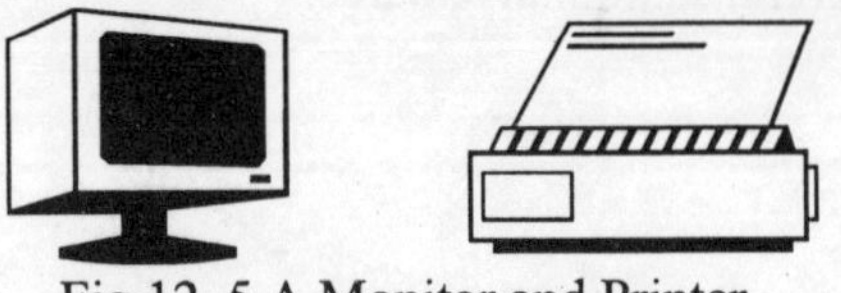

Fig 12. 5 A Monitor and Printer.

The Printer - which gives the printed outputs (hard copy).*The audio output* is provided by the speakers. Now, it is even possible to use the computer as a fax machine or even a telephone for exchanging verbal messages..

DATA STORAGE FORMATS

TYPE		CHARACTERSTICS
FLOPPY DISKS		
$3^{1}/_{2}$ diameter Thin flexible plastic disk in a stiff plastic case		Double-sided 700 to 800 K Double-sided, high density 1.4 megabytes
$5^{1}/_{4}$ diameter Thin flexible plastic disk in a stiff paper case		Double-sided, double density, 340 to 360K Double-sided, high density, 1 to 2 megabytes
HARD DISKS		
Varies—usually $5^{1}/_{4}$" or $3^{1}/_{2}$" diameter Metal or metal coated platters Internal or external to the computer	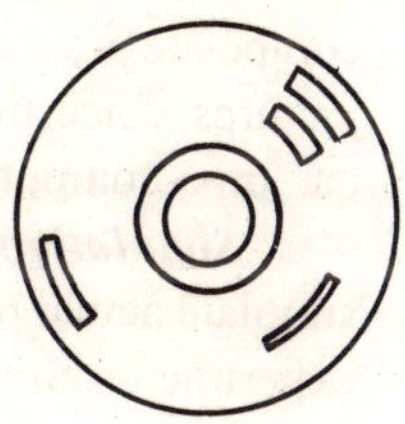	40 megabytes most common Up to several giga bytes available for some machines Available for all personal computers
COMPACT DISKS		
$4^{3}/_{4}$" diameter Metalicized disk coated with clear plastic	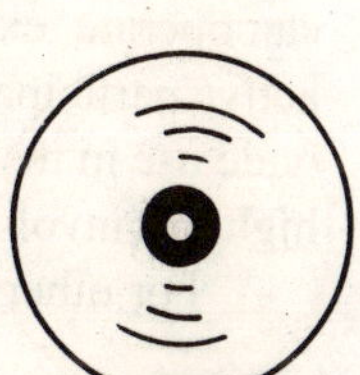	Approximately 550 megabytes Commony used with Macs, PCs, and Tandy Also used with special systems like CD-I

SOME COMMONLY USED COMPUTER TERMS

In computer application, many of the terms are used loosely with overlapping meanings. Here are a few tems every teacher should be familiar with.

Authoring System - An interactive system designed to simplify the programming process. With this system teachers can author CAI packages. The author is guided to proceed step by step filling out pre-designed screens with the content to be taught.

Clip Art - A library of ready shapes, sketches or cartoons available in the form of software. The user can import these images directly on the material being generated.

CD-ROM- A compact disc with read-only memory. This implies that the CD can be used only for reading and the information (digitally ecoded) can not be altered or erased.

CD-WORM - A variation of CD-ROM which allows the user to write once-read many times facility.

Computer Aided/Assisted Instruction (CAI) - An instructional system where teaching is carried out through computers. Learning materials are specially designed to incorporate all elements of instruction and evaluation. A corresponding system is CAL- Computer Aided/Assisted Learning which is more learner oriented.

Computer Based Training (CBT)- A system for imparting training through computers. The system is found to be very effective in learning skill oriented tasks.

Computer Managed Instruction - A system where the computer acquires the managerial or supervisory role of prescribing work schedules, carrying out assessment etc. A corresponding system is Computer Managed Learning (CML) which is more learner oriented.

Default - A term referring to preset values for a computer application when no alternative values are specified by the user e.g. the default font for MS Word programme is 10 points, New Times Roman.

Local Area Network (LAN) - A network which connects two or more computers located in one location such as an office, a university etc. A corresponding system is Wide Area Network (WAN) which is a network linking several LANs in a city, country or continents.

Multimedia - A system which permits a composite presentation of text, graphics, pictures, voice, music, video images, animation etc. on a computer.

Simulation - A programme designed to simulate actual processes or laboratory experiments. Simulation, in different forms, is becoming a vey important area in instruction specially in technical and medical instruction.

Virtual Reality - A computer generated, three dimensional environment where the user can operate, explore and feel the event as an active participant. The concept is yet to find wide use in instruction because of the very high cost involvement.

For other terms refer to glossary.

TYPES OF COMPUTERS -

The first computer came on the scene in 1946. It was a very basic machine with very limited possibilities. The next generation, appearing in 1956 were smaller in size, more powerful and could perform upto 0.1 million operations per second. Ten years later, in 1966, came the next generation using a silicon chip. It was more energy efficient and used higher programming languages. With the fourth generation (1975), the real potential of the machine was unleashed and since then, there has been no looking back. Progressively, the computers have become more competent, powerful and cheap allowing other media formats audio, video etc. to be mixed with it.

Although most teachers would be working with a version of PC, it is useful to know that computers are of different types. They can be classified into -

Mainframe Computer It is a centralised equipment to which other computers can be linked. It can operate upto 100 million instructions per second and is very expensive.

Super Computers: A computer with a capacity for operating upto 100 million instructions per second.

Midi Computers: A medium sized computer can carry 1 to 10 million instructions per second.

Mini Computers: A small sized computer and capable of carrying out half a million instructions per second
The microcomputer has a self-contained integrated circuit on a single chip. It usually works with a floppy disc as additional memory.

Personal Computers: These are stand alone units. Their ability is indicated according to the type of chip they are equipped with. It is possible to have PCs AT 286, AT 386, AT 486 or Pentium. Portable versions of PCs - notebooks or laptops are very popular because of the several special features they offer.

ABOUT BITS & BYTES ...

Although we type information in words, the computer has its own system for reading it. It reads in 1s and 0s known as the Binary numbers. The term binary digit was shortened as *bit*. Every single letter as well as simple maths operations such as +, -, - , etc, are converted into bits or different combinations of 1s and 0s. In computer programming, the bits are arranged in groups of eight and this group is called a *byte* .

For example :
the letter A is represented as 00110001
The memory of the computer is indicated in terms of bytes - as Kilobytes.

THE COMPUTER AS AN INSTRUCTIONAL TOOL

In instruction, the computer plays different roles. By itself, it is an *object of instruction.* Besides, thanks to the omnipresence of the computer in everyday life, it has become almost mandatory to be computer literate.

The computer has been recognized and hailed as a wonder *writing device*. In the teaching-learning environment, it is used as a multipurpose tool for typing, calculating, tabulating and presenting.

Today, computers are emerging as a major teaching-learning tool and have been found to be effective in all types of learning environments - formal classroom instruction, non-formal and distance instruction and individual programmed learning. Computers have been used very effectively in teaching physically and mentally handicapped learners. Many institutions and universities now have facilities for the faculty to teach directly with computers. Special rooms have been equipped with large projection screens where the teacher can conduct the entire lesson using a pre-prepared lesson on a floppy. Use of computers in different modes is discussed below.

* **Lecture Mode:** Using a large projection screen the teacher delivers a normal lecture. The great advantage is legibility and student participation.
* **Tutorial Mode:** Designed on the lines of programmed learning, small units of content are presented through question-answer mode. The student works by herself and is provided immediate feedback.
  Equally effective for individual learners and for small groups.
* **Discovery Mode:** Using the inductive approach, the learner finds her own answers through trial & error method. Specially effective for developing problem-solving skills in a learner.
* **Practice Drills:** The learner is provided opportunity to develop fundamental skills. Using the concept of 'doing' & 'repetition'.
* **Self-learning Mode:** Most effective mode. A complete package is developed which includes theoretical knowledge, exercises & responses to the exercises. With the emerging sophistication in multimedia and hypermedia techniques, such packages can be made highly interactive and interesting.
* **Laboratory Exercises:** Laboratory experiments which are very complex, time-consuming or hazardous to the student can be conducted through the computers. Research shows that if the same laboratory instructions and worksheets are used, it is possible to give the learner near real experience.
* **Simulation Exercises:** Excellent for skill acquisition and decision making. Simulation can also be used in regular classroom instruction. Simulation exercises help the learner in making decisions, see the evaluation of that decision and revise it effectively.
* **Tests & Examinations:** Computers can be used for evaluating performance by storing and retrieving questions (in the form of question banks); scoring and providing correct responses. Learners can take tests on the computers and computers can also be used to evaluate papers.

DEVELOPING COMPUTER-BASED INSTRUCTIONAL MATERIAL

Given the facilities, most teachers would want to develop their own material. Studies show that such a material is far more valuable than using a ready version of it. It becomes even more effective when students are also involved in the creation of such materials.

> ***The Teacher & The Computer***
>
> What can a teacher do with a computer? She can-
> * Create handouts using editing tools.
> * Plan an entire course lesson wise.
> * Prepare tests and examination papers.
> * Generate good transparencies for class room teaching.
> * Author support materials in self-learning mode for weaker students.

Whatever the nature of the material being generated, six major components are involved -

- Assessment of the learner
- Defining Goals
- Identification of specific learning tasks
- Structuring Instruction
- Planning learner interactivity
- Environmental implementation

These different components do not operate independently but interact with each other. The teacher, therefore, has to plan the final product as a whole which is much more than the sum of all these components

1. *Assessing the Learner-* The starting point for all programmes is to understand the learner. The products developed and the level of instruction should match the characterstics of this population. Although this seems obvious, research shows that lack of attention to this component is the major cause of failure in instruction both at the corporate level and at the formal school setting. Academic, cultural and experience background of the learner must also be taken into account.

2. *Defining Goals* - It is essential to identify whether the material is targeted towards - acquiring knowledge, perfecting a skill, solving a problem or modifying an attitude.

3.*Identifying Tasks* - It is essential to identfy the specific learning tasks to be accomplished. For example, applying punctuation rules to a paragraph is not the same thing as learning to write one. If the task is tiresome as in the case of many `training' tasks, additional motivational attributes - visuals, animation or puzzles may have to be added.

4. *Structuring Instruction* - CAI/CAL lessons are usually studied alone. It is therefore important to make instruction explicit, complete and precise. The human presence available in a normal classroom is missing and certain components should be built-in which make the learner feel supervised/attended to.

5. *Computer Application* - It is important to ensure that the learner has sufficient competency to use computers. Attention must be paid to factors impacting human-machine interaction. One important concern is that the computer processes information at a rate which may be too fast for the learner.

In a classroom situation, the instructor can repeat information as and when need arises but here the need has to be anticipated. Competencies at the linguistic level have also to be taken into account. For example, if someone is trying to learn how to fly an aeroplane by simulation, then he is also expected to follow instructions given by the control tower. A problem can arise if the learner does not understand the language very well.

6. *Environmental Implementation* - Several factors such as equipment, physical condition and the role of the instructor are important for the success of computer-aided instructional materials. While designing computer-aided instructional materials, the author should take into account the kind of equipment the learner is likely to have (there may be no mouse/sound card etc). The kind of learning setting in which the material will be used? Whether it be a laboratory, a factory or a large classroom ?

In addition to addressing these basic components of instructional design the materials should support iterative cycles of learning and evaluation of both the teaching point and the lesson as a whole. For every new author, it is essential to know that developing computer-based instructional mateials requires -

* Patience, perseverance and revision
* Compatibility with machines
* Basic knowledge about instructional design and evaluation.
* Basic knowledge about authoring systems and tools

MULTIMEDIA

The new generations of computers offer unlimited potential in designing high quality material using text, graphics, still pictures, sound and video clips. They can also control compact disc players and videodisc players. Thus a wide variety of media options can be packaged together to make learning more exciting.

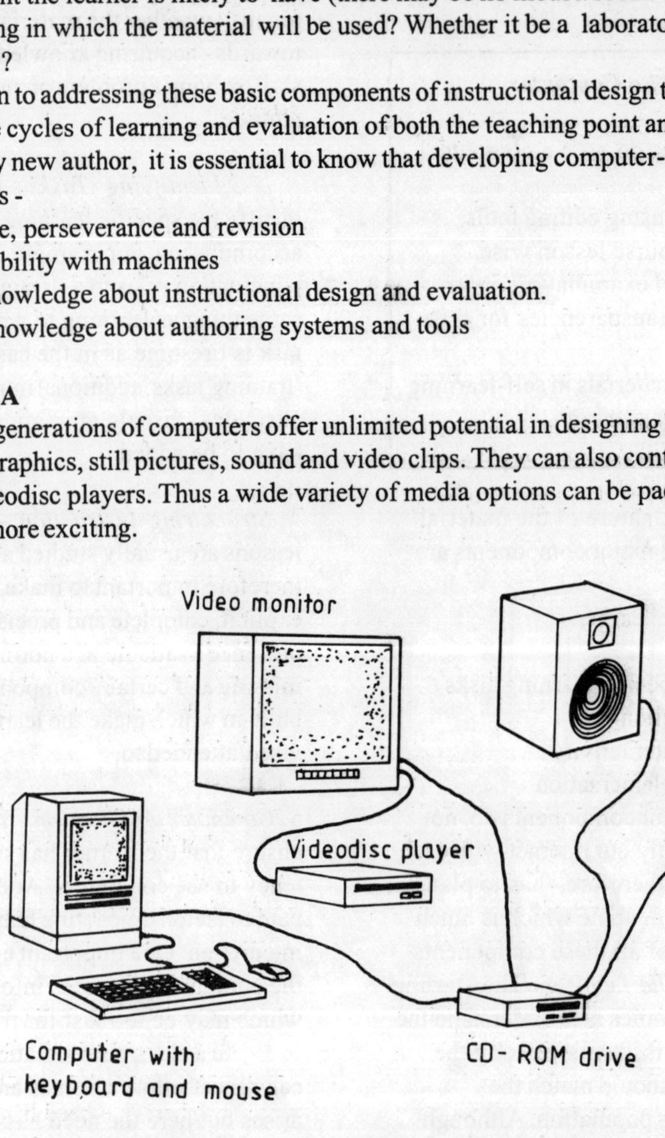

Fig. 12.6 A Typical Multimedia Workstation

The term **Hypermedia** refers to a *non sequential* document composed of text, audio and video information. The computer here serves to link and annotate related *blocks of information (nodes)* to larger networks or more popularly known as *webs.*

The term Hypermedia was coined by Theodor H Nelson in 1974 and its aim was to immerse users in a richly textured information environment. In a way, hypertext aspired to simulate properties of the mind, allowing one to assimilate a variety of sources and to create personalised learning.

The instructional objective here is to allow the user the possibility to move about within a particular set of information without any pre-determined structure or sequence.

Special Advantages of Hypermedia:

* Highly motivating
* Allows in-depth study
* Caters to individual learner differences
* Offers student autonomy
* Offers linkages with related ideas/topics
* Allows flexibility of time and pace
* Offers rich multisensory learning

Some Limitations:

* The lack of structure is not within the competency of *all* learners.
* Students can *get lost* in the Cyberspace.
* It expects the learner to be computer proficient with a fairly high level of computer competency.
* It does not invite student feedback.
* It is time consuming - The non-linearity feature along with the richness of information tempts the learner to spend too much time.

The learner thus *navigates* in a hypermedia environment as per her needs.
The concept of hypermedia is based on cognitive theories of how individuals structure knowledge and how they learn. Hypermedia works to organize information through concepts and their inter-relationships (links). With hypertext, one can present information using different formats. There is no continuous flow of text, as in a textbook.

The information is broken up into small units which are *linked* in a variety of ways. The concept of hypermedia is completely learner oriented. Here, the information is provided in layers.

For example, a typical lesson on Shakespeare's 'Merchant of Venice' in the hypermedia format will offer the learner to locate information on -

- Shakespeare's Life
- Shakespeare's complete works
- Shakerpeare's Comedies
- Elizabethan Theatre
- History of the play
- The town of Venice
- Plot of the Play
- Character sketches
- History of different performances of the play
- List of critiques on the play
- See a scene in action
- Listen to some famous lines delivered by a well-known actor/actress

And, many more aspects can be explored. The student, depending upon her need, decides to consult the item/s chosen in any order. She can very easily move from one topic to the other without having to close or open files.

Hypermedia is excellent for catering to individual differences in basic knowledge, capabilities, learning styles and interests. In addition, it is highly receiver oriented. It can be used in the nonlinear format giving the user full freedom to explore information.

The hypermedia format is highly interactive - the software is designed to keep the user and her needs in mind. Moreover, additional information can be made available in any desired form (audio, pictures, video etc.) on demand in any chosen order.

It offers flexibility of pace and path. All information is provided in the form of options and the user has the liberty to work in any order.

Before designing materials in hypertext mode, the following checklist may be verified :

* What information should appear on the computer screen ?
* Where should the student exercise choice or decision?
* What options should be available to the learner at these decision points ?
* At what point should a question be asked?
* What form should a test question take ?
* Need there be provision for review or remediation ?
* Is there need for audio/video support?
* What supporting material should be on paper ?

To develop materials in the hypertext mode, one needs to begin by identifying the authoring system that provides the necessary features. The actual programme is then constucted with the help of flow charts.

Fairly complex flow charts can be constructed with the help of a few simple symbols. Develop a flow chart by first listing all the steps in the instructional process then identify those steps which are decision points and would result in branches. Indicate these steps by using the standard symbols. The process will help you get a much clearer understanding of how the programme should be constructed.

Even if one is not actually writing out a programme, it is still important to know the symbols to understand a programme developed by a colleague or a commercial agency.

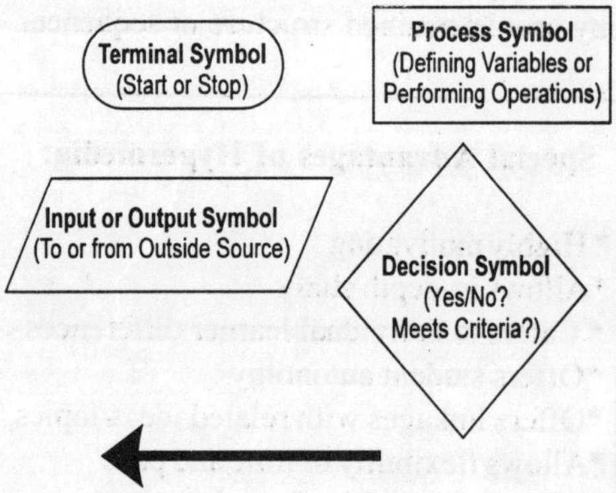

Direction of movement

* The *rectangle* represents a single step in the process,
* The *diamond* indicates a decision point at which a branch should occur.
* The *oval* is used to indicate a terminal or connecting point and should have only one input or one output.
* The *arrows* indicate the direction of movement through the flow chart. The arrows should point down but may point in other directions when other options are needed or to return to an earlier part of the programme.

THE INTERNET

No discussion about instructional media can be complete without talking about the *internet.* The youngest in the family of instructional media, the internet has somewhat revolutionised the very process of learning. It promotes what has been described as the *generative form of learning* - learning which aims at creating authentic real -life learning tasks. The system offers the most active form of learning there can be. The learner is encouraged to explore and locate information, ask questions and find solutions.

Created in 1969, by the US defense department, the internet (then called the ARPAnet) was initially designed to link different military sites for research purposes. In 1986, a better system National Science Foundation Network (NSFNET) was created as a non-commercial computer network. By 1995, most of the activities of NSFNET were replaced by commercial services and the usage of the internet had increased by 2800%.

The main reason for extraordinary growth of the internet is its increasing ease of use. Until recently, navigating the internet required knowledge of UNIX, a difficult computer language. With the coming of *World Wide Web* (also known as WWW, W3 or the Web) *Browser,* operating internet has become just a *point and click* game.

The user only requires the very basic familiarity with the *windows* operating system. The Web, designed in *Hypertext,* provides a multimedia environment with easy move within inter and intra topics. The most striking advantage of hypertext is its facility of nonlinear access. The information is organised in such a way that the user can hop around and select information like she would in a library.

The Internet and Instruction

* Student is autonomous
* Learning is active
* Learning is multisensory
* Trains the learner to be more focused.
* Learning is more collaborative and cooperative going well beyond the walls of a school or a university.
* Learner becomes aware of her own learning style and learns to optimise.
* Learning is contextualized - the learner can see and experience content in authentic contexts.
* The teacher-taught relationship becomes more mature.

Infrastructure required -

To have access to the internet the minimum infrastructure you will need is:

Hardware:	Computer - 386 or better Modem - 14.4 kbps
Software:	Netscape, Mosaic (for WWW), Pine/Eudora (for E-mail) Slip/PPP (for connection)
Internet: Service Provider	A commercial agency or a university offering SLIP or PPP

How does the internet work?

There are two different set ups:

a) *Individual connection:* A single user subscribes to the internet provider agency.

b) *Group connection:* The network (LAN) of an organisation/university is linked to the internet provider agency.

a) At the very simplistic level, the connection is as follows.

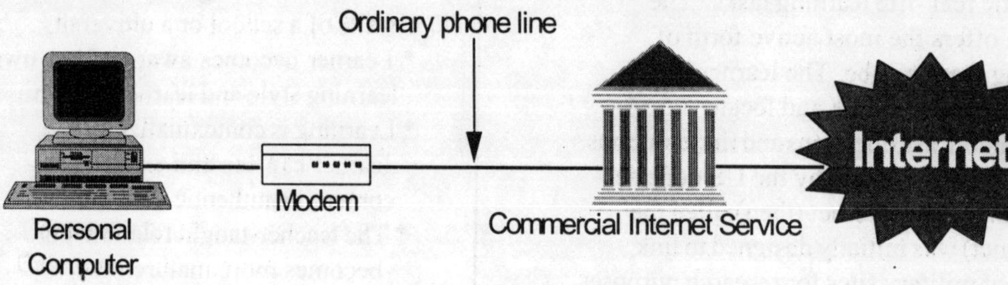

This system allows you to use ***e-mail, newsgroups, World Wide Web Browser.*** It also allows you ***download text, images and sounds.***

b) This system provides all the above-mentioned services at a much faster speed. Each PC in the link becomes an individual user.

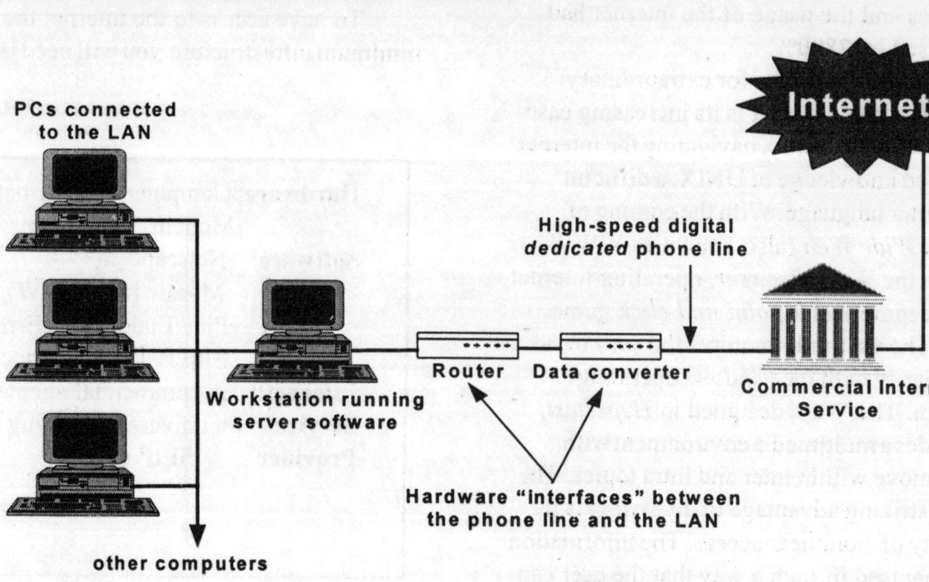

Fig. 12.7 Common Configuration for Setting-up the Internet

Locating information on the internet

The system incorporates clear signposts to guide the user in locating information. However, with the vastness of the space and the quantum of information available, users can get lost easily. Information on the internet is located with the help of ***search engins.*** Some of the popular links are: *Yahoo, Lycos, Find-it, Web index, Webcrowler, InforSeek, Deja News, El Net* and *Inktome.* All you have to do is to select a topic of interest to you and enter it in several of these search engines. You will begin getting the information (or *hits*). It is interesting to note how differently each search engine responds to the same query.

Sharing Software

The internet also offers facilities for sharing software. shareware.com (http://www.shareware.com) has a database of nearly 160,000 usable software files.

Useful sites for educators

A number of sites are available where teachers can locate vast amounts of information of special interest to them. These sources provides valuable *nuggets* of direct and indirect information which can be studied and downloaded if required.

Netiquette

As sharing is the main slogan of the internet, certain informal rules have emerged to guide good conduct on the net. Users are advised to refrain from ***shouting*** (overuse of capital letters); ***Flamming*** (e-mail attack on someone) and ***Spamming*** (posting the same message to many newsgroups).

Using e-mail for instruction

E-mail provides an inexpensive and quick means of obtaining and sharing information amongst learners, with teacher and with community at large. E-mail is an excellent tool for establishing difficult, cross cultural academic connections.

There is little doubt that the e-mail is a powerful tool to allow learners from various countries and cultures to interact. However, one of the major dangers of the internet is the possibility of the learner getting lost or wasting far too much time with little real academic gain. The teacher needs to ensure that such activities are well-designed and closely monitored. One possibility is that a list of questions is supplied and the responses are compared and contrasted bringing out the differences or/and similarities in the perspectives.

E-mail can also be used to acquire language competencies. Contacts may be established with a *e-mail pal* (like a pen pal) and short exercises exchanged for correction and commenting. Both parties can benefit by writing on the same topic in two different languages..

With the ever- increasing popularity of the internet, a teacher is presented with numerous instructional activities through mailing lists, Web sites and in Newsgroups. It is necessary to distinguish between those resources that provide activities mainly to promote the use of the internet for learning and those that can be directly used as teaching-learning materials.

Each activity should be carefully examined to determine how it may be adapted or restructured for direct use with the learners.

13

USING AVAILABLE MEDIA OPTIONS

Major Considerations for Selecting Media

Locating Instructional Resources

Validating Media for Learning Outcome

Validating Media for Audience Acceptance

USING AVAILABLE MEDIA OPTIONS

As a teacher desirous of using media options for your teaching, you have three choices for procuring instructional media.

i) You may plan and produce your own media.
ii) You may buy or rent ready-to-use commercially available materials, and
iii) You may mix the first two i.e take a ready option and adapt or modify it to suit your specific needs.

In earlier chapters, simple procedures for developing personalised materials in different formats have been discussed. However, given the abundance of material available, adopting available media options is also a very attractive option.

Selecting and adapting available media-based materials is not easy. We know that media enhances learning, certainly appropriate media does. But, how does one know what is appropriate? In order to make an intelligent choice, several different factors need to be taken into account.

To make successful use of any available material, you need to learn about :

i) locating appropriate media,
ii) selecting potentially suitable sections
iii) evaluating media
iv) adapting or supplimenting them
v) planning to use them effectively

These steps need to be carried out within the context of your instructional planning. As described in chapter 3, whenever the use of instructional media is considered, a number of factors need to be taken into account to ensure that the selected media fulfill their role.

Let us review these planning elements:

Major Considerations for Media Selection:

- Learner Profile
- Purpose and Objectives
- Mode of Instruction
- Media Attributes
- Available Time
- Available Infrastructure

Learner Characterstics:

Unless you have a good idea about the entry level and the *learning needs* and know something about the learners' characteristics, it is difficult to select appropriate instructional materials. Being familiar with the educational background, experience levels, knowledge of subject matter, as well as other abilities and interests of learners, can be helpful in guiding you in selecting the suitable media.

Purpose and Objectives:

The instructional environment within which you plan to use the media needs to be defined. For what major purpose will the media be used ? What specific objectives need to be achieved? Answers to these questions give clear directions for media selection.

It is a common practice for instructors to write learning objectives to specify the expected learning outcome. The *objectives* play an important role in the selection of media to be used. Once the objectives are specified, they must be examined carefully to indicate the elements of subject content, facts, concepts, and principles that need media support.

Mode of Instruction

In formal settings, instruction is delivered to different group sizes, generally ranging from 10 to 75 individuals. The group size and the chosen mode of delivery system greatly influence the selection of media. It is important to recognize that some types of media may be suitable, or preferable, for a particular mode of instruction. For example, printed materials or photographs are very effective for individual or small group instruction. On the other hand, overhead transparencies are more appropriate for a large group of learners.

Media Attributes

The capabilities of a medium to exhibit certain characteristics are known as media attributes. The instructor must be clear about the attributes required to serve a particular objective. Factors such as - whether a medium can show motion, or be in colour, or include sound, will affect media selection in terms of the required learning objectives. For example, if you need to discuss the principle on which a *fan* works, you may like to look for a suitable film clip or a videotape recording because it can show the fan in motion which definitaly makes learning more effective.

Time Requirement

This question needs to be addressed at three different levels :

i) How much time will be required to put the media option together;
ii) How much time will be required to show it during presentation; and
ii) How much time is required for carrying out the follow up activities.

Your decision to invest the time and effort must be taken in the light of the special contribution that a particular media option is expected to make.

You also need to decide how you wish to use it with the learners - whether you would like to show/use it all at once or break it up in smaller, more pointed segments. This will also help you to plan the support material required well in advance thereby giving you full control over the situation.

Infrastructure Requirement

A realistic evaluation of the availability of the required infrastructure is a pre-requisite for developing or using any media option. This is particularly important in developing countries where at times, even the minimal facilities like having a live socket in a classroom can be a problem. At the planning stage, a detailed list of equipment required should be drawn up so that a realistic approach can be taken. A personal inspection of the equipment and the venue where the media option is to be used is highly desirable, at least when it is being used for the first time.

Locating Media

A variety of sources are available around us. In fact, the unique problem of our times is that too much material is available and sifting it becomes a problem in itself. As you begin your search, two prime considerations will be *cost* and *time.* It is advisable to keep a list of venders and addresses of the media libraries/centres in your town readily available with you.
If a pointed search is carried out you are

bound to find that several different media options are available on the same topic with different sources.

Evaluating Media

Media option to be used in a classroom needs to be evaluated in two parts-

i) before use for its suitability, and

ii) after use for its effectiveness.

If you have personally designed and prepared the media option then most of the questions become redundant. However, if the media option has been procured, you need to carefully examine it.

Most commercially developed media options have relevant information available either on the packaging or seperately in the form of an accompanying brochure. This may not always give you a realistic estimate of its suitability for your particular set of students. *It is important to personally preview the material.*

While previewing both subjective and objective evaluations are essential. *Subjective evaluation* is related to the suitability of the material to the objectives and *objective evaluation* is about the design and production quality of the programme. It is useful to design a questionnaire for the purpose. A sample evaluation form is provided on the next page.

Media Evaluation Checklist

A. *Objective Components*

* Media form
* Exact scope of the subject treated.
* Number of learning segments.
* Duration of the programme.
* General subject area or topic treated
* Instructor's guide or documentation
* Production date
* Producer agency
* Purchase or rental source
* Purchase or rental cost
* Recommended pre-requisites
* Brief content overview

B. *Subjective Components*

* How well does the material achieve the learning objective ?
* How current and accurate is the content ?
* Is it appropriate for the knowledge level of the audience ?
* Is it appropriate for the experience level of the audience ?
* Is it free from any social bias ?
* What is the vocabulary level ?
* How good is the production quality ?
* Is the instructional guide/documentation helpful for using the material ?
* What are its strengths or weaknesses ?
* Should the material be purchased or rented?

Can someone else preview the materials? When the media is reviewed by someone else, one can, at best get a general summary of the content. Full analysis of subject treatment and other details important to the specific intention of using media may not receive attention.

Selecting Media:

The following quesions will clarify your thoughts and will help you through the selection process.

1. Is the media option cost effective?
2. Would the material appeal to the concerned age group?
3. Will they be able to appreciate the examples and visuals used?
4. Does the treatment of the topic match the instructional purpose?
5. Is the treatment open and without any bias?
6. Is the content suitable in terms of depth of treatment, accuracy and being up-to-date?
7. Will you need to develop further support material?
8. Is the treatment convincing?
9. Is the medium used appropriate in terms of delivery of content?
10. Is there provision for meaningful learner participation?
11. Does it lead to beneficial follow up activities/assignments?
12. Is the production quality in terms of colours, sound, legibility, continuity etc.acceptable?
13. Will it help one to save time?

Using Pre-prepared Media Options

The final success of a media option is not in what it contains but how it is used. A teacher can use the given media option innovatively. This again needs careful planning and preparation. To achieve the best results, the teacher must practice with the media option at least once to know the exact time requirement and to identify points of highest interest. She can then plan to develop short and simple games or quizes to focus on the main points.

A teacher can adopt different methodologies to use the preprepared materials. The selected media support can be used as it is i.e it can be shown or projected in totality from the beginning to the end. Alternatively, the teacher can work out the pauses for explaining, questioning etc. It is also possible to play around with the media option to get the desired result. For example, if in a given programme, explanations are not suitable, you can use a slide-tape programme without the commentary and provide the words yourself. To get the opposite benefit, audio may be used without projecting the slides.

MEDIA SELECTION FORM

Title:

Source:

Subject Area:

Key Concepts Covered

Target Audience:

Date of Production: **Duration:** **Cost:**

Instructional objective/s

Rating	**High**	**Medium**	**Low**	**Comments**
Match with curriculum	❑	❑	❑	
Accuracy level	❑	❑	❑	
Use of cognitive learning aids such as cues, advance organisers, summary etc..	❑	❑	❑	
Clarity of language used	❑	❑	❑	
Motivation/ Interest level	❑	❑	❑	
Learner participation	❑	❑	❑	
Technical quality	❑	❑	❑	
Objectivity of approach	❑	❑	❑	
Quality of print support material	❑	❑	❑	
Appropriateness of information flow	❑	❑	❑	

Strong Points:

Weak Points:

Evaluating Effectiveness of Media After Use:

After using the selected media option, it is essential to evaluate as to how well the media has served the objectives? It is important to take learner feedback on points such as - the clarity of explanations, communication value of illustrations, soundness of conclusions, and motivation for further study.

This is particularly important if one plans to use the selected media option subsequently with other learner goups. You should be looking for two types of feedbacks -

i) actual learning outcome, and

ii) the audience reaction.

Evaluating Learning Outcome:

An assessment of individual or group performance attained as the result of experience with the media should be made. This will indicate how far the media option used has been successful in enhancing learning.

Tests may be designed according to the topic to evaluate increase in knowledge or/and motivation. The testing material can be in the form of quizzez, multiple choice questions, true-false, short answers or long essays.

Audience Feedback

The second area to be evaluated is - how the media option used has made learning more enjoyable. Some of the questions one can ask are:

Did the learners participate actively?

Did the media option provoke curiosity?

Did it demand follow up study/action?

Did the learners enjoy viewing it?

Depending on the nature of the questions, a checklist, a rating scale or a questionnaire consisting of either open ended or multiple-choice questions may be devised.

Users' Opinion Form

* Did the materials meet the objectives?
* Was the time period used to present the information adequate?
* Were the examples well-chosen?
* Was the instructor skillful in using the media equipment?
* Was the introduction to the materials satisfactory?
* Were the follow up activities effective?
* Did the programme help in making the concept clear?
* Did the programme help in increasing interest of the learner in the topic?
* Did the design aid learning?
* Were the physical arrangements for use satisfactory?

Choosing Appropriate Media

Medium	Audience size	Cost involved	Preparation Difficulty	Impact	Easy Handling	Interactivity
1. Flip chart	Upto 30	Low	Low	Medium	V. High	High
2. Black board	Upto 45	Low	Low	Low	High	Medium
3. Overhead transparencies	Upto 60	Medium	Low	High	High	High
4. Audio programme	Upto 45	High	Medium	Medium	Medium	Medium
5. Slides	Upto 60	Medium	Medium	V. High	Medium	High
6. Film strip	Upto 100	V. High	V. High	High	V. High	Medium
7. Video	Upto 100	V. High	V. High	V. High	V. High	V. High

Glossary

GLOSSARY

Activator: Solution used to start action of developing agents built into photographic paper in photo-stabilization process.

Active learning: Learning which involves active participation on the part of the learner.

Advance organizer: Information and cues provided before beginning instruction in order to organize a learning experience which follows.

Affective domain: The domain of learning that involves changes in interest, attitudes, values, and appreciation within human behaviour.

Analog: A term used to describe information which steadily flows and changes. Most of the information which comes from the natural world is analogue: time, temperature and voltage, for instance.

Animation: A filming and video production technique that makes inanimate objects or drawings appear to move by quick sequencing of very brief or single-frame exposures.

ASCII: Pronounced as "eisk.ee", ASCII is a binary code in computers used for English letters and characters.

Aspect ratio: The width-to-height ratio of a media option - slides, film or video. For example, frames in video have an aspect ratio of four units of width to three units of height, and those in film a ratio of three to two.

Attention span: The time during which a learner can give his full attention to a topic, programme, etc..

Audible advance: A term used in slide-tape programmes. It refers to a synchronized sound/vision presentation with an audible synchronizing signal which indicates when the next visual should be shown.

Audio-notebook: A study guide and/or workbook with audiotape recording to guide the learner in self-studying a topic.

Audio track: The portion of a videotape on which sound is recorded.

Audio-tutorial system : An audiotape recording which provides information and directs the learner to learning activities using different resources.

Authoring language: A computer language which is designed specifically for developing computer-based learning/training materials..

Authoring system: A collection of authoring programs that allow users, without formal computer programming skills to design instructional materials. It takes the user step-by step through this process, often working in everyday language, and without having to learn tedious computer programming .

Beaded screen: A projection screen with a surface which consists of a very large number of tiny glass beads, which offer high forward reflection.

Behavioural objective: A precise statement indicating the performance expected of a learner as a result of exposure to given instructional material.

Bidirectional microphone: One that picks up sounds only from two opposite sides.

Bit: A binary digit, either 0 or 1, it is the smallest unit of information a computer can handle electronically. A computer's processing capability is usually reckoned in the number of bits which can be handled at one time. Personal computers, for example, contain commonly 8- or 16-bit microprocessors, while a minicomputer may have a 16-bit central processor.

Bit Map: An area in the computer memory that represents video images. Each pixel on a video screen is controlled by bits that set colour and intensity.

Block-format script: Directions for producing media that consist of visual descriptions of scenes written full-width across page with narration and other sounds indicated in narrow columns, centered below visual description.

Bloom's taxonomies: A set of taxonomies of learning objectives, compiled by Bloom and his co-workers, in which all such objectives are classified into three board groups, or domains – cognitive, affective and psychomotor.

Bounce: Light in photography, aimed at the ceiling or other surface to illuminate subject indirectly by reflection.

Branching programme: An instructional programme that makes use of branches. It contains options which are either selected by the learner. The learner has the choice of leaving out certain points and going ahead at her own pace. Such a programme, thus, consists of sequences that may be different for each learner.

Broadcasting: A simultaneous dissemination of information to a large number of receivers, usually via electromagnetic carrier waves as in radio and television broadcasting.

Byte: Short for 'By eight'; a set of eight bits (binary digits). A unit of measure for the number of bits required to store a single letter in computer memory. It generally takes six to eight bits (one byte) to form a single ASCII character. A computer's storage capacity, or 'memory', is reckoned in kilobytes, or K's. A typical personal computer might have an 8-bit central processor and 64 K of memory.

Camcorder: Videocamera and videotape recorder as a single, compact unit.

Camera ready: A term used in printing. It refers to the *Paste-up* copy of pages that are ready for reproduction with a process camera.

Captions: Titles or printed explanations for visuals in a media option.

Cardioid microphone: An instrument that picks up sounds in a heart-shaped pattern, namely with major sensitivity from one side. It has some sensitivity on the adjacent two sides, and almost none from the back side.

Carousel: A term generally applied to a slide projector using a circular tray to hold slides.

Cassette: A closed container of film or magnetic tape designed for loading and unloading into a suitable projector or recorder.

Character generator: An electronic device used to create titles, captions and simple graphics which can be translated into video signals on videotape.

Closed-circuit television (CCTV): A television system which limits distribution of the signal to those receivers or monitors which are directly connected to the point of origin by a coaxial cable, optical fibre or microwave link.

Close-up: A concentration of the camera on the subject, or on a part of it, excluding everything else from view.

Cognitive domain: Domain of human learning involving assimilation of knowledge and other related intellectual skills.

Colour bars: The colour pattern put in the beginning of a videotape recording that serves as reference for adjusting players and receivers for maximum colour quality when a videotape is played.

Colour standard: The way in which a colour picture is composed and transmitted. There are three distinct colour standards: PAL, NTSC and SECAM. These are not interchangeable.

Compact disc (CD): A 4 3/4 inch disc on which sound is recorded with laser beam as series of digital patterns. When played back, the digital pattern is read by laser.

Computer-aided (assisted) evaluation: An examination, assessment, or test that is constructed and/or administered and/or marked with the help of a computer.

Computer-aided/assisted instruction (CAI): The use of a computer as an integral part of an instructional system, the learner works with specially designed learning materials.

Computer-aided/assisted learning (CAL): Learning with the aid of a computer through computer-aided instruction materials. Simulation is an important component of CAL materials.

Computer graphics: Sketches, graphics generated and displayed by computers, either on a video display unit or as hard copy produced by an electronic or mechanical plotter.

Computer-managed instruction (CMI): The use of a computer in a managerial or supervisory role, the computer prescribing work schedules and carrying out assessment.

Computer-managed learning (CML): A term which is almost synonymous with computer-managed instruction. Here the focus is on the learner.

Condenser microphone: A microphone that transmits sounds through vibrations received though a plate which vibrates with the direct current it receives with respect to an adjacent fixed plate.

Concept film tape: A short sequence or a programme, recorded on film or tape, to illustrate a single concept or idea.

Constant angular velocity videodisc (CAV): Each video frame occupies one track, permitting still pictures, slow motion and rapid movement to any section of disc for branching programming.

Constant linear velocity videodisc (CLV): CLV: Constant Linear Velocity or 'long play' videodiscs. CLV discs assign a fixed track length to each frame and spin at a speed which gradually decreases as the disc plays. CLV discs are a good medium for entertainment, but are of little use interactively.

Continuous-tone subjects: Illustrations designed in shades of gray, varying from black to white.

Control track: A continuous series of signals placed along the lower edge of a videotape when recording. These are intended to regulate tape speed during playback and also useful during editing for locating scenes.

Copy stand: A vertical or horizontal stand generally used for slide making. The stand is designed to hold the picture or flat display in an accurate position while a camera fixed on the top, can capture it within a tight frame.

Courseware: A total instructional package comprising computer software, visual and audio media, and printed material. Generally this term is applied to teaching materials that store information in forms that are compatible with new sophisticated technologies.

Credit title: A listing of those who participated in the development of a media project.

Crystal microphone: It contains crystals or granules that produce electricity with the pressure of sound waves.

Cut: An instantaneous change from one image to another within a sequence of projected visuals.

Cut-away shot: The scene of a subject or action taking place at the same time as the main action, but separate from it, and placed between two related scenes which have a discontinuity of action.

Debriefing: Discussion conducted among the learner group after an instructional activity has been completed with the objective of summing up what has been learned.

Developer: A solution that chemically sets the photographic image by acting on silver salts, which have been affected by light during picture taking, in exposed films.

Diazo process: A method for preparing overhead transparencies requiring film containing one of a possible number of dye colours, which is exposed, in contact with an opaque original prepared on translucent or transparent paper or film, to ultraviolet light, and then developed in ammonia vapour.

Digital: A term applied to an information processing, storage or transfer system in which the signal is translated into binary code before processing, storage or transmission. Most of the new equipment and systems use this format.

Digital sound: Binary signals of low or high voltage level pulses recorded on tape or disc.

Dissolve: A special effect used in slide projection and video production. Here, two visuals are so superimposed that the second one gradually appears as the first one gradually disappears.

Documentary approach: A method of taking pictures or recording images without detailed script preparation.

Dolly shot: A videotape scene recorded as the camera is operated while in a fast moving trolley.

Drill: A technique of teaching-learning. The content is repeated in an ordered way with the intention of developing or perfecting a specific skill or aspect of knowledge.

Dropouts: The momentary loss of sound on an audiotape or horizontal flashes on a videoscreen due to dirt on the tape or loss of head-to-tape contact.

Dry mount press: A process used for dry mounting. It uses heat and pressure to seal flat materials to cardboard with a heat-sensitive adhesive placed between the two surfaces.

Dry mounting: A process used for framing visuals and pictures using a dry mount press.

Dry-transfer: Commercially prepared symbols for transferring from a sheet to the working surface by rubbing with a blunt object.

Dubbing: The transfer of a recording from one unit to another; commonly from record to tape, audiotape to audiotape, or videotape to videotape.

Dummy: Final layout of all elements for a page that serves as guide for paste-up used for printing.

Dynamic microphone: A microphone that employs a moving coil in a magnetic field to generate an electrical signal from sound waves.

Editing: The procedure for rearranging elements of an audio-recording or videotape recording, removing bad takes, and disturbing pauses.

Epidiascope: A device that combines the functions of an episcope and a diascope. It can project images held on both opaque and transparent materials on to a screen.

Establishing shot: A medium or long shot that establishes the context of a scene and orients the viewer.

Expository treatment: A straightforward informational programme presented by a presenter.

Fade-in: A visual effect in videotape recording in which a scene gradually appears out of blackness.

Fade-out: A visual effect in videotape recording in which a scene gradually disappears into blackness.

Feedback: The information received by a learner during a sequence of programmed instruction which indicates the correctness (or otherwise) of the response. Feedback can also refer to responses received by a teacher about the course etc..

Feltboard: A flat display surface covered with felt, flannel or similar material on to which pictures, symbols or shapes backed with the same or similar material will adhere. It is also known as a Flannel Board.

Fill light: The secondary light source illuminating a scene, which brightens dark shadow portions created by the key light.

Fixed microphone: A type of microphone which is attached to a stand and placed on a table or suspended from the studio ceiling.

Fixer: A solution in which the chemicals desensitize the developed film image to light and change all undeveloped silver salts so they can be removed by washing.

Flip chart: A set of large sheets of paper attached to an easel unit so that they can be flipped over the top of the unit into or out of view during the presentation progresses.

Flow chart: A diagram that illustrates the sequence/s of steps that a learner might follow in a computer-based or interactive instructional programme. It represents a computer programme in graphic form – usually as a series of variously-shaped boxes.

Frame: An individual picture in a filmstrip or videotape recording. Each separate presentation of a small basic unit of material. For example, a film runs at the rate of 24 frames a second; video at 30 frames a second in NTSC standard systems, 25 frames a second in PAL and SECAM systems.

Freeze: Holding a single image on the screen during a multi-image presentation, videotape or film sequence.

Frequency: The number of times a signal vibrates within a given time; usually measured as Hertz (Hertz) or cycles per second.

Fresnel lens: A large flat glass or acrylic lens under the glass stage of an overhead projector which spreads light evenly over transparency placed on stage.

Galley proof: The first copy of the press run of typeset material to be proofread.

Graphics: A term loosely used to represent visuals, graphics, captions or a brief message.

Halftone: A printed illustration consisting of uniformly spaced dots of varying size, which blend together and convey shades of gray.

Hard copy: Information printed, typed or otherwise reproduced on paper, as opposed to information temporarily displayed on a screen.

Hard Disk: An inflexible magnetic disk with greater storage capacity than a floppy diskette. A hard disk is sometimes sealed within a computer to provide a large memory.

Hawthorne effect: In learning, where improvement apparently brought about by the use of a new technique is wholly or partly due to the increased interest and motivation provided by the use of the technique rather than to the intrinsic properties of the technique itself.

High-angle shot: A scene photographed or recorded with the camera placed high, looking down at the subject.

High fidelity: A qualitative term used to describe a sound recording or reproducing system capable of handling the full audible range of frequencies.

Hook-and-loop board: A presentation board consisting of a cloth surface textured with minute nylon loops with which display materials backed with strips of tape having nylon hooks will intermesh and hold firmly.

Inaudible picture advance signal: An electronic signal used in a slide-tape programme. The signal is placed on tape and not heard, but which automatically activates a projector to change the picture.

Infra-red light source: A heat lamp used in processing thermal transparencies with the help of a thermocopier.

Instructional media: The physical tools of educational technology, including printed words, film, tape records, slides and the various combinations thereof.

Interactive learning: The interplay between a person and any media wherein the learner controls the pace and possibly sequential use of the media for instruction.

Interactive video: Combining video images with computer programming, such that the sequence of the programme will depend on user choices, answers to questions, and so forth. It is the convergence of video and computer technology – a video programme and a computer program running in tandem under the control of the person in front of the screen. In interactive video, the user's actions, choices and decisions genuinely affect the way in which the programme unfolds.

Interface: As a general term, the link between two pieces of separate equipment.

Keystoning: A distortion of image projected on the screen due to the fact that the projection is not perpendicular to the screen.

Language laboratory: A room equipped for language instruction in which tape-recorders, projectors, record players and other devices are used singly or in combination in order to present material, provide feedback, etc.

LCD (Liquid Crystal Display): A device for direct overhead projection of computer-generated data.

Lens diaphragm: The opening through which light enters a camera; its size is controlled by an adjustable diaphragm consisting of metal blades.

Linear program: Information and instruction presented in a fixed sequence which is the same for all learners.

Magnetic board: A flat sheet of ferromagnetic material (or steel) to which objects may be stuck with magnets for display purposes. Now a days, it is common to have magnetic chalkboards.

Master: An audio or video media option prepared from original material and then from which duplicate copies are made.

Memory: The place in which computer-based equipment stores recorded information, either permanently or temporarily.

Menu: In computer-based technology, a page on the screen which lists options available in people using the system for some purposes – such as prepapring an interactive video programme or working with one.

Microcomputer: Physically, the smallest of computers. Also known as a home or personal computer.

Microfiche: A transparent sheet of photographic film bearing a matrix of micro-images (usually pages of text) together with an eye-legible title strip.

Microfilm: A roll or strip of photographic film carrying a series of micro-images.

Microphone: A device which converts sounds into electrical signals, usually for feeding into an amplifying, mixing or sound recording system of some sort.

Microprocessor: A self-contained solid-state microcircuit unit that can be used to build more complicated devices such as computers and control systems.

Microteaching: Training of teachers, presenters in specific presentation skills using techniques such as video mediated self-confrontation and constructive criticism by peers.

Modem: Acronym for modulator, a modem is an electronic device that trranslates digital information for transmission overr telephone lines. It also translates analog information into digital.

Module: An organised, self-contained collection of learning experiences assembled in order to achieve a specified group of related objectives.

Montage: A series of short scenes in a videotape recording used to condense time or distance or to show a series of related activities or places.

Multicamera technique: Recordings of the same action with two or more cameras operated at the same time and located at different positions in relation to the subject.

Multi-image presentation: The simultaneous use of two or more separate images, usually projected.

Multimedia: A composite presentation of text, graphics, pictures, voice, music, animation, video images, etc. with the help of a computer.

Multisensory learning (teaching) aids: Learning or teaching aids which utilize or bring into play more than one of the physical senses.

Nondirectional microphone: A micophone that picks up sounds coming from all directions.

NTSC: The video system used in America. NTSC stands for American National Television Standards Committee and implies the colour standard use for broadcast with a 525-line screen, and a running speed of 60 fields/30 frames per second.

Open learning: An instructional system in which many aspects of the learning process are under the control of the individual learner, who decides what and how to study, usually under some form of guidance.

Optical pointer: An electrically-operated torch which projects a small arrow or spot of light; used in place of a conventional pointer during projection.

Optical system: The path that light takes in direct projection to reach the screen. Generally, light emanating from a lamp, is reflected to pass through condenser lenses, a heat filter, the aperture opening and the projection lens.

Output device: A video screen, plotter, or printer to display the information provided by a computer.

Overhead transparency: A transparent sheet of material (usually 18 cm x 22.5 cm in size) intended for use with an overhead projector or light box as a means of showing graphic, textual or other information. The mode is very useful for large groups.

Overlay: One or more additional transparent sheets with lettering or other matter that can be placed over a base transparency or an opaque background. A very effective way to build and display information.

PAL Phase Alternating (or alternate, or alternation) Line: The most widely applied of the three colour standards. PAL was developed in West Germany, and is employed in UK and across most of Europe, India, Africa, Australia and South America.

Parallax: The difference between the vertical position of an object in a filmed scene as viewed through a viewfinder and as recorded on film through the camera lens.

Paste-up: The combination of illustrations and lettering, each unit of which is rubber-cemented in position on paper or cardboard.

Path cord: An electrical wire used to connect together two pieces of sound equipment (such as tape recorders and record players) so that electrical impulses can be transferred between the units in order to make a recording.

Pedagogy: A term for educational science, that is, the study of classroom methodology and educational techniques.

Permanent mounting: Use of dry-mount tissue placed between the material and the mount surface, with heat and pressure being applied to seal the layers together.

Photo modifier: A large-size camera used to enlarge or reduce art work.

Picas: A printing measurement in which 6 picas equals one inch of line length.

Pixels: The arrangement of dots or picture elements that comprise a computer-generated graphics image. Pixels is an abbreviation of picture element.

Premaster: A high-quality, edited videotape recording from which master videodisc is prepared.

Psychomotor domain: A category of human learning that involves physical skills and coordination of skeletal muscles.

Rangefinder: A camera attachment that, upon proper setting, indicates the distance from camera to the subject or sets the lens in focus at that range.

Readability formula: A procedure to determine a grade level of difficulty for reading material. The formula proposed by Edward Fry, it involves counting the number of syllables and sentences for a certain number of words on a printed page.

Reinforcement: The result of success in learning that builds confidence in an individual to continue learning.

Resource material: A general term for resources and instructional materials used by learners or teachers.

Rule of thirds: A principle of composition for graphics and photographic in which the area is divided into thirds both vertically and horizontally. The centres of interest are located at the intersections of these lines.

Scanner: A computer device that converts an image on a piece of paper into an electronic form that can be stored in a computer file.

SECAM: 'Sequential couleur a memoire', the colour standard for video, developed in France, and subsequently adopted by the USSR and its satellite states, and in some parts of the Middle East and North Africa. It involves sending the three primary colour signals sequentially, rather than nearly simultaneously (as the NTSC and PAL systems do).

Shotgun microphone: A unidirectional type microphone that accepts only a narrow angle of sound and rejects most other noises.

Shutter speed: The interval between opening and closing of the shutter of a camera, measured in fractions of a second.

Simulation: A programme which attempts to emulate a realistic situation. In general, any operating representation of a real system or process or part thereof.

Single-lens reflex camera: A compact camera employing a mirror or prism for accurate viewing directly through the camera lens.

Slow motion: The technique of slowing down a motion picture film or a video clip in order to show an action slower than it is.

Special-effects generator: A device that allows the addition of various effects to visual images as they are selected and recorded on videotape.

Split screen projection: Showing of two or more different images on different parts of the same screen.

Storyboard: A series of sketches or pictures and any accompanying text used in the planning of an audiovisual programme.

Super VHS: The form of 1/2 inch videotape format that produces higher quality images than conventional VHS.

Systems approach: A term used to describe the systematic application of educational technology to an educational or training problem, starting with the input (entry behaviour) and output (terminal behaviour) and determining how best to progress from the former to the latter.

Tape-slide programme, presentation: An instructional programme or presentation in the form of a slide sequence accompanied by an audiotape, the two being synchronized by means of audibie

Telecine: Equipment used to make a videotape copy of a piece of film footage, transparencies or 35 mm slides from photographic slide film on to videotape.

Teleconference: A configuration for communication employing electronic transmission technologies (audio/video) to hold live interaction between geographically dispersed participants.

Telephoto lens: A camera lens that permits a closer view of a subject than would be obtained by a normal lens from the same distance.

Teletext: The generic term used to describe systems which use broadcast television signals to transmit digitally-coded information.

Thermocopier: A reprographic device that uses infra red heat to develop negative and positive overhead transparencies.

Thumbspot: A visible mark placed in the lower left corner of a slide to indicate the pope position for correctly viewing the slide.

Titler: An electronic device that creates lettering in a video camera and which can be recorded on videotape while a scene is being tape-recorded.

Tone-control Programmer: It uses audio frequency tones to control different dissolve functions in a multi-image slide presentation.

Tracking control: A setting on videocassette recorders to adjust video head speed to overcome minor variations that affect picture quality of a tape during playback.

Twin-lens camera: It includes a lens for viewing the subject and second lens for picture taking

Uplink: A ground station that transmits signals to satellite for transmission to other ground stations. At the other end, the signals are received by a **downlink** which requires a satellite dish, a decoder and a display screen.

VHS (Video Home System): A 1/2 inch video format used for domestic recording. The VHS format is not suitable for producing transmission quality recordings.

Visual literacy: Skills an individual develops in interpreting, judging, responding to, and using visual representations of reality.

White balance: A videocamera setting to fine-tune the camera for the particular light conditions under which the scene will be recorded.

Wide-angle lens: A camera lens that permits a wider view of a subject and its surroundings than would be obtained by a normal lens from the same position.

Wipe: A visual effect in videotape recordings in which a new scene seems to push the previous scene off the screen.

Workbook: A text produced as a study or learning guide, usually containing exercises, problems, practice materials, etcetera.

Worksheet: A sheet carrying instructions, information, etcetera relating to part of or some aspect of the work of an exercise. Such sheets often contain spaces where information, answers, results have to be filled in.

Zoom lens: A camera lens of variable magnification that permits a smooth change of subject coverage between distance and close-up shots without changing camera position.